THE HORROR OF HIMMLER'S DEATH SQUADS

THE HORROR OF HIMMLER'S DEATH SQUADS

THE EINSATZGRUPPEN AND THE HOLOCAUST IN THE BALTICS

NORMAN RIDLEY

FRONTLINE
BOOKS

THE HORROR OF HIMMLER'S DEATH SQUADS
The Einsatzgruppen and the Holocaust in the Baltics

First published in Great Britain in 2024 by
Frontline Books
An imprint of Pen & Sword Books Ltd
Yorkshire – Philadelphia

ISBN: 978-1-03610-670-6

Typeset by Lapiz Digital
Printed and bound by CPI UK

Pen & Sword Books Limited incorporates the imprints of Archaeology, Atlas, Aviation, Battleground, Digital, Discovery, Family History, Fiction, History, Local, Local History, Maritime, Military, Military Classics, Politics, Select, Transport, True Crime, After the Battle, Air World, Claymore Press, Frontline Publishing, Leo Cooper, Remember When, Seaforth Publishing, The Praetorian Press, Wharncliffe Books, Wharncliffe Local History, Wharncliffe Transport, Wharncliffe True Crime and White Owl.

For a complete list of Pen & Sword titles please contact:

PEN & SWORD BOOKS LTD
47 Church Street, Barnsley, South Yorkshire, S70 2AS, UK
E-mail: enquiries@pen-and-sword.co.uk
Website: www.pen-and-sword.co.uk

Or

PEN AND SWORD BOOKS,
1950 Lawrence Road, Havertown, PA 19083, USA
E-mail: uspen-and-sword@casematepublishers.com
Website: www.penandswordbooks.com

CONTENTS

Chapter 1

THE BIRTH OF BALTIC NATIONALISM

The Baltic countries of Estonia, Latvia and Lithuania were all part of the Imperial Russian Empire in the nineteenth century, but the Tsarist overlords in St Petersburg had always been acutely aware of the difficulties and dangers of trying to impose Russian culture on its vast and multi-ethnic empire. Nationalism was not by any means a driving force at the time but veneration for tradition and cultural identity gave ethnic minorities a dual allegiance. They had little choice but to 'give unto Caesar that which was Caesar's' but all the rest was theirs to hang onto. To consolidate its hold, however, Russia did employ the tactic of ensuring that anyone from the regions who wished to acquire a position within the Russian state apparatus, first had to show an understanding of and a veneration for Russian culture and must be able to write and speak the Russian language.

A law of 1906 decreed that 'The Russian State is one and indivisible. ... The Russian language is the common language of the State and is compulsory ... in all State and public institutions.'[1] Those who followed this path and rose to become the elites of their own communities inevitably became 'Russified' to a greater or lesser extent, but the rest of the populations retained much of its local cultural affiliations. That is not to say, however, that such tolerance of minority sensibilities led to any level of tolerance for opposition or breakaway movements. The Tsarist secret police kept a very close watch on any signs of dissidence. Poles and Jews, in particular, were seen as potentially dangerous and rebellious groups, and as such were particularly constrained by many laws and restrictions.

Unlike the Poles, the people of Lithuania, for a long time, seemed to show little resistance to Russian domination and were seen by

St Petersburg as destined to eventually become fully assimilated into Russian culture. This proved to be a particular inept assessment of the situation when Lithuanians joined the Polish rebellion against Russian domination in the 1863 Uprising. What Professor Andrzej Nowak, of the Polish Academy of Sciences, calls a deep-rooted tradition of 'freedom and citizenship' meant that Poles and Lithuanians would not 'agree to live with their heads bowed'. St Petersburg saw the danger of the nationalist movement spreading and came down heavily on the rebels, hanging the leaders and imposed restrictions on all expression of Lithuanian culture. They closed schools where instruction was given in the Lithuanian language and made the study of the Russian language compulsory in all elementary schools. Catholic monasteries and churches were shut down.

Lithuania's northern neighbours, the smaller nations of Estonia and Latvia had been thought to pose less threat to Russian power, and far enough from Polish influence to be mostly left to their own devices but St Petersburg, unnerved by the 1863 Uprising and the growing influence of Germany through the large and influential German-Baltic communities, began to introduce reforms to bring the Baltic peoples more into line with Russian standards. The growth in German culture and influence had become problematic as Germany had become significantly more powerful after the unification in 1871 and Russia was afraid that the gravitational pull of its much more modern economy would entice the Baltics into its sphere of influence.

Already the communities of the Baltics had started to see a growth of prosperity as a result of the land reforms that had started in 1804 and then after the Reform Laws of 1840 and 1860 the small farmers gained rights at the expense of the traditional German-Baltic landowners. When the Russian language was imposed upon Latvia and Estonia in all bureaucratic and administrative affairs as had been the case in Lithuania, and their judicial and educational system were brought under direct Russian control there was a strong reaction from the people who had felt a growing sense of nationhood arising from their increased prosperity. There was an upsurge in Baltic art, literature, and music, especially in Estonia and Latvia but the Lithuanians, who had been much more under Polish dominance, did not benefit to the same extent.

Despite Russian fears, this growth of identity politics did not, at first, seem to be accompanied by any great desire for independence. The very idea of separation from the Imperial Russian Empire was so revolutionary as to be almost unthinkable but a process had begun, which would go on to weaken ties between Russia and the Baltic states and see the growth of a sense of nationhood. History shows that this would inevitably lead to calls for independence but at the turn of the century few understood what a powerful force that desire, couched in the slogans of freedom, could become.

The Lithuanians got caught up in this movement when Polish cultural influence, though to be a major destabilising factor in their country, was met with a Russian crackdown. The Lithuanian alphabet was banned, and Cyrillic enforced, which was seen as a blatant attack on Catholicism, whose literature and litanies were in Latin script. This was a serious issue for deeply religious people like the Lithuanians. Hostility that had been focused on the Poles now widened to take in Russians. An underground book printing and reading culture erupted using the Lithuanian alphabet and more and more Lithuanians began to read literature as a form of protest. This inevitably led to a greater awareness of Lithuanian culture, which boosted the Lithuanian people's self-esteem and began to nurture a stronger identity, which then turned into a call for independence. In 1905, when protests broke out throughout Russia in reaction to Tsarist rule, Estonians and Latvians joined these protests but quickly found that the Tsar still had the upper hand and the protest movement was brutally crushed. The big turning point came with the First World War in 1914 and the Russian Revolution of 1917.

The Baltic states in 1914

The Baltic states in 2023

In these first few months of the First World War the Baltic area was very much on the periphery of the action in the east with the focus of events further to the south and west. Even so, by the end of September 1915, the Germans had taken control of all of Lithuania and about half of Latvia. Vilnius, the centre of Lithuanian nationalism, was in German hands and Rīga, occupying a similar place for the Latvians, was right on the front line against the Russians who had suffered more than 1 million casualties during the first year of the war. They suffered further massive losses right up until the February Revolution of 1917 when the Tsar abdicated leaving the Kerensky government in charge in Moscow. The new leadership launched fresh attacks against German forces but a German counterattack in July broke the Russian lines as the first Russian forces rebelled against their commanders. At the Battle of Rīga at the beginning of September, Russian forces were again driven back and weeks later the October Revolution brought the Bolsheviks to power in Moscow. The Germans now looked to be on the point of achieving one of their war aims, which was the annexation of all the Baltic provinces that lay within the Imperial Russian Empire.

Russia was weakened by war and in turmoil after the 1917 Revolution, which gave the Baltic states a narrow window of opportunity to assert their independence before Russia recovered and while the Germans were still heavily involved on the Western Front. The period of Russification that had begun at the turn of the century had, ironically, ended up fostering Baltic nationalism and the Baltic people took advantage of the opportunity to break away from the Imperial Russian Empire, completely at a time when it was in no position to retaliate.

Germany posed a harsher reality militarily, but that country was also politically weak with the Western Allies determined to prevent it from benefitting territorially in the east. It was a blow to them, however, when, on 3 March 1918, Germany forced a much-weakened Russia to sign the formal peace agreement between their two countries known as the Treaty of Brest-Litovsk that extended German influence over Finland, Estonia, Latvia, Lithuania, Belarus and Ukraine at Russia's expense.

It was to be a short-lived agreement. It was denounced by the Western Allies, ignored at every opportunity by the Bolsheviks, and soon formally annulled as part of the 11 November 1918 Armistice agreement.[2] German ambitions had been dramatically thwarted even further by the establishment of the state of Poland, which had swallowed up lands that had formerly been part of the German Empire, and recognition of the independence of the Baltic states. Under such circumstances, the post-war German government was compelled to change its approach and work towards establishing good working relationships with the new Baltic states of Estonia, Latvia and Lithuania essentially through the indigenous Baltic German communities.

Language is obviously an important part of national identity but up until the start of the twentieth century, the Lithuanian language was spoken almost exclusively by the peasantry while the educated class spoke Polish or Russian. This started to change as the country's elite became enthused by thoughts of independence and they began to speak Lithuanian as an expression of that ambition. At the same time, they sparked a resurgence of the study of Lithuanian history, recalling the pagan princes who had ruled as far south as the Black Sea. This was the beginning of a drive to educate the peasants and instil in them a nationalist fervour but there were significant obstacles.

The Lithuanian port of Memel was a German town in as much as it was controlled by Baltic German businessmen and embodied much German culture. The Lithuanina capital city Vilnius (Wilno in Polish, Vil'nia in Belarussian, Vil'na in Russian, Vilne in Yiddish) was predominantly Polish, albeit in a way that differentiated it in language and culture, sometimes called 'krajowcy', from that of the Polish people. There were many Poles who rejected the very notion of Lithuanian statehood and thought that the whole of Lithuania should become part of Poland. The Russians saw that Lithuania was a barrier to German expansion in the east and had its own designs on curbing nationalism to keep the country firmly in the Russian zone of influence.

Ironically, Vilnius became the centre of Lithuanian nationalist ambitions even though hardly anyone in the city spoke Lithuanian. For more than 150 years, it had been the centre of eastern European Jewish cultural life, but this was no obstacle to the nationalists who chose to see all those living in and around Vilnius as Lithuanians who just happened to speak Yiddish, Polish or Belarussian. Unfortunately, Belarussian nationalists saw Vil'nia as their capital too. When thousands of refugees poured into the city in 1915 it exacerbated the ethnic divide as Poles and Lithuanians competed for culture and political dominance but linguistically the city remained Polish.

Then on 18 September 1915, after German forces had invaded Lithuania, Chief of the German Military Administration in Vilnius, General Traugott von Pfeil, on his second day in place, outraged Lithuanians by putting up notices describing Vilnius as 'the pearl of the glorious Kingdom of Poland'.[3] Clearly the Germans had little understanding of local sensibilities and, in fact, had little idea what they would do with the occupied territories other than use them as a barrier to Russian expansion west. In talks with the Germans, Lithuanians made great use of the term 'ethnographic boundaries' and emphasised its right to Vilnius as its historic capital.

Its ambitions for independence, however, were hampered by having no specific borders or boundaries to define what would become the Lithuanian state. The region was defined essentially by people, language and culture that had been striving to create a national identity independent of the Imperial Russian Empire since the beginning of the century. It was hoped that this would be more achievable under the Germans rather than the Russians. By September 1917, the Germans, who had hitherto shown scant understanding of or interest in Lithuanian politics invited influential, authoritative, active and politically conscious Lithuanians of all classes to Vilnius for a conference.

Not surprisingly, the conference called for an independent and democratic Lithuanian state comprised of ethnographic Lithuanian land. A twenty-member *Taryba* (Council of Lithuania) was established and began negotiations with the occupying German authority to establish an Independent State of Lithuania with its capital Vilnius. This began the separation of Lithuanian lands from Poland and Russia and established close relations between Lithuania and Germany in respect of customs, finance, communications and military. The German government, however, caught up in a frenzy of nationalistic fervour across eastern Europe and unsure how to respond, hesitated to agree to Lithuanian independence causing the Council of Lithuania to act in a more radical manner.

On 16 February 1918, the *Taryba,* chaired by Jonas Basanavičius, unanimously adopted and declared the Act of Independence, which proclaimed the restoration of the independent state of Lithuania, founded on democratic principles, with Vilnius as its capital and 'spiritual centre',[4] and declared the termination of all the political ties that formerly bound this state to other nations. The *Taryba,* however, was unable to form a government, police force, or other state institutions due to the continued presence of German troops. Germany made no secret of plans for the total annexation of the territory prompting the Council of Lithuania to attempt to preserve their independence by creating a separate constitutional monarchy under Prince Wilhelm Karl von Urach, Count of Württemberg and 2nd Duke of Urach, as the King of Lithuania. It was a futile gesture as the whole landscape was to change irrevocably with German defeat in the war and the ensuing armistice. Crushed and demoralised by its military failures, on 20 October Germany recognised Lithuanian independence and promised to convert the German military administration into a civilian government allowing the Lithuanians to take over once they were able to do so.

The *Taryba* rescinded its invitation to Prince Wilhelm and adopted its first constitution, which organised the government on a provisional basis until the Constituent Assembly made a final decision. After Germany's humiliation at Versailles, the fragile balance of powers crumbled and the contest over taking possession of Vilnius became especially bitter, with the Poles looking to take over control by force. Meanwhile, the Communist Party of Lithuania held a congress on 1 October to organise a communist revolution in the country financed by Moscow to take advantage of German withdrawal. On 16 December, a provisional revolutionary government, following the Red Army as it advanced westward, declared the formation of the Lithuanian Soviet Socialist Republic (LSSR) as a puppet state of Soviet Russia under the leadership of Vincas Mickevičius-Kapsukas. The *Taryba* lacked any means of organising resistance to the Soviet forces who occupied Vilnius and more than half of Lithuanian territory by January 1919. In the occupied areas, the Soviets created revolutionary committees based on Russian models. The government of Lithuania relocated to Kaunas.

The Soviet advance was eventually halted in mid-February by a combined force of Lithuanian and German volunteers and then at the end of February, the Germans went on the offensive in Latvia and northern Lithuania. The Soviets decided to combine the weak Lithuanian and Byelorussian Soviet Socialist Republics but that had little effect on Polish forces who took Vilnius and Minsk during the Polish-Soviet War. Russia now formed an alliance with Lithuania and on 11 July 1920 signed the Soviet-Lithuanian Peace Treaty, which guaranteed Lithuania's neutrality in return for permission to move Soviet troops in its territory. Thus, Soviet Russia became the first country to recognise Lithuanian sovereignty and the treaty became a significant milestone in Lithuania's struggle for international recognition.

The tide had been turning in the Polish-Soviet War and the Soviets recaptured Vilnius but did not transfer the city to the Lithuanian administration, as had been agreed in the Soviet-Lithuanian Peace Treaty signed just two days before. Instead, the Soviets, buoyed by victories on the battlefield and its armies closing in on Warsaw, planned to overthrow the Lithuanian government and re-establish a Soviet republic. However, before they could do this, their army was repulsed at the gates of Warsaw when the Poles inflicted a massive defeat on them and forced them to retreat chaotically.

When the First World War broke out general mobilization occurred in Latvia and its forces were deployed in East Prussia where they suffered total defeat against the advancing German army. In the face of German advances, Russian relocated as much of Latvia's industrial plant as could be moved, and as many as 750,000 of its population relocated to the east in what the Latvians would call the *Beglu laiki*

(Refugee times). When the Germans plundered what was left, what had once been one of the most advanced industrial areas of the Imperial Russian Empire was devastated. The Germans advanced as far as the river Dvina (Daugava) in Courland as the Russians hurriedly organised nine *Strelnieki Regiments* (Latvian volunteer rifle battalions) and integrated them into the Russian army on the Rīga front. In November 1916, these had grown into regiments recognised for their comparatively high level of education and higher level of average discipline than the units of the Russian army.

Latvian units fought at Ķekava, Sloka, Ķemeri and Ikšķile in January 1917 when they had some initial success but failed to break through strong German defences and, with disappointingly poor Russian support, took heavy casualties. The hoped that their contribution to the Russian cause would show their loyalty and allow the Provisional Livonian Council, formed at Valmiera in March to demand total self-determination in return. It was not to be. When the first democratic elections to the Provincial Livonian Council were held, the Bolsheviks gained a majority. Against a determined German offensive towards Rīga in September, Latvian forces again took heavy losses as they held the line for a crucial twenty-four hours allowing the Russian 12th Army to withdraw without being encircled. It was becoming increasingly evident to the Latvian forces that they were being used to cover for the poor fighting qualities of the Russian army, which began to decrease morale.

Latvian nationalists now found themselves split between 'White' (nationalist) and 'Red' (Bolshevik) Strelnieki militias facing regular German forces and paramilitary *Freikorps* units, (which translates to free corps units – a group of right wing, mainly nationalist German soldiers and anti-communists), who tried to preserve whatever German control they could. One day the Latvians were fighting the Bolsheviks and the next day the Germans in what amounted, in all but name, to a civil war between nationalists and communists.

In Valka on 16 November 1917, nationalist Latvian politicians formed the Latvian Provisional National Council with the intention of separating Latvia from Russia and creating an independent state, but the council lacked the means to achieve this. After the armistice ended the First World War, however, the British gave de facto recognition to Latvia and the declaration of independence of the Republic of Latvia was made in Rīga in the Latvian National Theatre on 18 November 1918 when the Latvian Provisional National Council declared itself to be the only true representative of the will of the people. Although announcing Latvia as an autonomous, individual state entity, the Latvian Provisional National Council did not demand Latvia's independence yet simply because it did not control the Latvian territory and was de facto an underground organization mostly active in Petrograd. The German army ruled over Courland and Rīga, while Vidzeme and Latgale were in the hands of the Bolsheviks.

The Latvian Provisional Government, under Kārlis Ulmanis had no national army to defend the country and, as German forces withdrew the Bolsheviks moved in and occupied Latvia, and declared the Latvian Soviet Socialist Republic on 17 December which, under the leadership of Pēteris Stučka, brought in draconian laws and ruled with ruthless terror against the wealthy, the landowners, the clergy and anyone who was perceived as a threat. A Red Army force under its Latvian commander, Jukums Vācietis, occupied Rīga on 3 January 1919 forcing the Latvian Provisional National Council to flee to Liepāja and from there onto a Royal Navy ship. The legitimacy of Stučka's government rests on the extent to which it had popular support. The head of the US mission, Lieutenant Colonel Warwick Greene certainly thought it did and the Soviets, as one might expect, agreed that 'the communists in Latvia did not need any outside military support in order to restore Soviet power.'[5]

Arrests, kidnappings and torture were common as up to 6,000 people in Rīga alone were killed within a few months. The Latvians called on German irregular Freikorps units to battle the Bolsheviks and on 16 April a German-backed coup ousted Stučka, which saw a purge of communist sympathisers in yet another wave of violence as, on 10 May 1919, a puppet German-Latvian government was formed. German forces drove the Bolsheviks out and re-established German authority in Rīga instigating a killing spree of communists and suspected sympathisers. Red Latvians who could, fled to Russia where they joined the 200,000 ethnic Latvians living there alongside around 700,000 Latvian wartime refugees. Many achieved positions of power. Jēkabs Peters helped the Pole, Feliks Dzerzhinsky, to establish the *Cheka* (*Vserossiyskaya chrezvychaynaya komissiya* – Soviet political police that would eventually become the KGB), while Jēkabs Alksnis went on to lead the Soviet Air Force in the early 1930s. While many of these would fall in Stalin's purges quite a few were still around to enter Latvia with the Soviet forces in 1940.

The Latvians realised that they could not stand up to either the Germans or Russians without help and looked for support in the west. The Western Allies were certainly not happy to see Germany retaining so much control in the Baltic region, but their priority overall was to thwart the Bolshevik revolution by supporting White

Russian Tsarist forces whose ranks were being boosted by significant numbers of German volunteers. For the Western Powers, the question of independence of the Baltic states was essentially an irrelevance but in early 1920 an armistice was agreed between Latvian forces and the Bolsheviks, and a peace treaty was finally agreed with Moscow on 12 August 1920 in which Russia, without reservations, recognised Latvian independence and sovereignty, renouncing voluntarily and forever any claims to Russian sovereignty over the Latvian state. German assistance had been crucial to Latvia in its early resistance to Bolshevik occupation, but the Western Allies ensured that this did not result in German dominance of the country. The Estonians too played an important role in helping Latvia to defeat the Russians.

Estonian nationalism emerged at the start of the nineteenth century when scholars of German extraction began documenting its culture and language. Before this time, neither descent, religion or place of birth had been enough to create a sense of national identity but now there was a national cultural and political 'awakening' with the printing of newspapers in the Estonian language and the teaching of the Estonian language in schools alongside Russian. The emerging leaders of the ethnic Estonian people understood that they were very much a political minnow when compared to the imperial powers that surrounded them and so encouraged the development of a cultural identity to unite them and give them a sense of being separate people. To counter the dominance of the big German landowners and the political influence of Russia, the Estonians developed the characteristics of a 'small, hard-working culturally effective politically liberal' community.[6] This allowed them to thrive and gain enough self-confidence to begin contemplating sovereignty and independence from their neighbouring giants.

Chapter 2

POST-FIRST WORLD WAR CONFLICTS

At the end of the First World War, with the collapse of the three great Russian, German and Austrian empires, Latvia, Estonia and Lithuania were new states created on the shores of the Baltic Sea. These countries had never before really been masters of their own fate, and had been mostly battlegrounds over which bigger and stronger neighbours had vied for control. At first little seemed to change in that regard. For the Baltics, the war did not end in November 1918. Instead, it became a protracted theatre of both conventional and ideological disputes, involving the nascent armies of all three countries, White and Bolshevik Russians, regular German army and Freikorps, Poles, the Royal Navy, and volunteers from a number of different countries.

Economically, the Baltic states were bankrupt, destitute, and clearly not masters of their own destiny and, under these conditions, had little prospect of improving their circumstances. They had suffered years of ethnic strife, pogroms, civil war, wars of independence, and interstate conflicts. Bolshevik forces battled nationalist movements in a region where the imperial empires had disintegrated leaving a power vacuum across eastern Europe from the river Elbe to the Black Sea. Many of the political and ethnic tensions that underlay this period of internecine warfare had their roots in history going back long before 1914 but they were reignited in the context of Germany's defeat in war and the Russian communist revolution.

With the Germany army having occupied the region for most of 1918 and the Russians having ceded control under Brest-Litovsk the most likely outcome at this point might have been the formation of a single Baltic state aligned to Germany but on 16 February 1918, with a population of some 2 million, the Republic of Lithuania declared itself independent and challenged the authority of the governorates of Vilnius, Kaunas and Suwalki. A week later, the northern part of the Governorate of Livonia and the Governorate of Estonia declared itself to be the Republic of Estonia with a population of around 1 million people. Then the Republic of Latvia was created on 18 November out of the southern parts of the Governorate of Livonia, the Governorate of Courland, and the western parts of the Governorate of Vitebsk.

The Paris Peace Conference opened on 12 January 1919 to agree a peace settlement and the Treaty of Versailles was duly signed between Germany and the Allies on 28 June 1919. The treaty did not particularly concern itself with the Baltic states meaning that they were essentially left to negotiate their own relationship with the new Russian Bolshevik state. All the Baltic states made the most of the relative power vacuum that followed the end of the First World War and declared independence as a result. The Russian saw this as an opportunity to strip the Baltic German communities of their hereditary authority in the region and put their own people in charge. With the threat of a Russian invasion ever present, the three nations looked to international organisations to safeguard their independence. They were inspired by US President Woodrow Wilson's call for self-determination as one of his 'Fourteen Points' even though he had not particularly used the term in reference to the Baltics.

When the Baltic states declared independence, they slipped away from the German sphere of influence and deprived the Baltic Germans within their borders of their erstwhile status as the dominant caste economically, politically and socially. These Baltic Germans had fully endorsed the regional wartime expansionist policies of the Wilhelmine administration and they were now about to face the backlash and pay the price. Tension mounted between them and the ethnic Balts. The loss of German prestige and authority was a bitter blow while Latvian nationalists were ever more eager to strip them of what residual power they had. One of the biggest symbolic and humiliating acts was the transfer, in 1931, of St Jacob's Cathedral, central to the German Catholic faith to the Evangelical Latvian Church. Two major German craft guilds, albeit virtually moribund ones, were disbanded.

In Germany, the new post-Versailles Weimar government was also facing a crisis of self-esteem. They had been faced with the challenge of coming to terms with a significant decrease in population and territory as well as the loss of military might and the consequent sense of injustice and humiliation. They were inevitably going to have to quickly acquire some humility by compromising over their relationship with minor states in order to build trading links through the Baltics into Russian markets where their main hope of economic recovery lay. It was hoped that the German Baltic communities would play a major part in opening up the eastern trading routes.

The Germans had plenty of internal disputes to settle first, however, but they were united in their hatred of the Treaty of Versailles and their Federal Minister of Foreign Affairs Gustav Stresemann argued that the Treaty need not be permanent. The historian Fritz Fischer suggested that the idea of *lebensraum* (the territory required for natural development) had been around long before the Nazis employed it and that Stresemann's policies, particularly those towards national minorities abroad, were part of a continuous trend from pre-war Imperial Germany right through to the Third Reich. 'The creation of a state, whose political boundaries include all of the German people, who live within the borders of the areas of Central Europe settled by Germans and wish the union with the Reich, is the distant goal of German hopes,' he said, expounding on his ideas of a *großdeutscher Staat* (greater German state) although it is clear that, unlike future German governments, he advocated only peaceful means to bring that about.[1]

Geopolitical ideas were introduced into German schools to persuade the new generation that the emergence of new states in the east was unnatural and unjust and, therefore, their existence could reasonably be seen as temporary. Stable state borders, the young were told, were determined not by unstable artificial boundaries but by ethnic and geographic factors. Pan-German movements that defined a nation as the conceptual entity where state, people and territory coincide argued that millions of Germans continued to live outside the borders of the German Empire and needed to be brought within the fold. They seemed to have had success when the Treaty of Brest-Litovsk was signed in March 1918 but the treaty, in which the Soviet Union had ceded to them control of much of the Baltics, was effectively terminated later that year because of Germany's capitulation to the Allied powers. The German government was forced to temporarily abandon its claims in the Baltics, but Germany never ceased to consider the people in Memel, at least, as part of the German nation.

In 1923, however, in blatant disregard of the provisions of the Treaty of Versailles, Lithuania seized the Memel territory. German foreign policy makers now saw the vital importance of supporting the Baltic-German community to preserve and promote German culture in the east and strengthening the ties between the Baltics and the Reich. It was clear that pursuit of German territorial ambitions was the main concern rather than the welfare of the German Balts who, nevertheless, received significant economic and cultural support through subsidised schools, theatre and cultural exchanges.

Returning to their various homelands, Armenians, Georgians, Poles, Ukrainians, Balts and other eastern European soldiers released from what had been the Imperial Russian and Imperial German armies found only revolutionary and nationalistic turbulence that denied them a peaceful return to civilian life. It was not a difficult decision for many, with no prospect of work or means of sustenance, to transfer allegiance from national armies to paramilitary organisations. These paramilitaries would variously find themselves involved as adjuncts to state power or conversely revolutionaries against state power. They often became perpetrators of ethnic violence in conflicts over state boundaries and self-determination. For many the willingness to engage in further violent struggle was fuelled by a sense of shame and anger at having failed to achieve victory after the suffering of war and coming home to find only hunger, despair and political instability. It offered them a chance to overcome their humiliation.

Not surprisingly, it was ex-soldiers from the contested regions of the states now struggling to define their borders who made up a disproportionate percentage of conscripts to the paramilitary armies. They were joined by youths who had been too young to fight in the war but who were now fired up by nationalist and revolutionary ideals eager to emulate their older brethren. It is important to note that in the case of German paramilitaries, or Freikorps, many of the men were from the officer class whereas in other units such as the Lithuanians, the bulk of recruits were from the peasant or middle classes. While many paramilitaries were motivated by political resistance to communism, in the Baltic regions, especially, old enmities resurfaced with brutality in the form of violence against ethnic minorities and rival national states well outside the confines of what might be called purposeful action. There would be a durable legacy to these events in the perceived need to 'cleanse' communities of alien elements to achieve balance and harmony in society, which became 'the common currency of radical politics' and perpetuated the cycle of ethnic violence into the 1940s.[2]

Events that occurred in Lithuania will illustrate how the paramilitaries functioned across eastern Europe in the post-First World War chaos and go some way to explain how grievances and disputes rumbled on without resolution right through the following two decades and ultimately into the next war. The large-scale formation of non-Russian units in the Imperial Russian Army started in 1915 when nine Latvian rifle regiments were formed and saw a rapid rise after the Russian Revolution in 1917.[3] Lithuanian troops in the Imperial Russian Army followed suit and were allowed to form ethnic units albeit under Russian officers. In June 1917, this resulted in the establishment of the Union of Lithuanian Soldiers who called for a 'free and democratic Lithuania.'[4] Later when Lithuanian troops were demobilised from the Imperial Russian Army, they formed an independent battalion, which resisted all efforts to coax it to align with the newly established Bolsheviks Red Guard. The Soviets responded by cutting off all supplies forcing the battalion to disband. By the end of the First World War, there were six separate Lithuanian regiments in Smolensk, Rovno, Vibetsk, Siberia and Estonia.

Germany had recognised Lithuanian aspirations for independence in March 1918 hoping that this would encourage a close political alliance but the head of the *Taryba* (Council of Lithuania), Augustinas Voldemaras, preferred neutrality and refused to raise an army, only a security force to combat internal banditry that was rampant. Then, after the Armistice, as German forces started to withdraw from the east and the Russians threatened to move in to take their place, Voldemaras left the country for Germany in a move that the *Taryba* saw as dereliction of duty. They dissolved his government effectively firing him *in absentia* and replaced him with Mykolas Sleževičius. He started recruiting a volunteer army with the support of the German government who authorised a loan of 3 million Reichsmarks to equip it. Unfortunately, there was a poor response to the call for volunteers and full conscription had to be introduced on 15 January 1919.

The Vilnius 5th Infantry Regiment, founded in March 1919 by Kazys Škirpa, included large numbers of Lithuanian volunteers boosted by recruits of peasants from Russian-occupied Lithuania who were motivated by class rivalry and the prospect of a regular pay packet. They fought against both Poles and Russians but, realistically, the only forces capable of preventing a Bolshevik take-over of the country were the Germans. Unfortunately, their best troops had been drawn away to the Western Front and those that remained were racked by desertions and bombarded with communist revolutionary propaganda. It looked as if the Bolsheviks would have the field to themselves as the German forces started to fall apart. In many cases, their soldiers were either selling their weapons to the Bolsheviks and fleeing with the proceeds or, succumbing to their propaganda, joining up with them.

The German government saw that its eastern European strategy was, once again, disintegrating but they were not willing to abandon east Europe to the Bolsheviks. As a desperate measure, with the rapidly falling morale of the regular German troops, special volunteer units were rapidly formed to replace the disappearing regular army troops. In early December 1918, German Minister of Defence Gustav Noske set up the *Anwerbestelle baltenland* (German Recruitment Office for the Baltic Lands) which started recruiting *Freikorps* units in Berlin. He called for 'those who are unable to adjust to the transition from the military to civilian life' and offered them regular pay.[5] Desperate for help to stall the Bolshevik advance, the Latvians promised the *Freikorps* local citizenship and, crucially, right of settlement while the Lithuanian government offered to buy from them all the war booty they could acquire. The positive response encouraged the Lithuanians to petition the German government to withdraw all of its unreliable and troublesome regular forces whose presence was threat to public order and the internal security of the Lithuanian state.

As part of the *Freikorps* initiative, the first group of volunteers who were known as 'The Saxons' were recruited from Dresden and Leipzig but proved to be a major embarrassment. Many had signed up because they were homeless or jobless and had no inclination to fight. When they arrived in the Baltics many simply sold their weapons and other army material on the black market and 'from the early morning they spent their time in the stuffy public houses of Kaunas, playing cards and chasing women.'[6] They were very quickly disbanded and repatriated with a second recruitment drive providing a better contingent that proved invaluable in supporting Lithuanian forces at Jieznas, Alytus and Kaišiadorys in early 1919 when the Red Army invaded from the east and the anti-Bolshevik German-Russian troops of General Pavel Bermondt-Avalov came down from the north. This defence gave the Lithuanians enough time to get organised and it was they who expelled the Russians later in the year.

In Latvia, meanwhile, the Red Army had occupied most of its territory by mid-January 1919 and were threatening to move south. The government of Ulmanis had fled to the last remaining German-held area at Liepāja. There was some initial support for the Bolshevik occupation force but Pēteris Stučka who had been placed in charge by them, was a fervent and ruthless revolutionary who initiated a reign of terror against the middle classes, subjecting them to property requisitions and ritual humiliations. The Western Allies, eager to prevent the spread of the Bolshevism beyond the borders of Russia, looked on anxiously from afar but were unwilling to commit troops of their own so they chose to make do with the only other military resources available on the ground which, at the time, was the German army and its irregular *Freikorps* units.

All German forces in the Baltics comprising Baltic Germans, White Russians and Latvians, had been placed under the command of German firebrand General Rüdiger von der Goltz, who was adamant that Germany had not lost the war in the east and he was determined to restore German honour with the help of *Freikorps* drafted in from Berlin. These Freikorps units of hardened war veterans, eager like von der Goltz to see German pride restored whatever the cost, were later described by one of them, Ernst von Salomon, as ready to 'march over burning fields, to stamp over ruins and scattered ashes, to dash recklessly through wild forests, over blasted heaths, to push, conquer, eat our way through towards the East.'[7] This made for a strong defence against the communists but was hardly a prescription for long-term stability in the region.

Von der Goltz saw no reason for restraint and moved against the Bolsheviks ousting the Latvian Ulmanis' administration at the same time and installing a puppet pro-German government under pastor Andrievs Niedra. Stučka ordered arbitrary executions of alleged opponents, and the nearer von der Goltz got to the city, the more of Rīga's citizens were shot. The city fell to the Germans on 22 May when they unleashed a wave of reprisals every bit as brutal as Stučka's campaign of terror. Von der Goltz pressed on and moved against Cēsis where he suffered defeat at the hands of a combined Estonian-Latvian force supported by Britain and was forced to fall back allowing their pursuers to occupy Rīga at the mouth of the Dvina river where it meets the Baltic Sea. By July the Western Allies, committed to supporting a Latvian army with British instructors, officers and munitions, were not too disturbed to see von der Goltz brought down a peg or two. He was too far out of anyone's control fighting his own personal war in the Baltics.

War had brought devastation to the towns and cities of Latvia. In Rīga, hunger haunted the streets of the city. One British observer reported: 'We gave away biscuits and everything we could spare but it was simply terrible to see a struggling, cursing mass of men, women and children fighting for scraps which one in 'Blighty' would not have given to a dog.'[8] A huge American-led relief operation followed to feed the city. The Allies sent the British Lieutenant Colonel Harold Alexander to try and establish control with a combined force of *Landeswehr* (Baltic Germans' Territorial Army), who had been persuaded to break with von der Goltz. They simultaneously threatened economic sanctions against Germany if it did not withdraw their *Freikorps* units who were wreaking violence wherever they went and were operating with minimal control.

Von der Goltz could not ignore calls from his government to withdraw but he allowed many of his men to join up with a new force of White-Russian volunteers commanded by the comic-opera figure of Bermondt-Avalov. Bermondt-Avalov had invented for himself a false persona of royal descent and was renowned as 'something of a ladies' man, popular with the nurses of the Russian Red Cross.' His military colleagues knew him to be a 'poseur who had never been involved in a real battle … a dashing, inspirational figure with big ideas, who was neither a good organizer nor a talented military mind'.[9] When von der Goltz was recalled to Germany, it was Bermondt-Avalov who was left in charge of the plan to re-take Rīga, depose the Latvian government and open up the road to Petrograd, hoping to present the Western Allies with a fait accompli.

In October, Bermondt-Avalov's Germans were able to occupy the Rīga suburb of Torņakalns on the west bank of the Dvina, but found the bridges too well defended to cross the river. Their bombardment of the city intensified but the Latvians counterattacked under covering fire from British warships. Bermondt-Avalov's army withdrew but not before some *Freikorps* went on a killing spree that one described as follows:

> We ran across the snowfields and broke into the forest. We took them unawares and raged and shot and killed. We hunted the Letts [Latvians] across the fields like hares, set fire to every house, smashed every bridge to smithereens and broke every telegraph pole. We dropped the corpses into the wells and threw bombs after them. We killed anything that fell into our hands, we set fire to everything that would burn. We saw red; we lost every feeling of humanity.[10]

Bermondt-Avalov had never gone anywhere near the action and when the attack failed, he fled to Germany where he lived out his paranoid fantasies as an exiled reactionary, raging against Weimar, Versailles and the Western Powers.

Then, during bitterly cold weather in January, a joint Latvian, Landeswehr and Polish offensive drove the last remaining Bolsheviks out of Latvia and the Treaty of Tartu was signed in February 1920. The Landeswehr troops were absorbed into the Latvian army and six months later, Rīga was a peaceful city in a country of some 1.5 million people, able to welcome foreign visitors once again. While Germany's war aim had been the eventual annexation of the Baltic provinces, after November 1918, the young German Republic had been faced, instead, with the task of building up friendly relations with these small states. The new Polish state, hostile to Germany, now covered what had been German territory and the German government was anxious to obtain good relations with the Baltic states as a means of indirect access to Russia as well as a counter to Polish influence. Many Latvian riflemen fled to Russia after the war and formed an important part of the leadership of the Red Army. Many Latvians also became prominent members of the Cheka.

Estonia saw little fighting right up until the last year of the war when either German or Russian dominance seemed to be the only two possible outcomes for the country. Anti-Russian sentiment was strong. About 100,000 Estonian men had been conscripted into the Russian army and they fought mainly in what is now Poland, Belarus, and the Baltic states. Some 10 per cent of them had been killed with many more wounded. Unrest in Russia after the Russian Revolution of 1917 had repercussions in the Estonian-Russian community. The new Bolshevik administration in Moscow was rocked by a massive demonstration in Petrograd calling for Estonian independence and caved in by granting a measure of autonomy and the appointment of an Estonian, Jaan Poska, as governor general and mayor of Tallinn. This did little to calm things down and simply escalated tensions as Russians in the administration were replaced by Estonians and the Russian language was relegated below Estonian. Many Estonian-Russians, however, were not enamoured of Bolshevism and were not too unhappy to see a reduction in Russian influence in the country but workers favoured the revolutionaries and saw economic advancement for themselves under communism.

The Northern Baltic Committee had been formed in Tartu to help refugees and support the Russian army but was also active in spreading Estonian nationalist ideas. It was the Estonian proletariat who had tried to seize power on 27 October when news of the Bolshevik revolution in Russia had filtered through. Viktor Kingisepp, Vice-Chairman of the Bolshevik Estonian Revolutionary War Committee ousted Poska but his administration was opposed by many and he was forced to take extreme measures to retain power. Planned elections were cancelled. The German Estonians appealed for help to Germany which brought the wrath of the communist government down on them as many were deported to Russia.

Germany responded to stalled peace talks with the Russians by occupying Estonia on 24 February 1918 in Operation *Faustschlag* and the provisional government declared Estonian independence from Russia. The Germans had not acted in the interests of promoting Estonian independence, however. It was more a case of putting up a challenge to the Bolsheviks. They threw the newly elected Prime Minister Konstantin Päts into prison, political parties were banned, and strict censorship was introduced. This lasted until the Germans were stunned by the crushing terms of the Armistice signed on 11 November 1918 when all their ambitions for dominance of eastern

Europe seemed to evaporate. Two days later Russia felt emboldened enough to rub salt into the German wound by annulling the Treaty of Brest-Litovsk and prepared for offensive action in the Baltic region. As the Germans withdrew, the Russians took Võru, Valga, Tartu, and most of southern Estonia.

On 28 November, the Estonian War of Independence started. With British help, on 6 January 1919 the Estonians counterattacked driving the Russians out of their country. By February, Estonia was free of Soviet forces but Estonian Bolsheviks continued internal agitation and Soviet artillery continued to bombard Narva from over the border. The communists attempted another uprising in Tallinn in December 1918 but failed again. To the south-east the Soviets counterattacked and retook Petseri in March but could not hold it. By mid-May the Estonians were in complete control and their army formed an uneasy alliance with Russian anti-Bolshevik forces who had made very clear their opposition to Estonian independence. Together they took Pskov, Jamburg, Gdov and Luga reaching the outskirts of Petrograd. In the south, Estonian forces took Aluksne in Latvia on 28 May 1919, and Jekabpils a week later. However, they initially failed to take Cesis against Baltic German forces that had ousted the Latvian government only weeks beforehand. The battle raged until 23 June when the town fell to the Estonians on what they came to celebrate as Victory Day.

The Soviets were desperate to start peace talks and concentrate on stabilising the situation in their own country but Western governments applied pressure to ensure that the Baltic states did not respond. Estonia's allies, the White Russians were soundly beaten by the Bolsheviks in November and forced to retreat into Estonia where many of them joined the Estonian army. The Western Allies realised that their bid to defeat the Bolshevik forces was doomed to failure and now they actively encouraged peace talks. At the start of December, they started up again in Tartu and on 31 December 1919 an armistice was agreed. The Treaty of Tartu was signed on 2 February 1920. The Germans had played very little part militarily in the move towards the independence of Estonia which was essentially achieved by the Estonians themselves against Bolshevik opposition.

Chapter 3

THE INTER-WAR YEARS

In the first years of independence for the Baltic states, political parties were formed on the left and right and competed for power in elections. Estonia and Latvia were dominated by left-wing parties who were eager to move far away from type of the autocratic rule they had known under the tsars. Initially they tried to emulate the Weimar constitution with its progressive policies including extended female franchise knowing full well that none of the great powers would do very much to protect their fragile democracies. The Western powers had no real understanding of the politics of eastern Europe and showed little inclination to learn. All they cared about was holding back the Bolsheviks. It was left very much to the small states to make their own accommodation with Russia and this they did when it was clear that the Versailles agreement had passed them by.

Initially it was the League of Nations to which the Baltic nations turned. Membership was granted in September 1921 on condition that the three states gave guarantees for their ethnic minorities; guarantees that had not been demanded of any of the other members. Previous attempts to bind all five Baltic states, Lithuania, Latvia, Estonia, Finland and Sweden, into a Baltic League foundered when Polish and Lithuanian relations were soured by the Polish occupation of Vilnius in October 1920 and all that came out of talks was a narrow defensive alliance between Estonia and Latvia both of whom were accepting of the post-Versailles political map. For these two, Poland was seen as an important ally in the struggle to hold off the Bolsheviks but for Lithuania, Poland was seen as an existential threat.

For their part, the Bolsheviks, continuing to create mischief to advance their own agenda, courted Lithuania by recognising Vilnius as its capital currently under the illegal Polish occupation. Moscow saw the Baltic region as a sphere of major concern throughout the whole inter-war period and a region that was vital to their national security interests. With the degradation of St Petersburg during the civil war and their economy in ruins, the Soviets looked for trade access to the Baltics through Memel, Tallinn and Rīga, which had been part of the Imperial Russian Empire. It was also their ambition to export communism to the Baltic coast as a revolutionary springboard to the west and as a means of re-establishing control of the Baltic states.

External threats failed to create internal consensus, however. In Estonia, the communists attempted to seize power on 1 December 1924 when 300, mostly Russian, conspirators working on the transit base at Tallinn, on the Gulf of Finland, tried to seize communications and call in Soviet troops massed on its border, but it was poorly planned, and rebels were arrested within hours. The ethnic Poles and Germans who had held the reins of power in the Baltics for generations now found themselves stripped of their wealth as new reform bills redistributed their lands to the peasant class. Many Germans emigrated. New forms of democratic government saw progressive legislation enacted but power struggles ensured that the political system remained febrile.

In all three countries the new authoritarian regimes drew their principal support from the well-to-do peasants and from the armed forces and home guards. Opposition remained limited. Peasant strikes and workers' demonstrations occasionally occurred, particularly in Lithuania, but they never posed serious danger to the regimes. The rural populations and business interests favoured the authoritarian regimes. Political repression remained mild, consisting for the most part of temporary imprisonment of opponents, especially those from the extreme left. Foreign trade showed a steady increase, and there was a rise in prosperity.

Estonia

In Estonia, there was a slow and steady move to the right politically. This manifested itself in 1926 with the emergence of the *Eesti Vabadussõjalaste Liit* (Union of Participants in the Estonian War of Independence) which became the *Eesti Vabadussõjalaste Liit, vabadussõjalased* (Estonian War of Independence Veterans' League) in 1929 under the leadership of Andres Larka and Artur Sirk. The movement had its roots as far back as the nineteenth century in the Baltic German communities but only attained real political influence when it took on the role of a self-help organisation for the veterans of the 1918 struggle for independence supporting their rights under the land reform acts. It would play a significant part in Estonian politics right up to the start of the second Soviet occupation in 1944 but its historical significance had been distorted according to the political agendas of both communist and Western powers who tried to fit it into their narratives around Nazism.

The Estonian constitution, drawn up in 1918, followed the example of many other newly created states after the war by establishing what it saw as the foundation of democratic government. This made no provision for a presidency that many feared would lead to dictatorship and instead favoured a multi-party system that would elect a prime minister to govern. Unfortunately, this encouraged factionalism and corruption in a political structure that had no historical ballast or traditional means of reaching consensus and when the Great Depression struck, resulting in unemployment, and falling agricultural prices, there was no resilience in the system to prevent social trauma. Coalition governments came and went in quick succession as political infighting took precedent over the welfare of the population. Political corruption became the rallying cry for the league demanding the introduction of a new constitution with strong executive power under a dominant leader but crucially one still elected under a democratic system.

Opponents of the league accused it of trying to introduce dictatorial government in a one-party authoritarian state despite evidence showing that all the league's proposals favoured democratic processes both to install and remove the leadership. There was huge popular support for the league, which prompted those politicians and business leaders who were profiting from corruption to take strong action to preserve their position. On 11 August 1933, Jaan Tõnisson's government declared a nationwide state of emergency and banned all political meetings. This led to increased support for the league that won a huge majority in a referendum to change the constitution and became the only one of all the fascist groups to succeed in legally obtaining the absolute majority vote of the people, but many Estonians began to see the lack of a strong leader as the key problem and looked to constitutional reform for an answer. Konstantin Päts saw himself as that leader. He had courted the league in its early days to gain support from the public but now came with a mission to 'put the ex-servicemen in their place.'[1] Tõnisson's government now banned the league calling it a threat to public order but it remained a powerful force despite having no public platform. When the league's support was evident from the results of a general election, Tõnisson was forced to resign in favour of Päts.

A new constitution was introduced in 1933 creating a presidency and gave sweeping powers to the office.

When canvassing for the presidential elections began the de facto prime minister and presidential candidate, Konstantin Päts, leader of the Farmers' Party, allied with the Socialists and with support from the police and army, declared a state of emergency on 12 March 1934 claiming that the league was planning a coup d'état with the help of Nazi Germany or the Soviet Union. The majority of the Estonian political elite, state officials and the media, approved of the event.

Opposition leaders were arrested, the political activities of all parties were forbidden, elections were postponed and Päts assumed dictatorial powers. Evidence shows that Päts had received financial support and encouragement from Moscow to stage the coup.[2] The Soviet media also helped by printing stories about support for the ex-servicemen coming from Berlin and even that the movement was led from there. The British Foreign Office, which was starting to take an interest in German ambitions in the Baltics, had initially been of the opinion that the league was decidedly anti-German because of the historic dominance of Baltic Germans in the country but early in 1934 had recorded 'strong suspicions' about German involvement and recommended 'putting a stop to this foreign penetration.'[3]

Ironically, given that Päts had made much of alleged Nazi links to the coup, he received open support from Berlin, which was anxious to see stability in the region. Modern historians such as Andres Kasekamp have found no evidence that the Nazis had given moral or material support to the veterans and argue that the movement showed no inclination towards violence or anti-Semitism, above the normal levels prevalent throughout eastern Europe at the time and lacked the essential characteristics of fascism. Indeed, their early manifesto included calls for a 'just wage' an eight-hour working day and health and unemployment benefits.[4] Their creed may well have embraced nativism, authoritarianism and populism, but it also sought power through the democratic process.

Leading powerbrokers in Estonia now created what they hoped would be a unity party, the *Isamaaliit* (Patriotic League) but, operating from exile in Finland, Sirk only now hatched a plot to overthrow Päts' authoritarian rule but it was too late. All the momentum was with Päts. His secret police uncovered the plot and arrested many of Sirk's activists in Estonia. Sirk fled to Luxembourg and later died in 1937 after falling from a window. It has never been ascertained if it was suicide or murder. The complete lack of evidence that Sirk plotted a coup before the 1934 elections suggests that Päts had fabricated the threat in pursuit of his own dictatorial ambitions. His new powers now enabled him to elect judges and enact law by decree which were way beyond anything that the Veterans' League had envisaged.

When elections eventually took place, only candidates of the 'National Front for the Implementation of the Constitution' were allowed. Päts' ruling party won sixty-four out of eighty seats in the newly created lower house of the Estonian parliament. He was nominated for president and was sworn in on 24 April 1938.

Latvia

The Baltic Germans in Latvia had opened themselves up to retribution by their open enthusiasm for German annexation during the First World War and it was not long in coming after independence. On 2 October 1920, the Latvian government instituted agrarian reforms that broke up the big German estates leaving none bigger than 50 hectares. The confiscated land was redistributed to Latvian peasant families. Then German industry came under the spotlight and the state made further moves to strip the Germans of their wealth. These measures proved to be a severe blow to German prestige, power and cultural identity and it was only through politics that they were able to retain some of their former influence.

The Latvians had been determined to introduce a democratic system of representation which, in the unprecedented new environment saw a burgeoning of political parties many of which could muster no more than a single elected representative in the parliament. The Germans were much more organised and cohesive as a group and, although their representation under the new system was small, they had common purpose and understood how to manipulate the system.

Independence brought its own problems for Latvia, not least its woeful economic situation. The country desperately needed foreign investment for machinery to modernise its industry and it was here again that the Germans were able to exert a disproportionate degree of influence. Berlin saw not only a way to prop up its German allies in the country but also realised that Latvia, as a sphere of influence, would be a means of opening trade with Soviet Russia, a market that was coveted by all the Western powers. German Trade Minister Crohn-Wolfgang put it succinctly when he said in January 1921, 'Latvia is perhaps the most important area on the edge of Russia if not the most important transit area for future trade with Russia.'[5]

Berlin understood that its influence in Latvia was through the German community there but since independence a distinction had been created between Reich Germans and Baltic Germans. Many Germans had opted to become citizens of the new Latvian state and could no longer look to Berlin to represent their interests but as a group they were encouraged to support policies adopted by the Reich Germans in the country who had retained their German nationality. For Berlin, this combined German influence formed part of a greater strategy of the *Bund der Auslandsdeutschen* (Union of Germans Abroad), which was to become an important factor in the rapid economic recovery and commensurate resurgent political prestige of Germany.

Through links with foreign German communities, especially in eastern European, Berlin hoped to utilise the greater business acumen and relatively better education of these minorities to promote trade policies favourable to Germany. The *Bund der Auslandsdeutschen* was most concerned in the Baltics to encourage all those Germans who had fled during the war to return and resume their economic activity by cooperating loyally with the state they were returning to. Their economic importance to the new independent states would allow them to orientate trade towards Germany, which would benefit not only the state and German industry but would create political affinities also.

Latvia had formally achieved its independence from Russia on 11 August 1920. Article 2 of the formal peace treaty stated that Soviet Russia 'unreservedly recognises the independence and sovereignty of the Latvian State and voluntarily and forever renounces all sovereign rights ... to Latvian people and territory.' This agreement was reinforced on 5 February 1932 by the signing of a non-aggression treaty based on the 20 August treaty which 'unalterably and for all time [formed] the firm basis' of the relationship of the two states. The country was admitted to the League of Nations on 22 September 1921. It had already agreed a trade deal with Germany a month earlier, which restored peaceful relations, but a formal commercial treaty was delayed until December 1926 while Latvia pursued a claim for war damage and Germany sought compensation for infrastructure it had installed during its wartime occupation.

A new *satversme* (Latvian constitution) was approved by the Constituent Assembly on 15 February 1922, providing for the democratic election of a 100-seat *Saeima* (parliament) and a president, Jan Chakste, who took office on 14 November. German capital began to flow into the country in 1923 with investment across the whole economy in textiles, chemicals, metallurgy, timber and paper, but especially the banks. By this time, every German firm that had an interest in the Soviet market had a branch or subsidiary in Latvia.[6] The Weimar Republic was once more being eased back into the ranks of 'respectable' nations and this also allowed the Baltic states to be more accepting of German trade and influence to the extent that in 1925, the President of the Finance Commission of the Latvian *Saeima* was a German, J. Hahn. By and large, the Germans had pursued their own political agenda and remained aloof from local pollical squabbles. By 1928, numerous Latvian government commissions had German representatives on them.

The German trade agreement worked well up until 1932 when Germany imposed tariffs on the main Latvian export, butter. This became critical after the Nazis came to power and banned the import of Latvian butter completely in protest at an early move by Jewish businesses in Latvia who had boycotted German goods in protest at the Nazis introduction of anti-Semitic legislation. The dust soon settled, and trade resumed after only a few days but in the meantime, Britain had stepped up to become Latvia's main trading partner.

The Latvian Communist Party had been banned. Many of its leaders fled to Moscow where, with Soviet support, they worked ceaselessly to prepare for their return, but those who stayed behind organised an underground network of activists briefly seeing the light of day in the guise of the Workers' and Peasants' Party. Instead of allowing them to campaign freely and expose the paucity of their popular following, the authorities made the mistake of closing it down in 1933 and arresting its leaders thus giving it victim status and allowing it to claim injustice.

Kārlis Ulmanis, who had studied agriculture at the University of Nebraska, had dominated Latvian politics for a decade or more as leader of the Agrarian Party supported by the Aizsargi (which translates to guards) anti-Bolshevik vigilantes, he was elected prime minister on 16 March 1934. The Aizsargi, along with the ultra-nationalistic Pērkonkrusts played a prominent role in Latvia's transition from democracy to authoritarian dictatorship but there are debates over the full extent of that influence.

The Aizsargi had been set up in 1919 with local self-defence volunteers but grew into a nationwide paramilitary force with multiple roles, including policing, in every Latvian township. They were essentially apolitical but their role as adjuncts to the military and their links to the landed classes gave them a distinct right-wing character. Ulmanis, along with Minister for War Jānis Balodis, the Rīga Garrison Commander Krišjānis Berķis and Aizsargi leader, Alfreds Berzins staged a coup d'état on 15 May 1934 by dissolving parliament, disbanding political parties, and declaring a state of emergency all without any semblance of constitutional authority. A quarter of all *Saeima* deputies were arrested. Valdis Lūmans claims that it was the Aizsargi who provided the 'muscle' for the coup.[7] This is disputed, however, by Pēters Vecrumba who says that it was the army and the police who were behind Ulmanis and his subsequent assertion of Aizsargi complicity was little more than a ploy to suggest that his action had popular support.[8] Vecrumba's assertion may well be supported by the fact that twenty-eight Pērkonkrust activists were rounded up at the same time.

Ulmanis asserted that the coup had been necessary to counter political instability in the country caused by factionalism within the democratic system but Brūno Kalniņš a Social Democrat politician in the *Saeima* saw the motivation for Ulmanis' action as having stemmed from his visit to Germany a year previously.[9] Amongst the political parties that had been outlawed previously was the fascist group known originally as Ugunskrusts (Fire Cross), which had been set up in 1932 by Gustavs Celmiņš and banned one year later by the government. It re-emerged, however, via a virtually moribund group called *Tēvijas sargi* (Guards of the Fatherland), as the ultra-nationalist, anti-German, anti-Slavic and anti-Semitic *Pērkonkrusts* (Thunder Cross) party whose slogan, predictably, was 'Latvia for Latvians.' Surprisingly one of its main targets were the Baltic Germans and not the Jews.

Ulmanis banned the *Pērkonkrusts* and the *Tēvijas sargi* and put Celmiņš on trial after which he was given a three years' prison sentence before being banished from Latvia to Finland. Troops occupied all the major government locations in Tallinn, banned the sale of alcohol and leaders of the extreme right parties were arrested on charges of conspiracy against the state. Having established links with fascist groups all across Europe, in Helsinki Celmiņš proceeded to set up a 'foreign liaison office' of *Pērkonkrusts* but rejected an offer of financial assistance from the German National Socialists in order to preserve independence of action. It is still disputed whether Celmiņš was got out of the way for being a potential rival to Ulmanis or sentenced for being a real fascist threat to the country which, at the time, had a reputation of being sympathetic to Jews fleeing from Germany. Ulmanis justified his action by claiming that the previous administration had been moving towards a state of fascism similar to that in Germany.

As in Estonia, it was it was not right or left extremists or the army that destroyed democracy, but the democratically elected leaders themselves. One consequence of the coup was the closing down of some Jewish newspapers and the arrest of leading Jews in the community, despite Ulmanis declaring that anti-Semitism would not be tolerated. It was not clear if the fascists had been supressed or if they had assumed power.

Another was the suppression of the press by the government. It had been brought in to ensure absolute neutrality and avoid provoking either the Nazis or the Soviets but had the uncomfortable effect of keeping the Latvian people ignorant of international developments and the nature of the two neighbouring totalitarian systems that they would shortly have to deal with.

Lithuania

Of the many complicated boundary disputes arising from the collapse of the three east European empires in 1918, two were of special relevance to Lithuania, plus Vilnius and Memel. Both dogged Lithuania's relations with its three powerful neighbours; Germany, Poland and the Soviet Union and its failure to resolve the two issues left the country very much as a pawn in the power politics of eastern Europe. Referring to what became known as Klaipėda (Memelland), Article 99 of the Treaty of Versailles stated,

> Germany renounces in favour of the Principal Allied and Associated Powers all rights and title over the territories included between the Baltic, the north-eastern frontier of East Prussia as defined in Article 28 of Part II (Boundaries of Germany) of the present Treaty and the former frontier between Germany and Russia. Germany undertakes to accept the settlement made by the Principal Allied and Associated Powers in regard to these territories, particularly in so far as concerns the nationality of the inhabitants.

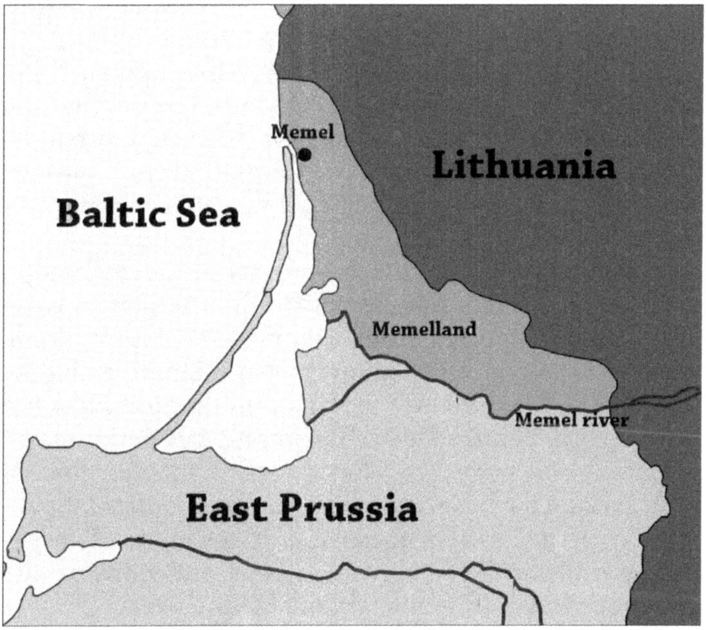

Memelland, 1923–39

For a few years, nobody knew what to do about the administration of Klaipėda that was left to various temporary agencies of the Allied powers. The large German population wanted to reunite with East Prussia, an ambition that Berlin supported, or get the same free status as Danzig, an option favoured by Poland. A small number of Lithuanians naturally wanted union with Lithuania which, in turn, was keen to get control of the port of Memel. This stand-off was interrupted in January 1923 when Colonel Polowinski led a small Lithuanian force to invade Klaipėda and took over the government representing the revolt as a genuine uprising of the local population against German oppression. The League of Nations, unwilling to give much time to the issue, gave its blessing to Lithuanian control of Memel within an autonomous Klaipėda under a Chamber of Representatives. Lithuania's occupation of Klaipėda had the effect of weakening its economy resulting in significant unemployment. Local hostility towards the Lithuanian government increased especially amongst the German nationalists.

In September 1930, Germany brought the issue up at the League of Nations claiming that Lithuania had repeatedly violated the terms of the Memel agreement. Wishing to avoid the intervention of the League, Lithuania compromised by accepting Otto Böttcher onto the directorate, but he was soon removed by the Klaipėda governor for holding secret talks in Berlin. Böttcher had been active in the *Sozialistische Volksgemeinschaft des Memelgebiets* (Socialist People's Community of the Memel Region, SOVOG) and had become involved in political agitation on behalf of reunification of the region with Germany. Against international law German money was coming into the region paying the wages of civil servants and teachers who supported unification with Germany.

The Germans persisted with more claims of judicial malpractice the following year. At this stage, Adolph Hitler was more concerned with consolidating his power within Germany and desisted from overt interference in other countries although his ultimate ambitions had been clearly set out in *Mein Kampf*. Hitler and Rudolf Hess formally denied any involvement in the Memel unrest, but Berlin maintained a close interest in events there and quietly approved the Socialist Peoples' Association whose approach was less confrontational than that of the Union of Christian Socialist Workers of the Memel Region (CSA).[10] It was in the best interests of Nazi ambitions to keep the Klaipėda controversy simmering without boiling over.

Lithuania feared that Nazi machinations in Klaipėda were an excuse to interfere in Lithuanian politics in an increasingly disruptive manner and so looked to its Baltic neighbours and the Soviet Union for help. The recent German-Polish Non-Aggression Pact was seen as a direct threat with the possibility of a secret deal whereby Poland would be given a free hand to expand its borders east in exchange for returning the Danzig Corridor to Germany. The Soviets responded by offering Lithuania an extension of the 1932 Non-Aggression Treaty, but the other Baltic nations were reluctant to discuss collective security given Lithuania's long-running disputes with Germany and Poland that could erupt into conflict at any moment.

The extent to which Germany was involved in the struggle to win over the hearts and minds of the Lithuanian population has been hotly debated. The most recent evidence has come from Soviet archives of trials held in Germany between 1934 and 1945 to prosecute more than 100 Lithuanian agents charged with anti-German activities. These documents shed light on German involvement over a decade since the 1930 elections when the Memel Germans were given 10,000 Reichsmarks via the *Deutsche Stiftung* (German foundation) to help with electioneering. A letter confirming this was intercepted by the Lithuanians and for a time forced the Germans to step back from their involvement in Memel politics.

Lithuania responded by accusing the German national socialists of helping the far-right CSA to foment revolution. The Lithuanian Security Police (LSP) had successfully infiltrated the CSA and SOVOG. The leaders Pastor Theodor von Sass and Dr Klaus Neumann were arrested and put on trial in a military court for subversion. It was not the first mass indictment of Nazis but it was the first public one. This time, German forces were mobilised along the border and Berlin sent many protest notes. Evidence shows that SOVOG at least had been actively plotting a coup which for some unknown reason was abandoned.[11] On 13 August 1934, both political parties were banned. When heavy sentences were handed down to the CSA accused, Germany lodged strong protests and demonstrations were held in German cities.

Fearing Nazi infiltration of its own national Socialist movements, Lithuania clamped down on German activists and imposed martial law in Klaipėda. More than 500 German officials; judges, police, and teachers, were dismissed from their posts and the use of the German language in schools was banned in some areas. Germany responded by instituting an import ban of Lithuanian butter and pork. When Germany protested, the League of Nations suggested that they re-join and discuss the matter at the council, but Hitler had no intention of re-joining over such a relatively minor issue. He would deal with it in his own way. Lithuania simply brushed off accusations of oppressing their German population.

Eventually the League of Nations was forced to intervene and reprimand Lithuania threatening action if they did not desist taking illegal measures in Klaipėda. Lithuania backed down and dismissed some of its Klaipėda administrators instructing others to be more conciliatory in their dealings with the German community. This proved futile since the German population objected to the new directorate and refused to talk to them. Hitler ramped up his rhetoric in the Reichstag and kept up the pressure by one niggling complaint after another that denied Lithuanian politics any chance to stabilise. Leading Nazis went public with warnings about dire consequences if Lithuania did not desist what they called provocative policies.

Ever since 1923, it had been the policy of Germany to maintain a sense of Germanness within the Klaipėda region by illegal subsidies to farmers as well as financing the building of schools and pro-German newspapers. Radio sets that had been modified so they could not pick up Lithuanian broadcasts were provided by the German *Kulturbund* (cultural assosiation) ensuring that the listeners were subjected to a steady stream of pro-German propaganda, especially during elections.[12]

The head of the Polish State Józef Piłsudski had been born in Lithuania and harboured ambitions to see that country and Poland allied in a federal relationship in which Vilnius would be recognised as its capital. Piłsudski's vision, however, was not shared by the majority of Poles who simply wanted to see Vilnius annexed. The Lithuanians were happy to see Polish influence remain in Vilnius but only as one part of a multi-ethnic community in a city which was 'the capital of ethnographic Lithuania.'[13]

The Poles, however, were embroiled in a war with the Soviet Union who were threatening to take Vilnius by force. Both sides tried to tempt Lithuania to support them by giving assurances about Vilnius. The Bolsheviks occupied Vilnius, which gave the Lithuanians hope that they would be allowed to take control of the capital, but very soon the Poles counterattacked and drove the Soviets out, and refused to recognise Lithuanian borders. Piłsudski ordered Polish troops to masquerade as rebel forces and occupy Vilnius, which gave him the excuse to send in 'legitimate' Polish forces to defend the city.

By January 1922, the Poles had begun ejecting Lithuanian intellectual activists s from Vilnius and in April, a swathe of 'Middle Lithuania', which included Vilnius, was annexed into the Polish state. Naturally, Lithuania refused to accept these new borders and the issue remained a prime concern of the state that persisted over the coming decade in looking for ways to put the issue back on the international political agenda. Both Soviet imperialism and German revisionism made use of the conflict over Vilnius as a factor, which hampering efforts of the Baltic states and Poland to create an effective system of collective security.

Soviet diplomats eagerly forged ties with Baltic politicians and business leaders while conducting secret talks with the Poles to agree a mutual border and partition the Baltics into separate Soviet and Polish spheres of influence. When the Poles walked away from talks, the Soviets turned to Germany to forge political ties and relegated Poland to a hostile state, taking the Lithuanian's side over Vilnius. Then the Soviets tried to pre-empt any attempt to form a Baltic alliance by negotiating treaties with each in turn. This would have the added bonus of reducing British influence in the region. Lithuania was warned that the Soviets were merely manoeuvring to take control of Lithuania. Eventually the Soviets ran out of ideas and by the early 1930s seemed to have reached a stalemate. They expected a Lithuanian-Polish alliance, which they thought, was 'something pre-determined by the laws of history.'[14] When they eventually persuaded Latvia and Estonia to sign treaties, primarily by scaremongering over Polish intentions, the Soviets found new diplomatic ways to proceed.

They sent arch negotiator, Karl Radek to Warsaw to offer the Poles a deal in the Baltics that included supporting Polish claims to Vilnius. This was intended to prevent Poland turning to Germany but Germany, now under the Nazis, was already gaining influence in Latvia and Estonia, which unnerved the Poles. The power balance was shifting away from Poland but not yet decisively in favour of Germany. Moscow saw a chance to ingratiate itself with the Balts and their efforts resulted in a treaty of conciliation and cooperation between Latvia, Estonia and Lithuania signed in Geneva on 12 September 1934 that openly encouraged military cooperation and was seen as a steppingstone towards a Soviet-Baltic treaty.

Fearing that this was drawing them too closely into the Soviet camp, the Baltic states now tried to develop closer ties with Germany, but the Soviets raised the stakes by offering unprecedented military aid to them in 1936. The Soviet priority was now to ensure that the Baltic states remained neutral in any future war with Germany. While this may well have been the policy of the diplomats, the Soviet military made it abundantly clear to all that, in the event of war, Baltic sovereignty would not be a factor in their calculations and would not prevent Soviet boots marching across Baltic soil. The reign of state terror and executions that was sweeping through the whole Soviet leadership, including diplomats who had been dealing with the Baltics for the previous fifteen years, meant that Soviet delegates at talks held on one day might become an entirely new team on the following day. Any agreement not yet signed might be repudiated in a moment and it was clear that the Soviets could not be relied to maintain a consistent approach to negotiations.

In early 1938, the earth shook in Germany when Minister of War Werner von Blomberg and Wehrmacht Commander-in-Chief Werner von Fritsch, were unceremoniously cast out and Hitler placed himself at the head of the armed forces in another inexorable step towards total dictatorship. At the same time the cautious and moderate Foreign Minister Konstantin von Neurath was replaced by the sycophantic hard-line Joachim von Ribbentrop. Then on 13 March, German forces entered Austria and annexed the country into the Reich in the Anschluss. The whole of eastern Europe felt the aftershocks of this event and countries braced themselves to see what Hitler's next move would be.

Poland looked to establish a middle-European bloc as a defensive measure against further German aggression and saw the occupation of Lithuania as a first step. The Poles delivered an ultimatum to Lithuania on 17 March demanding the restoration of full diplomatic relations and the relinquishing of any Lithuanian claims to Vilnius. The Baltic states turned to Britain and France who saw no reason to get involved. Berlin and Moscow enraged the Lithuanians by advising them to comply. They did so within hours. For the Soviets, the Baltics had now become pawns in negotiations with the Western powers. Soviet diplomatic notes were handed to Estonian and Latvian officials advising them not to accept any further German influence in their countries, which would be against the terms of their agreements. Hitler responded a day later by threatening to occupy Memel if the Poles tried to take Lithuania by force.

German-Lithuanian relations were riven by riots as elections loomed in Memel. Lithuania felt pressure to be conciliatory and released political prisoners including Neumann who immediately resumed his pro-Nazi activities in Memel. Hitler demanded that the state of martial law be lifted. Lithuania tried to get agreement for a non-aggression pact with Germany, but von Ribbentrop would not hear of it. They eventually had to agree to lifting martial law in October, just weeks before the elections. Local Nazis now took to the streets in huge torchlit parades with Nazi flags. German troops massed on the East Prussian border, but it was just political pressure. Germany, which relied on Lithuanian butter, meat and grain, could not afford to alienate Lithuania completely at this stage and was hoping to get the leverage it needed in Klaipėda, if not legitimately at least by peaceful means. When the elections took place on 11 December the Lithuanian vote was split between four parties, but the Memel Germans had united behind the United Memel German Party and consequently won twenty-five of the twenty-nine seats in the *Landtag* (parliament).

Neumann made rapid progress with moves to have Klaipėda Nazified and incorporated into the Reich. Lithuania was resigned to losing Memel. They withdrew their security forces, recognised the German language to be the official one and allowed German propaganda in schools. Large numbers of the Jewish community emigrated from Klaipėda. Neumann made ever louder demands and then, inevitably, von Ribbentrop demanded, under threat of invasion, that Klaipėda be returned to Germany. Lithuania turned to Britain and Poland both of whom ignored them. They did not bother to ask the Soviets for help, Soviet boots on Lithuanian soil was the last thing they wanted.

On 23 March, Minister of Foreign Affairs of Lithuania Juozas Urbšys and von Ribbentrop signed a treaty stating that Lithuania was voluntarily transferring the Klaipėda Region to Germany. Immediately work began transforming Memel into a fortified naval base which certainly made the Soviets sit up and take notice. Up to this point they had maintained a vigorous anti-nazi and anti-capitalist rhetoric without ever exerting any effort for containing the aggressive expansion of the German Reich.

Fearing isolation and Soviet aggression, Latvia and Estonia signed a non-aggression pact with Germany on 7 June 1939 which put Moscow on the spot. To move in and occupy the Baltic states pre-emptively or come to terms with Berlin. On 23 August, the world had its answer to that when German Minister of Foreign Affairs Joachim von Ribbentrop and Soviet Foreign Minister Vyacheslan Molotov put their signatures to the Nazi-Soviet Treaty of Non-Aggression (Molotov-Ribbentrop Pact). Five days later Molotov and the German ambassador to Moscow, Friedrich-Werner Graf von der Schulenburg, signed a secret supplementary protocol, which put Lithuania in the German sphere of influence and Finland, Estonia, Latvia, Lithuania, Bessarabia and Northern Bukovina in the Soviet one. This was clearly in violation of Article 10 of the Covenant of the League of Nations and Article 1 of the Kellogg-Briand Pact. Both countries agreed to 'recognise Lithuania's interests in the Vilnius Region'. The alacrity with which Germany agreed to Soviet demands over the Baltics shows just how eager Hitler was to secure a deal with Stalin.

There has been much analysis of why the Soviets agreed a treaty with the Nazis in the first place. Geoffrey Roberts denies any overt aggressive intent by the Soviets. The treaty, he said, was a 'dramatic, last-minute improvisation' in response to British and French efforts to provoke a Soviet-German war.[15] Roberts also claims that when the Soviets invaded Poland in September 1939, they were merely taking advantage of the German attack to redress age-old territorial grievances and later when they occupied the Baltic states in 1940 they were claiming territory ahead of the expected peace talks after the fall of France and aimed to Sovietise the Baltics from within through the local communist parties. This interpretation, however, flies in face of Stalin's remark in September 1939 to the Latvian foreign minister that 'There are no communists outside Russia [only] Trotskyists. If they give you any trouble, shoot them.'[16]

The Soviets had long expected any invasion of the Soviet Union to come through Estonia and Latvia or even as far north as Finland. In the early days of the revolution it was thought that Polish forces would spearhead such a move with naval support coming from Britain and France but after 1935 it was clear that Germany was the real threat and an overland assault became the most likely scenario. This much wider front convinced the Soviets that neutrality of the Baltic states could not be respected in the event of war. The Soviet military theorist Mikhail Tukhachevsky proposed that any move against the Soviet Union by Germany should be met with immediate Soviet occupation of the Baltics. Stalin took that one step further and contemplated occupation before a German attack to close off invasion routes in the north. The Molotov-Ribbentrop Pact took him one step closer to realising this ambition.

Berlin now put secret pressure on Lithuania to make aggressive moves towards Poland by massing Lithuanian troops on the Polish border whilst simultaneously publicly urging them to remain neutral in the event of any future conflict 'between Germany and any other nation.' Again, Berlin dangled the prospect of reclaiming Vilnius in front of the Lithuanians but Kaunas bluntly refused to be bullied or blackmailed and re-stated its desire for neutrality. There would be no help from the Soviets since the Molotov-Ribbentrop Pact of 23 August had effectively secured German guarantees of Soviet neutrality and set the scene for the German invasion of Poland. By implementing the Molotov-Ribbentrop Pact, the Soviet Union then, by use of military force, coerced the signing of the Soviet-Lithuanian Mutual Assistance Treaty with Estonia on 24 September and with Latvia on 5 October.

Lithuania had emerged from the First World War and its subsequent wars of independence as a liberal democracy in which the legislative held considerable power and minorities were granted rights to an extent which was viewed as exemplary by contemporaries. In a very short time, however, this liberal democracy was replaced by an authoritarian regime.

During these inter-war years, Lithuania had seen the emergence of two fascist organisations. The first Geležinis Vilkas, led by Voldemaras who had been elected as head of state on the day the First World War armistice was signed. He assumed for himself the two cabinet positions of Ministry of Foreign Affairs and Ministry of Defence. When he left the country on 21 December 1918 in the face of Soviet aggression, he had been replaced as prime minister by Mykolas Sleževičius. Voldemaras was elected to the *Saeima* again, however, in 1926 when he called for dictatorial government like the Italian fascist model. In that same year he and Antanas Smetona staged a successful military coup d'état against a newly elected left-wing government which saw Voldemaras again installed as prime minister. His new government was not exactly fascist but more conservative and nationalistic in character and one in which the pluralistic structure of government was preserved.

In January 1928, Voldemaras signed a border treaty with Germany, in which Germany agreed to Lithuanian control of Klaipėda. The 1922 constitution was abandoned and a new one was imposed on the country. At this time, what was registered as a youth sporting organisation calling itself *Genzinis Vilkas* (Iron Wolf) was formed by right-wing army officers and students and it was soon clear that it would be used by the prime minister as a clandestine tool of repression of his opponents. Its secretive character meant that Voldemaras could not bring it onto the streets in for mass demonstrations that fascist movements worldwide are so fond of.

After an unsuccessful assassination attempt against him, Voldemaras increasingly shunned contact with cabinet colleagues and spent more time developing *Genzinis Vilkas* as his power base. Knowing Voldemaras as he did, Smetona feared the worst and decided it was time to get rid of him. On 29 September 1929, while Voldemaras was out of the country, Smetona removed him from office. *Genzinis Vilkas* continued as an underground organisation and even attempted a futile coup against the Smetona government in 1934. Voldemaras had flown into the country in anticipation of taking power again but instead he was given a long prison sentence that was amnestied in 1938 when he was exiled to France.

The inter-war period had been one of experimentation with democracy, but democracy cannot be easily achieved under such conditions as prevailed at the time. Almost inevitably the political system in all three Baltic countries devolved into dictatorships which curtailed democratic freedoms but, at least, brough a measure of political and economic stability which, after a long period of political turmoil and economic hardship was welcomed by the vast majority of the populations. There followed a period of relative affluence and cultural awakening in all three Baltic states which, for the first time in centuries were free from foreign rule.

Chapter 4

THE FIRST SOVIET OCCUPATION, 1940–41

When the Bolsheviks took power in Russia in 1917, they refused to accept that they were bound by the 1907 Hague Regulations which they described as a 'bourgeois' legal instrument. Indeed, both the Soviets and the Nazis would egregiously ignore its provisions all through the 1930s and 1940s. Soviet communist doctrine meant that they would refuse to recognise the existing capitalist institutions of occupied states or territory and instead would set about changing them into 'dictatorships of the proletariat' which was a completely new type of state. Neither did they accept that the Baltic states as they existed in 1940 were the ones, they had conducted peace treaties with in 1920 and anyone who had participated in what they called the illegal Baltic governments between 1917 and 1940 were considered to be 'unreliable'.

A Soviet dictatorship could only be created after destruction of the bourgeois state machine, of the bourgeois army, of the bourgeois bureaucratic apparatus, and of the bourgeois police. The NKVD (*Naródnyy komissariát vnútrennikh del*, Soviet People's Commissariat of Internal Affairs) order No. 001223 of 11 October 1939 demanded the preparation of 'mass dissolution of the anti-Soviet and anti-social elements in the Baltic states.'[1] The Lithuanian Constitutional Court in 2014 suggested the Soviet repressions that attempted to 'exterminate the basis of the political nation of Lithuania' directed at the 'most active political and social groups' had been tantamount to genocide. Instead of respecting the sovereignty of occupied territories following the conclusion of the Nazi-Soviet Non-Aggression Pact and the invasion of eastern Poland, Sovietisation and complete control over the occupied territories were the clear objectives.

Apart from native-born Baltic Germans there was a sizeable Baltic-Russian population who had only recently found themselves inside the borders of the new states after independence. Estonia included Jamburg, Pechera, Isborsk and Ivangrod, four regions with strong Russian heritage, while Latvia found itself master of three Soviet-speaking territories, Pytalovo, Pskov and Vitebsk. The transfer of the Pytalovo rail junction was of particularly importance to Latvia in as much as it was vital to the economic integrity of the new state. All seven regions retained full cultural autonomy and to all intents and purposes were entirely Russian in character except that they were now controlled from Rīga and not Moscow. Soviet sponsored political parties from these regions did have representation in the Latvian parliament, however, and Russian schools along with Russian theatre ensured that Russian culture was preserved to the extent that Russian was an official language of the country alongside German and Latvian.

After the Germans launched their invasion of Poland on 1 September 1939 and the Soviets grabbed their share three weeks later, both German and Soviet governments worked towards the total destruction of the Polish state by eliminating all vestiges of statehood including all its leading politicians and intellectuals. The Soviets, however, proved to be much more accomplished at suppressing resistance. The NKVD employed far more sophisticated methods than the German Gestapo, often turning resistance groups to work for the Soviet side without its members realising what was happening. In this way they hoped to uncover links between Polish underground movements and the Polish government-in-exile and to its British and French allies. In Poland, also, the Soviets had placed Jews in positions of apparent authority without actually giving them any power at all which exposed them to vilification within the occupied population. Catastrophically for them, these Jews would lack the resources or opportunity to flee when the Germans attacked the Soviet Union in June 1941.

During the first months of 1940, many thousands of Jews fled Soviet-occupied Poland to Lithuania which, despite being governed by a right-wing dictatorship under Smetona, did not exhibit overt anti-Semitic characteristics. In comparison to other east European states, Lithuania was seen as a refuge from persecution. This was especially so in the city of Vilnius which had, with German consent, once again come under Lithuanian control in October 1939. Latvia was similarly governed by a right-wing authoritarian, but not noticeably anti-Semitic, regime. Jewish political parties thrived there, and the country also became a refuge for many German Jews fleeing persecution in their homeland.

Even before becoming part of the Soviet Union, inhabitants of the Baltic states began to experience what life would become under Stalinism. After June 1940, local communist parties were given power with the formidable backing of Moscow and the Red Army to rapidly bring the formerly independent states in line with the Soviet model and suppress potentially dissident elements. Large businesses, and industries were taken over by the state. Oppression of the population during the first Soviet occupation was most apparent in the Bolshevik reliance on deportations, which began in June 1940 with the imprisonment of thousands of highly placed military and public officials on trumped-up anti-Soviet or anti-communist charges.

At the start of 1939, the NKVD officers were predominantly Soviets with Ukrainians contributing 17 per cent of the total. Jews having previously contributed some 40 per cent were now down to no more than a tenth of that.[2] The NKVD were experienced in mass killing and deportations in ways that the Germans had not even dreamed of yet. They had shot twice as many Poles inside the Soviet Union while preparing for war than the Reinhard Heydrich's *Einsatzgruppen* (murder squads) shot when German forces invaded Poland in 1939. That was quite a feat given that, by the end of 1939, the seven *Einsatzgruppen* had murdered some 50,000 Poles, including 7,000 Jews and infuriated the German High Command of the regular Wehrmacht with the brutality of their actions.

The Soviet system of deportations started with the Politburo who approved the quotas and then the NKVD worked out the details for each area which were handed down to the district level. Local administrators drew up lists of 'enemies of the people' which were handed over to NKVD who carried out the roundups. Even at this stage, they had discretion to add to their lists any other victims allowing them to overfill their quotas and claim 'revolutionary vigilance.' Having rounded up entire families and robbed them of all but the few possessions they were allowed to take with them, the NKVD auxiliary militias would hand them over to the NKVD railway police. They would now count them and compare their tally against the lists supplied by the local secret police authorities. The railway troops were issued with enough food for twenty-five people per rail car but often crammed twice that number in which allowed them to steal half of the rations for their own consumption or for sale on the black market.

This inevitably resulted in hunger for the deportees. Then at the end of the trip to the eastern and northern parts of the Soviet Union, the railroad NKVD would surrender the victims to local NKVD officers who would again count them and either escort them to their place of resettlement or often just dump them in the middle of nowhere and leave them to fend for themselves. Overcrowding of the cars was actually strictly against NKVD Ivan Serov's orders so the manipulation of numbers recorded for each transport resulting from the overcrowding of cars means that any surviving documents cannot be relied upon to give an accurate figure of how many deportees were on each one.[3]

When the Germans launched their much-anticipated attack against France and the Low Countries on 10 May 1940, Stalin prepared to take advantage of Hitler's attention being momentarily focused elsewhere. By early June the French were in full retreat and the British were licking their wounds after Dunkirk. It was an opportune moment for the Soviets to tighten their grip on the Baltics. Ultimatums were prepared. Lithuania, Estonia and Latvia would be accused of secretly plotting to form a military alliance against the Soviet Union. There is no evidence to suggest that this was ever the case.

The Soviet annexation of the Baltic states in 1940 lacked any grounds in international law, and a significant segment of the international community refused to grant formal approval. In each of the three Baltic states occupied, the Soviets installed three plenipotentiaries. The first was political whose responsibility was to bring about complete Sovietisation of the political and economic affairs. Then there was military and the third was security which in effect prepared for purges and deportations. In all three Baltic republics Moscow's representatives operated under the authority of the Politburo, an institution of the Communist Party, and not the Soviet government. Special agents were installed to create administrations based on the Soviet pattern, Andrei Vyshinsky in Latvia, Andrei Zhdanov in Estonia, and Vladimir Dekanozov in Lithuania.

Alfred Senn says that they acted rather more cautiously than the Soviets had done in Poland and instituted a slower, more careful, more systematic transition to socialism.[4] In his book *Intermarium; The Land Between the Black and Baltic Seas*, Marek Jan Chodakiewicz, however, thinks that Stalin subjected his captive peoples to a particularly harsh, crash course in social engineering that had taken twenty years to implement in the Soviet Union.[5]

They confiscated all state property, community and private possessions of all ethnic groups and all private property. The countryside was increasingly collectivized with the authorities demanding food quota from the villages. Many of the industrial plants, cargo warehouses, and department stores were looted, and their contents shipped to the Soviet Union. They systematically concentrated political power in their own hands by undermining established institutions and creating new ones paying particular attention to restructuring the educational system to control the political education of the young. Many teachers, mostly Poles, were removed, arrested, or even executed. Within weeks, new parliaments were created in in all three republics with members to be elected according to strict Soviet practice of single party participation.

Lithuania

Immediately after Germany had invaded Poland, Berlin had urged the Lithuanians to march on and occupy Vilnius and there were many in Lithuania who would have gladly done that, but the Lithuanian government insisted that they remain neutral and not get involved in the fighting war. Then on 16 September all German efforts to persuade the Lithuanians to take Vilnius stopped abruptly and the next day it was clear why. On that day the Red Army invaded Poland from the east and by 23 September had 'liberated' Vilnius declaring that it would be incorporated into a new state of Western Belarus, and it might even become the capital in place of Minsk. That was pure propaganda. The Soviets never had any intention of doing so. It was merely a ploy to scare the Lithuanians and force them to be compliant with Soviet occupation.

Even in retrospect, Soviet objectives in summer 1939 are difficult to ascertain. The Soviet leader Joseph Stalin was a pragmatic *Realpolitiker* who based his decisions more on an assessment of current circumstances rather than doctrinal imperatives. He was very much concerned by the possibility, or even inevitability, of a German attack against the Soviet Union but various theories have been presented to evaluate exactly how he planned to counter it. In a sense, Moscow's actions, ever since 1917, can be seen as a need for a *cordon sanitaire* against the west and that required a delicate balance between gaining influence in the Baltics and generating hostility through overbearance. The transfer of Vilnius to the Lithuanians in 1939 might be seen in this context since Stalin's predecessor Lenin had said almost two decades previously, 'We consider this not as a renunciation of the Sovietization of Lithuania, but as a delay and as a variant of the form of its Sovietization'.[6]

On 28 September 1939, the German-Soviet Boundary and Friendship Treaty was signed in Moscow which adjusted the terms of the 28 August Treaty. Under this new agreement those parts of Lithuania that had been grabbed by Germany were transferred to the Soviet sphere of influence after they agreed a payment of $7.5 million (gold). Then Soviet troops moved into Vilnius, still theoretically under Polish authority but, in reality, neither Germany nor the Soviet Union any longer viewed Poland as a viable state.

The Kaunas government now came under extreme pressure from the Soviets. Still theoretically neutral, they were given the option of getting Vilnius back in return for allowing the Soviets to establish five military bases in Lithuania, a Soviet military presence of 18,000 soldiers and an airbase in Ponary just outside Vilnius. Clearly, agreement to such terms would be a precursor to full occupation, but Kaunas did not have the means to resist and had little choice but to sign the Soviet-Lithuanian Mutual Assistance Treaty on 10 October.

The Soviet claws were sharpened and extended and now began to curl in on their prey. Under order No. 043 of 26 September 1939, the Leningrad military district had been instructed to start building up troops on the Estonian-Latvian border. On 13 August, the Novgorod Army Operational Group had been established in the Leningrad military district and became the 8th Army with 100,000 troops and an additional corps. This allowed for a total of 135,000 troops to be deployed at the Estonian border. Over 169,000 troops from the 7th Army stationed in the Kalinin military district were placed under the command of the Leningrad military district and deployed at the Latvian border. Their task was to occupy Tallinn and Tartu and Rīga. The Soviet navy prevented the Estonian fleet from retreating to Finland or Sweden. The Soviet 3rd Army, with 169,000 men and 1,078 tanks, was mobilised on the Lithuanian border.

Stalin made clear Soviet strategy when he said, 'let's create the conditions for the Baltic states themselves to fall into our lap.' By implementing the Molotov-Ribbentrop Pact, the Soviet Union had earlier, by the threat of military force, coerced the signing of the Soviet-Lithuanian Mutual Assistance Treaty with Estonia on 24 September and later with Latvia on 5 October giving them the right to establish Soviet bases there also. During talks, Molotov had issued clear, unambiguous threats by telling Baltic ambassadors, 'I beg you not to compel the Soviet Government to use other, more radical methods of safeguarding its security.'[7] By the time the treaties were ratified, the Soviets had 66,946 men, 1,065 tanks, 1,630 cannons, and 526 aircraft on Baltic soil.[8]

At the same time, Molotov tried to allay international fears of the Soviet action by saying on 31 October before the Supreme Soviet of the Union of Socialist Republics for the world to hear that

> All these treaties of mutual assistance strictly stipulate the inviolability of the sovereignty of the signatory states and the principle of non-interference in the affairs of others ... we declare that all the nonsensical talk about Sovietization of the Baltic countries is only in the interest of our common enemies and of all anti-Soviet provocateurs.[9]

This was clearly a lie given the secret protocol of 23 August.

With Soviet approval Lithuanian troops marched into Vilnius and Kaunas on 29 October 1939 to peacefully replace Soviet forces and celebrated the recovery of 'what belonged to [them] by the national, cultural, historical and economic right.'[10] The Polish government in exile fiercely objected to what it called the illegal occupation of Vilnius region in which Lithuanians were a clear minority. It was no easy matter for the Lithuanians since the large Polish population in the city, as well as Polish troops still at large in the region, meant the ever-present threat of revolt against the occupation.

The Poles encouraged the organisation of secret, underground political organisations in Lithuania but urged them to stay their hand for the moment. Orders were to cooperate and maintain good relations with the Lithuanian authorities, but Poland had no intention of giving up on Vilnius. They saw Lithuanian occupation of the city and outlying region as no more than a temporary setback. The Lithuanians had no illusions about the difficulties they faced if they tried to replace Kaunas with Vilnius as the country's capital and the Poles, unable to contain their anger, were quick to remind them. When a Lithuanian administration took over the city, the Polish population rioted and had to be forcibly suppressed. While the recovery of Vilnius had been high on the Lithuanian agenda for two decades, they really had no idea what they were going to do now that it was in their hands and so few of its population accepted them as its legitimate authority.

As a first step of social engineering, local street names were replaced by others commemorating Lithuanian historical figures and heroes. Other measures included the replacement of trade, industry and other signboards by ones in the official Lithuanian state language. The wearing of Polish uniforms was forbidden. A Lithuanian curriculum was introduced in the schools and where some teachers objected, they were dismissed. The Polish Stefan Batory University, that had become a magnet for Polish refugees, was closed.

All this, and the absence of any constructive policy, found the Lithuanian administration in Vilnius forced into a confrontational stance with ever more restrictive policies when dealing with the Polish community. Eventually they were obliged to make special provisions to accommodate Polish complaints but that only alienated the Jewish and Belorussian communities who were not given the same privileges. The new administration expected to hold democratic elections but feared that the huge influx of Polish refugees that has come into the city since the German invasion of their country threatened to swell the anti-Lithuanian vote. To counter this, all refugees that had entered the region since the start of the war were denied citizenship, whatever their nationality, meaning that they would be unable to vote.

While Lithuania might have thought that things were going their way with the occupation of Vilnius, the Soviets had only just started their murderous strategy. On 25 May, they accused Lithuania of kidnapping Soviet soldiers and mistreating them, and Soviet troops began concentrating on the Lithuanian border. In a meeting with Antanas Merkys on 7 June, which the Lithuanian prime minister must have found extremely discomforting but not altogether unexpected, Molotov accused his country of establishing anti-Soviet alliances with fellow Baltic countries and holding secret talks with Germany. He demanded that Lithuanian state officials be handed over to face trial for the 'acts of provocation' committed on 25 May and insisted on free access for Soviet troops to enter the country. In doing so, the Soviets breeched the Moscow Peace Treaty of 1920, the Soviet-Lithuanian Non-Aggression Pact of 1926, and the Soviet-Lithuanian Mutual Assistance Treaty of 1939.

On 10 June 1940, Soviet forces comprising the 11th Cavalry Corps, six divisions and three tank brigades in full combat readiness were deployed in the border region between Druskininkai and Ashmyany, near Lithuania's eastern border. The 3rd Cavalry Corps, five rifle divisions and two tank brigades were stationed in the area between Ashmyany and Daugavpils. Including those already in the Baltics, altogether the Soviets had 435,000 men, 3,000 tanks, 8,000 canons and 2,061 aircraft deployed. The Lithuanian military leaders considered resistance unfeasible and chose not to mobilise.

On 11 June, Soviet Colonel General Dmitry Pavlov, Belarusian Special Military District Commander, convened a meeting in Lida to plan for the Soviet attack. The troops would reach combat readiness by the evening of 13 June and the attack would go in at 09.00 hours on 15 June. Molotov, with customary disdain, told Lithuanian Foreign Minister Juozas Urbšys 'Irrespective of your answer [to our ultimatum], our troops will anyhow enter Lithuania tomorrow.'[11]

Soviet troops crossed the Lithuanian border at 15.00 hours on 15 June 1940. By 19.00 hours, Red Army tanks had already reached Kaunas and surrounded the Office of the President, the government, the Bank of Lithuania and other governmental institutions.

Lithuanian President Smetona fled the country and by the next day, the country was under complete Soviet control but the transfer of power had been engineered so as to appear a voluntary decision by the Lithuanians. Smetona, by fleeing, was deemed to have resigned and his deputy appointed the Soviet nominee, Justinas Paleckis as president with V. Kreve-Mickevicius as prime minister. On 21 July 1940 the Sovietized parliament, renamed the People's Diet, approved of and declared Soviet rule and on 3 August, the Lithuanian Soviet Socialist Republic became the fourteenth Republic of the Soviet Union.

It is worth looking at the text of the Treaty of Tartu 1920 between the Soviet Union and Estonia, which was repeated similarly for Latvia and Lithuania and included the following:

> On the basis of the right of all peoples freely to decide their own destinies, and even to separate themselves completely from the State of which they form a part, a right proclaimed by the Federal Socialist Republic of Soviet Russia, Russia unreservedly recognizes the independence and autonomy of the State of Estonia, and renounces voluntarily and for ever all rights of sovereignty formerly held by Russia over the Estonian people and territory by virtue of the former legal situation, and by virtue of international treaties, which, in respect of such rights, shall henceforth lose their force. No obligation towards Russia devolves upon the Estonian people and territory from the fact that Estonia was formerly part of Russia.[12]

The Soviet government had also concluded non-aggression pacts with all three Baltic states, Lithuania on 18 September 1926, Latvia on 8 February 1932, and Estonia on 4 May 1932. Each one included the following:

> Each of the High Contracting Parties guarantees to the other Party the inviolability of the existing frontiers between them, as defined by the Peace Treaty signed on August 11, 1920, and undertakes to refrain from any act of aggression or any violent measures directed against the integrity and inviolability of the territory or against the political independence of the other Contracting Party, whether such act of aggression or such violent measures are undertaken separately or in conjunction with other Powers, with or without a declaration of war.[13]

It is clear that Molotov's threat had violated the very spirit and essence of all major treaties then in force between the Soviet Union and the Baltic states and by issuing those threats, the Soviet Union violated its obligations under the non-aggression treaties it had concluded with the Baltic republics.[14] However, even though the governments of the Baltic republics did not protest in public against Soviet threats and their presidents even formally approved the new 'Soviet-friendly' governments, the decision of the Baltic governments to yield to the Soviet ultimatums did not bestow legality upon the Soviet occupation of those states.[15]

To try and legitimise the subjugation of the states, the Soviets tried to organise mass demonstrations to demand a communist revolution but the communist parties in all three countries were pitifully small and their calls for revolution were ignored by the vast majority. The Soviets persistently argued that The Baltic states had joined the Soviet Union 'of their own free will' despite their Decree on Peace by Lenin in 1917 that 'every unification of a small and weak people with a large and strong State, without the exact, clear and voluntarily expressed wish or consent of this people' was unequivocally annexation.[16]

According to a secret decision made by the Latvian state on 17 May 1940, 'In the event of an emergency, the powers of the government were to be conferred on Kārlis Zarinš, Latvian Minister in London' with Latvian Ambassador to Washington Alfred Bilmanis as his substitute. On 2 June, Lithuania had done something similar by designating a senior diplomat, former Minister of Foreign Affairs and then Ambassador to Italy, Stasys Lozoraitis, as head of the Lithuanian diplomatic service with the right to appoint replacements in case that government was no longer able to function. Estonia had made no such arrangements but Estonian Acting Consul General Johannes Kaiv who was in charge of the legation in New York wrote on 23 July 1940, 'I regard the above-mentioned elections [in Estonia] as null and void, as well as all acts passed by this unconstitutionally elected Chamber of Deputies, in particular the decision about the union with the USSR.'

Immediately, a great number of resistance organizations were formed: the Union of Free Lithuania, the Movement of Lithuanian Activists, the Lithuanian Security Guard, Lithuanian Army Fighters, the Lithuanian Rescue Circle, the Lithuanian Liberation Committee, the Lithuanian Liberation Union, the Lithuanian Freedom Army, the Union of Lithuanian Freedom Fighters, the Society of Lithuanian Lovers, the Committee to Save Lithuania, Union of Lovers of the Country, Union of Lovers of the Fatherland, Brotherhood of All Lithuanians, Partizanai, Saugūnas, Iležinis vilkas and Kaunas Partisan Unit.

Lithuania was forced to cut all its international ties but some Lithuanian diplomats, including Lithuanian representative to Germany, Colonel Kazys Škirpa, formed a prototype government-in-exile, the Lithuanian National Committee, with the aim of organising a broad anti-Soviet front and preparing for the restoration of Lithuania's independence in the event of a war between Germany and the Soviet Union. This was the precursor to what became known as the *Lietuviu Aktyvistų Frontas* (Lithuanian Activist Front, LAF) formed on 17 November 1940. In Berlin, Škirpa had the support of both the Nazis and the German military intelligence service, the Abwehr, and he appealed to the Wehrmacht and Ministry of Foreign Affairs on 19 May 1941 to help unite the Lithuanian people as an independent nation and to unite the Lithuanian nation and 'cleanse the Lithuanian soil [of] fiends and Jews.'[17]

The LAF was quickly to become the main contributor to the image of the Jew as a Bolshevik collaborator. The myth of a special role played by the Jews in the establishing of the Soviet regime in the country took root not only in the consciousness of common Lithuanians, but in that of politicians, prominent intellectuals and the leaders of the Church as well.[18] To the Jews Škirpa proclaimed, 'your history in the Lithuanian land that has lasted for five hundred years is now over. Have no hopeful illusions! The Lithuanian people, arising for a new life, consider you traitors and will treat you as a traitor should be treated.'[19] He urged Smetona to 'sow the ideological seed of national Socialism on the soil of Lithuania,' but Smetona refused to recognise the LAF's legal authority.[20]

Despite all the political and diplomatic efforts by Škirpa to persuade the Third Reich to recognise Lithuanian independence with him as prime minister, the Germans would make no promises that Lithuania would have an independent existence in the new Europe of their ambitions. Up until 1926, Škirpa had been known for his left-leaning views, his anti-Polish stance and his pro-Russian geopolitical orientation and would have been keenly aware that Prime Minister Mykolas Sleževičius had come to a 'gentlemen's agreement' with the Soviets aimed against Poland and partially against Latvia as well. It was in 1934 that Škirpa radically revised his political philosophy and adopted a pro-German stance. In early 1939, Smetona had considered expelling him from the diplomatic service for carrying out his own completely independent foreign policy.

The creation of the underground resistance movement emerged from the destroyed Lithuanian Riflemen's Union's attempt to keep their organizational structures viable. It should be noted that during this period underground organisations were weak, under-developed and operating independently of each other. Once the Berlin LAF was established, however, the various underground organisations in Kaunas and Kretinga worked more closely with Berlin and each other, and saw new ones forming and new members recruited to them. In Kretinga, Osvaldas Žadvydas, Jonas Ramanauskas and Petros Bortkevičius were the vital links between the Lithuanian underground and Berlin LAF. In Vilnius the LAF was led by Major Vytautus Bulvičius while in Kaunas Pilypas Žukaukus-Naritus formed a unit of mostly students.

The LAF's foreign-based leadership planned a revolt when conditions were right and began accumulating arms and its propaganda became infused with anti-Semitism. 'Smetona', said Bronys Raila, the LAF's chairman of propaganda 'had turned Lithuania into one of the most Jewish states in Europe' and he called for a state purified of 'Jews, parasites, and traitors [who supported the Soviet occupiers]. A directive sent out to activists said,

> We must create an atmosphere that is so stifling for the Jews that not a single Jew will think that he will have even the most minimal rights or possibility of life in the new Lithuania. Our goal is to drive out the Jews along with the red Russians. The more of them that leave at this time, the easier it will be to get rid of the rest later.[21]

In December 1940, the LAF condemned Smetona's government for having failed to curb 'Jews and similar elements who brutally exploited Lithuanians for their own benefit.' By summer 1941 Smetona, now living in the United States, was clear that his government had placed 'too much belief in Berlin's [good intentions] towards Lithuania.' Still the only legitimate president of the Republic of Lithuania, Smetona assured Ray Atherton, head of the US State Department's European division that he would never recognize the legitimacy of Soviet rule in Lithuania and would in no way recognise the legitimacy of any other government formed in German-controlled Lithuania.

The English-born Lithuanian John F. Mazionis, who was an employee at the US legation in Kaunas, reported to Washington that there was, within the country, a 'general spirit of … expectancy and eagerness for war between the Soviets and the Nazis,' which they hope the Nazis would win.[22] The Soviets also anticipated war and began arresting and deporting to Siberia as many as 20,000 'anti-Soviet elements'. Jews were blamed for collaborating in the deportations and the LAF responded in predictable fashion by publishing a leaflet saying "The crucial day of reckoning has come for the Jews at last. Lithuania must be liberated not only from the Asiatic Bolshevik slavery but also from the Jewish yoke of long standing … All Jews, without any exception, are strictly ordered to immediately leave Lithuania.'[23]

The LAF was organized in units of five sworn members and led by a reserve officer who liaised with the centre. Armed combat units were set up in institutions, companies, universities and the army. In Vilnius it was hoped that support would come from the 29th Rifles Corps of the Red Army, which had been formed out of units of the Lithuanian army in August. An armed uprising was planned to erupt in several cities simultaneously and leadership of the struggle would fall upon whichever group was having the greatest success. The LAF suffered a major setback, however, when some members were arrested and interrogated by the Soviet security service for distributing underground literature in Vilnius. This led to the arrest of some 400 activists and leadership passed to the Kaunas rebels.

Latvia

Baltic Germans had lived in Latvia for 700 years prior to the start of the Second World War and had been a dominant force in Latvia's politics but they almost vanished in a matter of weeks. Despite making up just 3 per cent of the population, Baltic Germans had owned 17 per cent of the factories and almost 30 per cent of Rīga's large-scale apartments. There was a Baltic German party in the *Saeima,* they had their own unions, corporations, schools and even a university, the Herder Institut in Rīga but this all changed dramatically for the 62,000 who lived in the country at the time of independence.[24] They had felt themselves to share a common identity with the Latvian people but that started to change to some extent after independence when their power and influence became increasingly under threat challenge.

The German character of the state was slowly being replaced by Latvian culture. German schools had their autonomy revoked and anyone speaking the German language in public was seen as un-Latvian. The disbandment of two centuries-old German craft guilds, the Great Guild and the Small Guild, even thought they were no longer influential, was a bitter blow to German pride and self-esteem.

The signing of the Molotov-Ribbentrop Pact sent shockwaves through the Baltic nations and then after the German-Russian invasion of Poland, the agreements forced on those countries by the Soviet to allow bases in Latvia signalled to many Baltic Germans that it was time to leave, and Berlin made it clear that it would do all in its power to aid repatriation. Translocation agreements were signed between Germany and Estonia on 15 October and Latvia on 30 October resulting in long queues forming at designated repatriation points such as the House of the Black Heads in Rīga. The demand was huge and immediate but German authorities applied strict 'racial hygiene' tests before granting permission to leave.

In Estonia, the people had to be on the list of the German Cultural Autonomy Administration or be in possession of a certificate from the Ministry of the Interior confirming their German nationality. They were allowed to take all their movable possessions and a limited amount of cash and valuables. By the end of the year, 10,849

Germans and 900 other nationalities had left Estonia. In Latvia a special commission was set up to represent the interests of emigrants in relation to the state. It negotiated which assets would be allowed to leave the country and set up an organisation to oversee transportation of movable property. Nazi officials were sent to Baltic capitals and a special bureau was set up in Berlin with branches in Gdynia and Posen to resettle the emigrants. The Baltic governments were powerless to prevent the loss of so many of its wealthier and better educated people not to mention its commercial assets. More than 6,000 head of cattle were exported from Latvia alone.

Latvia was divided into forty-five evacuation districts. In some instances, whole villages were empties of their population taking sick and aged with them. Special trains were laid on. There was soon a shortage of packing material resulting in huge piles of suitcases, trunks, crates, and baskets accumulating on the dockside at Rīga and Reval. In what had taken on the characteristics of an evacuation, whole new companies were set up in the ports of Ventspils and Liepāja to handle furniture and other possessions that families were hauling onto ships heading for Danzig, Gothenhafen, Swinemünde and Stettin in Poland, a land with which they had even less connection than the one they were leaving.

Upon arrival the sick and elderly were taken to hotels in the now-empty Baltic holiday resorts of Heringsdorf, Ahlbeck, Bansin and Misdroy. The rest were housed in schools, meeting halls and other such places. A Central Office of Immigration made identification and health checks before registering and photographing them. Each head of family had to complete forms requiring, for each family member, the name, status, place and date of birth, occupation, religion, Aryan antecedents and parentage. All now became full citizens of the Reich with all the privileges and duties that entailed. Then began the task of finding permanent residence for them. As far as possible, families and even communities were kept together. This was not too difficult since there were large tracts of land that had been cleared of the indigenous Poles after the German occupation. Once settled they were not allowed to move again.

Ulmanis' government made no effort to restrict the flow of fleeing Germans hoping that it would ingratiate them with Berlin in the face of Soviet aggression. They even compensated the emigrants for property left behind in Latvia, but they were less pleased about the many non-German Latvians who left the country at the same time and warned them, that they would never be allowed to return. The 46,921 Germans and 887 of other nationalities who left Latvia between 7 November and 16 December left a gaping hole in its economy.[25] Many wealthy Germans had left. Whole streets where they had lived were abandoned. Property values plummeted. Businesses crashed for lack of workers but worse was soon to follow when those who had fled were relieved that they had done so.

In the early morning of 14 June 1940, the Latvian Foreign Ministry was asked by an envoy in London if he had any idea why Latvian currency had suddenly stopped being quoted on the Stock Exchange. They had no idea. Then came a signal from London asking if it was true that Soviet troops had crossed the Latvian border. 'Old wives' tales,' the foreign minister wired back to London.[26] As it happened on that morning, Soviet troops had attacked three border posts in and around the village of Maslenki in eastern Latvia, killing three border guards, captured ten others and twenty-seven civilians, and took them to the Soviet Union.

At 14.00 hours on 16 July, Ambassador of Latvia Fricis Kociņš, who was in Moscow was given a note by Vyacheslav Molotov. It called on the Latvian government:

> (1) to form without any delay a government in Latvia that would be capable and willing to guarantee proper implementation of the USSR–Latvia Mutual Assistance Pact.
>
> (2) to guarantee without any delay unhindered entrance of Soviet troop detachments into the territory of Latvia in order to be stationed in the most important centres of Latvia in numbers sufficient to ensure the implementation of the USSR-Latvia Mutual Assistance Pact and to prevent possible acts of provocation against the Soviet garrison in Latvia.
>
> (3) The Soviet government shall expect the reply from the government of Latvia by 16 June 23.00 [hours]. The failure of the Latvian government to submit a reply by the stipulated deadline shall be regarded as a refusal to fulfil the above-listed requirements of the Soviet Union.

It cannot have been a complete surprise to the Latvian government but the speed with which events had moved left them no time to react and they unconditionally signalled acceptance of the provisions of the ultimatum at 22.30 hours. Soviet tanks rolled into Rīga at dawn on the next day meeting no resistance. Vyshinsky followed a day later and brought with him a full compliment of cabinet members to be installed in government. Ulmanis and the Latvian army Commander-in-Chief, General Balodis, were placed under house arrest and then on 19 June Ulmanis agreed to the formation of a new Moscow-approved cabinet and resigned in favour of Augusts Kirchenšteins.

Two days later, General Ludvigs Bolšteins, commander of the Latvian border guard, shot himself leaving a note saying 'A foreign power wants to force us to tear [our state] down. I cannot take part.'[27] In late June 1940 foreign ambassadors, including those of Britain and the US sent telegrams to Kirchenšteins congratulating him on becoming the prime minister. Ulmanis would be later taken to the Soviet Union where he died in 1942.

The arrival of Soviet forces was announced as the enforcement of the Soviet-Lithuanian Mutual Assistance Treaty, also called the Agreement on Military Bases ratified on 4 October 1939, which, the Soviets claimed, was being violated by the Latvian government.

> This selfless assistance granted by the peoples of the Soviet Union to the working people of Latvia and the far-sighted foreign policy of the USSR saved the working people of Latvia from the threat of imperialist intervention and disrupted the intention of the counterrevolutionary bourgeoisie to unleash a civil war, they said.[28]

The months of Soviet occupation would be later remembered as *Baigais Gads*, The Terrible Year. The Soviets, however, would not only deny having committed any crimes against humanity attributing its own crimes to 'traitors of the fatherland' or 'Nazi collaborators.'[29] In the first week, the occupation government ordered the disarmament of the Latvian Aizgari which was later abolished completely on 10 July. A new High Command of the Latvian army was formed under the ideological control of Red Army political commissars and incorporated into the Red Army as the 24th Territorial Corps on 8 July. Latvian officers were replaced by commanders from the Red Army. The most senior Latvian officers were ordered to report to Moscow where they were either shot or deported to Gulags. On 14 June 1941, the remaining officers, while on an alleged training mission, were disarmed, arrested and deported to Siberia, where they were sentenced to death or long-term imprisonment.

The Soviet interpretation of history maintained that the post-1917 governments in the Baltic states were not the legitimate ones with which they had negotiated peace treaties in 1920. Accordingly, everyone involved in governing the Baltic states between 1918 and 1940 was seen as having been involved in illegal acts against the Soviet Union. Now, having regained control over the Baltics, the Soviets wasted no time in reorganising the societies and economies along communist lines, which involved a systematic repression of the political, administrative, military and economic elites of the countries.

Repression of the civilian population was carried out by the NKVD and the Cheka. Thousands of government officials, leaders of industry, clergy, publishers and civil servants were arrested and later deported to camps in the Narym marshes of central Asia. Further arrests by 'Black Raven' secret police continued throughout the following year and a house called the 'White Villa' was set up in the Rīga suburbs as an interrogation centre. Residents close by frequently heard shots in the night and mutilated corpses were later found in the surrounding woods. Cellars in the building had one-man cells so small that inmates could not stand up.

Soon the number of Soviet troops in Latvia easily outnumbered the Latvian army. Two central tenets of communist ideology were implemented immediately. Private property was nationalised, and farming was subjected to collectivisation. The Latvian economy was now directed from Moscow and served the interests of the Soviet state but it suffered from inflation, increased taxation and replacement of local currency by roubles. Food shops, once richly stocked, saw empty shelves and the small number of luxury items were quickly bought up by occupying Soviet forces. The only commodity that was available in quantity was vodka. Ironically, the Russian population of Latvia was particularly badly hit. Russian libraries and bookstores were closed, and all Russian literature was confiscated. Russian societies were suppressed.

In the religious sphere, churches, synagogues and other places of worship were deemed to be potential centres of resistance to communism and were closed down. Religious holidays were forbidden and religious education in schools was ended to be replaced by atheist teachings and Marxist doctrine became a mandatory subject of study. All news media were taken over by the communists and strict censorship was imposed on all forms of communication and entertainment. Article 58 of the Criminal Code of Soviet Russia under which anyone could be accused of anti-Soviet activities was applied retroactively to include counter-revolutionary crimes committed before Soviet rule had been established. Pictures of Stalin went up in towns and cities across the country.

Ulmanis' government had chosen not to resist the Soviet occupation telling the people to 'remain in their place just as he would remain in his' but others took a different view.[30] The loss of Latvia's independence, so recently won, together with the wave of terror the occupiers had spread, the dramatic fall in living standards and imposition of Marxist ideology in all walks of life fuelled resistance movements particularly in the young. At more than twenty educational establishments underground groups and organisations were set up by students to oppose the occupation. In the adult community a number of larger, essentially non-violent, resistance organisations such as *Tēvijas sargi* (Guards of the Fatherland), *Jaunlatvieši* (Young Latvians), *Jaunlatvieši* (Latvian National Legion), *Kaujas organizācija Latvijas atbrīvošanai* (Military Organization for the Liberation of Latvia) and *Latviešu tautas apvienība* (Latvian People's League) were established and led by people from various social groups.

The problem for these groups was that non-violent resistance is a more nuanced and sophisticated movement than its violent cousin. The methods of non-violent struggle were largely a matter of spontaneous improvisation and not the result of careful planning and preparation. Groups lacked clear organisation and clear guidance to avoid untoward actions that might lead to reprisals especially under a regime that was actively collaborating with the Soviets and had been complicit in Latvia's incorporation into the Soviet state. Normally this would be achieved by the emergence of a charismatic and competent leader but, unfortunately, in the case of the Baltic states none arrived. Where leaders appeared at local level, none had sufficient status or reputation to move up and act in a national role. There was also a question of what non-violent resistance actual entailed. What sort of peaceful action would undermine the occupation? The risk was that it would be both ineffective at the same time as provoking retribution. Ulmanis' repressive administration had already created an effective secret police force that was now pressed into service on behalf of the Soviet occupiers so many of those likely to join the resistance would already be known to the authorities. Cheka agents and collaborators had ensured that the boldest fighters had been quickly rounded up.

Realising that opposition to the occupation could well prove counter-productive, the main priority of most of the resistance groups was to prepare for armed action in the event of a war between the Soviet Union and one of the western countries. Until that time, the forms of resistance employed included the printing and distribution of pamphlets urging actions such as the boycotting of elections where the only candidates were approved by Moscow.

No matter how many chose not to vote the outcome of elections was always 100 per cent support for the Soviet candidates. Other leaflets tried to support morale by calling for patience while waiting for the return of liberty and democracy. Underground newspapers tried to keep the public abreast of events outside the country. *Tēvijas sargi* managed to publish six issues of its bulletin *Ziņotājs,* which included rejoinders such as; 'Come, Latvians: the old appeal rings out again. No matter, who you are, let's stand shoulder to shoulder again. We'll have the chance to go our separate ways, once we're free again.' Instructions were passed on to encourage the population to stay safe, 'Latvians! Keep your heads and don't let yourselves be provoked ... Let's save our strength and build up our hatred. How valuable every Latvian heart, glowing with hatred against the enemy, and every hand will be, when the alarm bells ring.'[31]

When resistance took the form of displaying the national flag, singing the national anthem or laying flowers at the national monument on 18 November to commemorate Independence Day, the Soviet-backed newspaper, *Cīņa*, called it 'antics by layabouts.'

The leaders of resistance to the Soviet occupation were jailed and preparations were made for elections to 'express the will of the people.'[32] In usual fashion, elections returned a near 100 per cent vote for the Moscow-approved candidates. Contrary to the Latvian constitution, the *Saeima* now declared Latvia to be a Soviet Socialist Republic and petitioned for permission to be admitted to the Soviet Union.

This was granted and on 5 August 1940, the Supreme Council of the USSR declared Latvia as the fifteenth Republic of the Soviet Union. Having served his purpose as Moscow's puppet, Kirchenšteins was quietly removed from office as prime minister and made chairman of the of the praesidium of the new republic. This action of the *Saeima* was completely illegal and in no way complied with the 1922 Latvian constitution because the government of the LSSR became the executor of Moscow's decrees and orders without the authority to act on its own. This was in contravention of:

Article 1	Latvia is an independent democratic republic.
Article 2	The sovereign power of the State of Latvia is vested in the people of Latvia.
Article 77	If the Saeima has amended the first, second, third, fourth, sixth or seventy-seventh Article of the Constitution, such amendments, in order to come into force as law, shall be submitted to a national referendum.

Deportation, the exile of thousands of people without trial to Gulags or so-called reformatory labour camps in remote districts of the Soviet Union, had been a widely applied form of repression by the Bolsheviks since the end of the Russian Civil War. Approximately 275,000 ethnic Poles had been deported from the Western territories of Ukraine and Belorussia by the end of June 1940.

The first waves of Latvian deportation had taken place in summer 1940 but in general, as one NKVD man put it, the people had been 'handled with kid gloves' to avoid open rebellion but deportations were accelerated after 14 May 1941 when the Soviet Council of People's Commissariat for State Security (NKGB) passed a top-secret Resolution No. 1299–526 calling for deportations from the Baltic states, Moldavia and Belorussia. This was on top of the 16 November 1940 move to allow punishment of Latvian citizens under Soviet Law after which the NKVD and NKGB of the LSSR identified many thousands of 'socially dangerous' elements on the basis of archive materials of Latvia's Ministry of War. Subsequently the Soviet authorities passed the law 'On Measures to Cleanse the Lithuanian, Latvian and Estonian SSRs from Anti-Soviet, Criminal and Socially Dangerous Elements.' Specifically:

- Active members of counterrevolutionary parties and members of anti-Soviet.
- Nationalist white-guard organizations.
- Former Home Guards, gendarmes, police and prison personnel, as well as
- Acting rank-and-file police and prison personnel on whom there is compromising material.
- Former large landlords, factory-owners and high-ranking civil servants of the former Lithuanian, Latvian and Estonian state apparatus.
- Former officers of the armies of Poland, Lithuania, Latvia and Estonia and the White Army on whom there is compromising material.
- Criminal elements that continue to engage in criminal activities.
- Family members of the persons listed above who share a household with such persons or are their dependants at the moment of their arrest.
- Families of the members of counterrevolutionary nationalist organizations whose heads have passed into illegal status or are in hiding from authorities.
- Families of the members of counterrevolutionary nationalist organizations whose heads have been sentenced to capital punishment.
- Repatriates from Germany and ethnic Germans who, having applied for repatriation to Germany, have refused to depart and on whom there is material on their anti-Soviet activities and suspicious contacts with foreign intelligence services.[33]

On the night of 13 June 1941, in simultaneous raids all over the Baltics, some 15,500 Latvians, mainly family members of state officials, including 2,400 children under 10 were peremptorily arrested. They were given one hour to collect as much as they could carry then herded into boxed-in railway carriages, some still filthy after transporting animals. People were deported without having any charge brought against them, without a trial or a chance to defend themselves. At the stations, the men were forcibly separated from their families and transferred to Gulag camps in Vyatlag, Norillag, Sevurallag and Usollag. Family members were sent to Krasnoyarsk Krai and Novosibirsk Oblast. The train in Tukums station stood for two days, fully loaded with deportees before eventually moving off.

Soviet records show that the total number of deportees was 14,476 while the deportee remembrance book *Aizvestie* gives a figure 15,424.[34] On the long journey to the central Soviet Union, many sick, elderly and very young children died. All along the route, hundreds of corpses were thrown out of the boxcars. Then on 22 June, the Nazis launched Operation *Barbarossa,* their attack on the Soviet Union. This prompted further deportations of political prisoners and executions of others who could not be deported. The victims were buried in mass graves at Baltezers, Rēzekne and Ulbroka. Ironically, the Jews who were part of the June deportations would be shown to have a better chance of survival than those left behind to face the Nazis.

The new Soviet elites, especially in rural communities, being generally poorly educated, arrogant, and fully dependent on orders from central authorities, had completely failed to gain the support of their communities.[35] When the Germans struck on 22 June, these elites were quite incapable of offering any leadership. They rapidly lost control over the situation and many of them fled along with the Red Army soldiers.

Many parishes, mostly devoid of any information about what was happening in the wider world, came under the control of hastily formed armed groups of Soviet activists as law and order broke down. Shops and warehouses in places were looted by both locals and Red Army units who had abandoned their heavy weapons and fled wreaking havoc as they went. It was about two weeks before the country resolved its administrative dilemma by setting up a centralised system with only broad guidelines from the German authorities.

During these first few days, however, groups of men had formed under the leadership of local anti-communist activists. They acquired weapons from wherever they could get them, mostly from straggling Soviet soldiers. Some of these groups consisted exclusively of Latvian military personnel. Within weeks there were several thousand people in such groups who proved to be more than capable of curbing looting and criminal activity in general. It has been estimated that politically motivated murders during this time was no more than a few dozen.[36] These Latvian armed units were quickly utilised by the Germans as intelligence units, police officers or guards and even, in some regions, as temporary auxiliary troops of the Wehrmacht.

Modern Latvian historians have examined certain assumptions that had prevailed over the years and asked whether the Jews were, in fact, happier than any other section of the Latvian population at the arrival of the Soviet forces. The answer seems to be that the Jews were relieved to see the Soviets come in because it was felt that this would offer protection against invasion by the Nazi Germany with all the consequences that might flow from that given the experience of Poland.

Estonia

In September 1939, the Germans had invaded Poland and a few months later the Winter War followed when the Soviet Union invaded Finland. Estonia now became of vital importance to the Soviet military who, accompanied by direct threats, demanded the establishment of military bases for the Red Army in Estonia. Brutal demonstrations of power to secure agreement included a Soviet navy blockade of Estonian sea borders violation of Estonian air space by Soviet aircraft, concentrations of troops along the border and, in a false flag operation, the sinking of the Soviet steamship *Metallist* in Narva Bay by a Soviet submarine claiming it was an act of provocation by the Estonians.

Receiving no support from the Western powers, the Estonian government, and the *Riigikogu* (parliament) were forced to accept a treaty allowing the Soviets to establish military bases in their country. The treaty was signed in Moscow on 28 September 1939 and foreign troops, which exceeded the regular forces of the Republic of Estonia several times, were brought to the bases in October 1939 and Soviet naval forces occupied the ports of Paldiski and Tallinn.

On 12 October 1939, a new government was formed, headed by Prime Minister Jüri Uluots. Immediately, the Soviet military began exceeding the agreed numbers of troops stationed in the country and during the war with Finland, Soviet bombers used Estonian airfields, which was a gross violation of Estonian sovereignty. When the Soviets punished Estonia for its reticence by sinking the Estonian merchant ship *Kassari* in the Baltics on 10 December 1939 the Estonian government was suitably impressed and remained silent.

The Soviets presented an ultimatum to Lithuania on 13 June 1940 demanding that a new government be formed, and Soviet troops be allowed to take up positions in strategic locations. If there was no agreement within twenty-four hours Soviet troops would enter the country and crush all opposition. Soviet forces then invaded Lithuania isolating Estonia and Latvia from the rest of Europe. On 16 June at 15.20 hours a similar ultimatum with an eight-hour deadline was presented to Estonia, accusing it of violating the mutual aid pact and demanding permission for 100,000 men to enter the country ostensibly to protect the Soviet troops there from alleged danger. The ultimatum included the request for the formation of a new pro-Soviet government. Troops crossed the border even before the ultimatum expired.[37]

When the Estonian Commander-in-Chief of the Armed Forces, General Johan Laidoner, met with the Soviet army General Meretskov on the morning of 17 June to sign the agreement, Soviet forces were already on the outskirts of Tallinn. Andrei Zhdanov, the special commissioner of the Soviet government, arrived in Tallinn on 19 June and met the Estonian president to inform him that the writer Johannes Vares-Barbarus would be appointed as prime minister in place of Uluots. To make clear to the population that changes were afoot, two days later Soviet intelligence agents staged fake demonstrations in which a large number of Soviet migrant workers took to the streets of Tallinn demanding a change of government.

Captain Nikolai Trankmann, a traitor who had sold the plans of military objects at Narva to the Soviets was freed from Patarei Prison along with other common felons. Then on 14 July elections were held under the supervision of the occupation forces. The Estonian nationalist parties put up seventy-eight candidates for the eighty parliamentary seats but Zhdanov demanded that Vares' government remove all non-communist candidates from the electoral list except one: Mr Jüri-Rajur Liivak, a farmer from Raasiku. London newspapers printed the results of the election several hours before they were officially declared in Estonia.[38]

After the elections, the Riigikogu agreed to Estonia joining the Soviet Union. On 6 August 1940, the Supreme Soviet of the Union of Soviet Socialist Republics legalised the annexation of Estonia and it became the Estonian Soviet Socialist Republic. By the end of 1940, 1,082 persons had been arrested including General Johan Laidoner and President Päts. Sixty-eight members of the last *Riigikogu* were taken into custody and thirty-six were shot. The terror peaked on 14 June 1941 with the first mass deportation of 9,267 people, including children, to the Kirov and Novosibirsk regions in accordance with the decree of the NKVD No. 288 of 28 November 1940.[39]

The political leadership of Estonia did not resist the Soviet occupation and neither did it advocate underground resistance. There was no attempt to maintain the country's legal continuity by, for instance, evacuating political and military leadership and forming a 'government in exile'. The only rather feeble political response was to nominate opposition candidates in the *Saeima* elections but that was short-lived because their names were immediately removed from the voting papers. Any illusions of democratic process and independence were quickly shattered.

Public servants who had been thrown out of their jobs to do manual work did not cause trouble either because of their fears of arrest and punishment. Members of the armed forces were compelled to continue their service in the Red Army but some, at least, tried to hide caches of arms during the handover to the Soviets. Such protest as there was came from mainly young people in the form of displaying national colours in various ways and heckling public pro-Soviet speakers. The international football match between Estonia and Latvia on 18 July 1940, turned into a mighty patriotic demonstration, which at the end of the game had taken the shape of demonstration of sympathy for President Päts. When Soviet history and constitution was introduced as a compulsory subject in schools, children took little notice or attempted to ask teachers embarrassing questions that they could not answer satisfactorily.

Silent protests turned significantly more provocative when the Soviets began destroying monuments of the Estonian War of Independence. Flowers were placed at the foot of the demolished monuments and people stopped for a few moments to pay their respects when they passed by. Throughout Estonia, underground resistance groups were formed primarily by students and ex-students who had certain social status but they were fragmented with no central guidance.

At first, they restricted activities to political discussions and distributing subversive literature but occasionally weapons were collected and stored for future use. When an embryonic organisation, the Rescue Committee, emerged it was exposed and liquidated by the Soviets. There was also a group of mostly older people who had contacts in Finland, but the Soviets soon became aware of their activities through informants. As soon as the first few were taken in for interrogation and torture, it was not long before whole networks were uncovered. Remarkably, some cells survived and went on to play a part when the Germans attacked and drove the Soviets out.

In autumn 1940, a second wave of arrests saw 'speculators' rounded up. These were people who had taken advantage of the change-over from a market economy to a demand economy in which the central governmental authority dictated the levels of production that are permissible and the prices that may be charged for goods and services. The resulting shortages of essential commodities encouraged black marketeering for which punishment was soon ratcheted up from fines to incarceration in a concentration camp.

After 9 June, mass mobilisation of young men into the Red Army was introduced to try and remove potential troublemakers and prevent them being utilised by the Germans if and when they chose to invade. Once under Soviet control, these conscripts were used more like forced labour units than soldiers and were brutally handled to keep them under control. After the German attack, the head of the Political Administration of the Red Army, Lev Mekhis, realised that they were not going to be of any use militarily and he allowed conditions for them to deteriorate rapidly with the result that about one third, over 10,000 young men, died in the camps through hunger and diseases or in many cases murder.

In the winter 1940–41, the Stalin's commissioner Andreĭ Zhdanov issued top-secret 'Directive on the Deportation of the Socially Alien Element from the Baltic Republics, Western Ukraine, Western Belorussia and Moldavia.' It was not before June 1941, however, that this was implemented. During the early hours of Saturday, 14 June, tens of thousands of Estonians were woken up and had deportation orders read out to them. These orders declared them to be subject to deportation without any legal process or court decision.

All their property was declared to be subject to seizure. They were given an hour to pack. Loaded onto trucks, the young, the elderly, the sick and the pregnant were all taken to railway siding and transferred to almost 500 boxcars only recently used for transporting cattle. Estimates put the number of those under the age of 16 at around 2,500. Further deportations were halted when the Germans launched Operation *Barbarossa* on 22 June. In the Soviet Union prison camps, hundreds of deportees were shot for 'crimes' against the state while others were subject to forced labour. Less than half of those deported ever returned to Estonia after the war, only about 300 of whom were adult males.

The arrival of German forces in the Baltics forced the Soviets to compromise if they were to have any chance of mobilising the populations to resist the German occupation. With breathtaking disingenuity, they suddenly appealed to the historic unity and friendship between the Soviet Union and the Estonian people who now had to work together to defeat the 'fascist barbarians'. This allowed the resurrection of nationalist military units, previously banned in 1938, and the acceptance of nationalist partisan units willing to cooperate with the Soviets, who had to grit their teeth and accept a brief resurgence of Estonian nationalist fervour. Throughout the years of German occupation, the Soviets had to balance this forced identity as the 'older brother' in a family of equals who offered protection from the bully against their ambitions to recover lost ground and eventually bring the subordinate states back under the yoke of oppression which would, as a primary objective, destroy all nationalist ambitions. It offered the Baltic states theoretical rights that the Soviets had no intention of allowing them to enjoy.[40]

Special Soviet 'destroyer' battalions had been established and given extensive freedom to act according to their own whims and commit murders all within a broad context of consolidating Soviet power in what Stalin called the unruly 'western borderlands' of the Soviet Union. They had been active in the Baltics all through the Soviet occupation and were still very active when the Germans attacked and now vented their murderous spleen on political prisoners who could not be evacuated to the Soviet Union in time. These were executed without trial in Tartu Vangla (prison) on 8 July and in Kuressaare Castle on the island of Saaremaa in September.

There were isolated groups, mostly young men, who had gone into hiding during the Soviet occupation, but they were not yet active as armed resistance or partisan fighters. They had gone into hiding to avoid persecution by the Soviet occupiers but when deportations began on a massive scale in June 1941, the numbers of those fleeing into the forests greatly increased. The Soviets had created the 22nd Rifle Corps of the Red Army out of members of the Estonian army and large numbers of young men were mobilised to join them. Those who refused faced summary execution as 'bandits' and had no choice but to disappear into the forests and join other partisans in what became known, under the command of the Latvian army major, Friedrich Kurg, as the *Miško Broliai* (forest brothers) although women were also part of the resistance movement too.

Partisan bands ranged in size from a few members to several hundred. Some lived in the forest all the time, while others lived a normal life during the day. They depended heavily on sympathetic civilians to supply them with food and used abandoned German or Lithuanian army equipment as well as weapons captured from the Soviets. Eventually, these disparate groups came together in something like a disciplined way and, in the east of the country, began attacking Soviet forces who were retreating from the German invaders.

In the light of subsequent attitudes towards the Jewish community, it is worth quoting a Lithuanian security report of 21 July 1940, which stated that 'Anti-Semitism is growing extraordinarily. This is happening not just among the peasants but also among the workers.'[41] To see why this came about it is necessary to understand the Soviet means of political control. Together with arrests, deportations and executions they stimulated conflicts between individuals and groups in the time-honoured way of 'divide and conquer'. To destroy the old regimes and develop new ones they looked especially to the minority nationalities. And it was the Jews who offered the greatest potential in this regard. The Jews of Lithuania, especially, had seemed to them to be the most dissatisfied with their social and economic conditions and under Soviet rule they felt much greater physical security with the cancellation of all restrictions and discriminatory measures that had been in place against them.

The deportation of large numbers of Jews from the Belorussian and Ukrainian territories seized from Poland did not seem to dent this enthusiasm. Despite misgivings about the Bolsheviks' militant atheism, their persecution of Zionism, and nationalization of property, many Jews welcomed the Red Army as a liberator, especially the young men who were eager to fight the Nazis.[42] The Jews who supported the new regimes gained an unprecedented prominence in public life in all three Soviet republics. Young Jewish men were quick to exercise their new authority, and this was resented by the majority populations who now saw the Jews as the new executive elite that was implementing Soviet policy and destroying the social institutions of the national states. There is no doubt that the Jewish communists in Lithuania, whose number was estimated at 900 were very active in expropriating properties and in the process of choosing the deportees. They were helped by Jewish members of the NKVD, who arrived together with the Red Army.[43] Many viewed the Jews who welcomed the Red Army as traitors. An American diplomat who visited Soviet Lithuania in March 1941 reported 'a strong, anti-Semitic feeling in the whole country'.[44]

Pro-German propaganda was quick to turn popular resentment into a call for vengeance against the Jews. From Berlin, the LAF send a loud and clear message that 'one must create in the land a heavy atmosphere against the Jews so that no Jew could even dare to think that in the new Lithuania he could have even minimal rights and the general possibility of making a living.'[45] Such rhetoric gave the Jewish populations of Lithuania and Latvia every reason to fear the prospect of German invasion.

When the Soviets had moved into Estonia, political arrests began immediately. The Soviets had prepared for this moment and had lists already drawn up and as soon as they had control they set about arresting all the members of the former governments, higher state officials and judges, higher military personnel, former politicians, members of voluntary state defence organisations, members of student organisations, persons having actively participated in anti-Soviet armed combat, Russian émigrés, security police officers and police officers, representatives of foreign companies and in general all people having contacts abroad, entrepreneurs and bankers, clergymen and members of the Red Cross.

On 17 July the commander of the Estonian Defence Forces, Johan Laidoner, and his wife were exiled to Penza and a week later Konstantin Päts, and his family were exiled to Ufa. Neither was to return. Of the 8,000 people arrested for 'political' crimes only a few hundred survived their incarceration.[46]

The numbers of deportees from the Baltics during the period 14–22 June 1941 has been estimated at 34,000 for Latvia, 60,000 for Estonia and 75,000 for Lithuania. Each country marks 14 June in their calendar. In Estonia it is the *14.juuni küüditamise mälestuspäev* (Remembrance Day of the 14 June Deportation), in Lithuania it is the *Gedulo ir vilties diena* (Day of Mourning and Hope) and in Latvia it is *Komunistiskā genocīda upuru piemiņas diena* (Remembrance Day for the Victims of Communist Terror).

Chapter 5

GERMAN INVASION

Germany would attack the Soviet Union, of that there was no doubt in Stalin's mind, and he knew that the Soviet military was in no fit state to stand up to the Wehrmacht even though by June 1940 the country's industry was on a virtual war footing. The two horns of his dilemma were that his strategy of mobilising the armed forces to prepare them for a German attack was denuding industry of manpower and so slowed down the production of military hardware. Furthermore, the military had seen two thirds of the entire officer corps of the Red Army wiped out along with the 'flower of [the] foreign intelligence services' in the state trials and executions as Stalin's paranoia held him in an iron grip. Jonathan Haslam is clear that 'walled in by distorting mirrors of [his] own making' these were 'actions that could in no way be seriously represented as the actions of a rational and level-headed mind.'[1]

Still not secure in his position and fearing plots all around, he used his security apparatus with extraordinarily brutal efficiency to root out real and imagined enemies amongst his rivals, sparing only those like Lavrentiy Beria whom he relied on to carry out the executions. With his biggest rival, Leon Trotsky, still at large, albeit out of the country, Stalin would countenance no internal vestige of opposition to his rule. How great must his insecurity have been to continue purges of his military leaders even as German Panzers were rolling over Poland. He assumed that Hitler would not make the fatal mistake of fighting on two fronts and, after *Fall Gelb* (German war plan for the Battle of France) when the Panzers turned west across the Low Countries, he would no doubt have been reassured that he had a valuable breathing space to bring his forces up to strength especially with production of the T-34 tank in which the Red Army had invested such faith. The dislocation and disruption of the European political balance of power also provided him with the opportunity, as Soviet President Mikhail

Kalinin pointed out, 'to expand communism' by tightening his grip on the Baltics.[2]

Despite, or perhaps because of, multiple intelligence warnings of a German attack all through April, May and early June of 1940, Stalin held onto the opinion that 'Germany would not attack the Soviet Union in the very near future.'[3] He also got repeated warnings from the British and US governments about German intentions, which he interpreted as blatant attempts to spark a German-Soviet war.

With Wehrmacht forces massing along the English Channel, Stalin rightly concluded that Hitler would achieve no strategic advantage by launching an attack against Britain even though British armed forces were shattered after Dunkirk. He banked on Hitler conserving his energy in preparation for the inevitable attack against the Soviet Union, but it was a gamble that involved second-guessing the German leader over just how much time he would take to get ready and that would feed into his own judgement over how much time his own forces would have to prepare. Any miscalculation over the implementation of aggressive military preparations would have serious consequences, not least a possible provocation that Hitler might respond to it by disavowing the Molotov-Ribbentrop Pact, which Stalin believed was still having a significant restraining influence.

Evidence points to the fact that what Stalin needed was time, and more time to manufacture tanks and heavy weapons, time to train recruits, time to build border defences. It is hard to say just how much of his decision-making was underpinned by little more than a 'cross your fingers and hope for the best' strategy. Stalin was not blind to the truth, however, and he did the most he thought could get away with without giving the appearance of gearing up for an imminent war. During May 1941, 800,000 reservists were called up and 28 divisions were moved up to the western border. To a large extent, the blame for the Soviet failure to meet the German attack effectively can be laid at the door of his coterie of close advisers, Lavrentiy Beria, Georgy Malenkov, Lazar Kaganovich and Vyacheslav Molotov. Having built their carers on slavish obedience to the leader and spent years exercising a chronic obsession with internal politics and intrigues, their understanding of military matters was lacking, to say the least. They were certainly no match for the career generals of the Wehrmacht. Molotov's remark to Admiral Kuznetsov around mid-June to the effect that 'only a fool would attack us' is a clear example of what was wrong.[4]

Furthermore, inexperienced officers promoted to fill the ranks made vacant by the purges proved incapable, through fear or incompetence, of giving Stalin an accurate assessment of Red Army preparedness for war in terms of resources and training. Stalin's assessment was also severely handicapped by a serious lack of hard intelligence about German military capabilities and intentions. There was no organised collection and analysis of intelligence and where it came through it was not used efficiently. The Intelligence Directorate had no links with the military High Command and failed to provide the Red Army with information on foreign armed forces' organization, condition, armaments and preparations for deployment.[5]

Stalin's statement, as reported by the Soviet news outlet Tass on 14 June, was an attack on the British ambassador for spreading malicious rumours about an impending German-Soviet war. Some historians have taken this to show that Stalin was in denial about German intentions, but others have seen it as having been for purely foreign consumption. In one sense it was a warning to Germany that Stalin was perfectly aware of German preparations for an attack and the Soviet Union was preparing to defend its borders; what Stalin would later refer to as 'a conciliatory request containing a veiled threat' but it was pure bluff to which Stalin had no realistic follow-up if it failed.[6] Nikita Khrushchev would later condemned Stalin and his clique of military advisers for 'criminal negligence and incompetence' over their unpreparedness to face the German invasion on 22 June 1941.[7]

The Soviet plan to meet a German attack had been drawn up by Chief of the General Staff, Marshal B. Shaposhnikov, in April 1940 and presented to Stalin in September of that year. Stalin objected to Shaposhnikov's expectation of the main line of attack being through the centre and amended the plan to prepare for a German attack through Ukraine and this seems to have been sound planning when, in May 1941, General F.J. Golikov, head of General Staff of the Armed Forces of Russia (GRU) intelligence, reported that German troops were massing on the border facing Kyiv. An operational plane drawn up as the results of Soviet war-games held in December showed that an effective defence required that all armed forces to be put on alert with immediate mobilisation of reserves and huge reinforcement of border troops. Since the Soviet military was committed to a counterattacking response to German invasion, however, none of these proposals was implemented.

German preparations for their attack made it difficult for the Soviets to understand what was happening and did not give them sufficient time to respond when it became clear. During the month before the attack, German infantry divisions had moved up at a rate of up to two divisions every twenty-four hours, mostly during the night and Panzer divisions had been held back right up until mid-June before racing to the border. This put Soviet military planners entirely on the back foot but still Stalin refused Semyon Timoshenko's mobilisation request of 13 June. It was not so much the result of incompetence of the Soviet military command as the stubborn, iron control Stalin held over all functions of government. Initiative and improvisation had been outlawed in the military and few outside Stalin's inner circle had a complete understanding of Soviet plans, preparations or capabilities let alone those of the Germans.

Notwithstanding the somewhat egregious dislocation between intelligence and military, on 20 June 1941, Soviet Intelligence sent a report to Stalin entitled 'On Signs of Inevitability of the German Attack on the Soviet Union in the Next Several Days'. The biggest fear of the Germans was that when attacked, the Soviets would implement a strategic defence but, in reality, the Soviet High Command had no doctrinal affiliation to such ideas. The Soviet Marshal Georgy Zhukov would later write in his memoirs that, '[Soviet] military strategy in the pre-war period was based mainly on the assumption that only offensive actions could defeat the aggressor and that the defence would play a purely supportive role, helping the [offensive] groupings to achieve their goals.'[8] The consequence of this would be that the Soviet High Command lost control of many of its units in the immediate aftermath of the German invasion. Zhukov would also admit that 'the General Staff failed to realise the changed tempo of modern warfare.'[9]

In summary, Stalin's strategy was based upon five assumptions:

- The Soviet Union must delay the German attack until 1942 at the earliest to give it time to prepare a defence.
- Two hundred divisions would be placed on the border to implement the Soviet counterattacking plans when the Germans attack.
- Soviet intelligence would give adequate notice of the movement of German mobile forces.
- After the coup in Yugoslavia which brough an anti-German government to power, Hitler would be tied down in the Balkans until 1942.
- Once combat is joined there would be ample time to mobilise reserves.

When analysing how this played out it is clear that Stalin was determined to delay a German attack as long as possible, failed to make the necessary preparations due to a fear of provoking Hitler and failed to anticipate when the attack would take place.

Much has been written about the original date for the German offensive of 15 May being delayed by the situation in the Balkans and the late spring thaw in eastern Europe that left whole tracts of land waterlogged and inhospitable to mobile forces. This should be viewed against the spectacular success the Germans achieved during the first six weeks which 'had had achieved all the necessary preconditions' for victory.[10] The Soviets required four years and massive assistance from their Western Allies to recover from the first few weeks of the war.[11]

During the early hours of 22 June, thirty specially selected Heinkel bombers flew over the Soviet border and struck at more than ten Soviet forward airfields at the very moment, 03.00 hours, that an artillery barrage signalled the start of the German attack against the Soviet Union. The Soviet aircraft were conveniently parked wingtip to wingtip, row upon row. The German Luftwaffe had already accumulated a great deal of combat experience by 1941 and this combined with technical and tactical superiority accounted for huge losses of Soviet aircraft in the first days of the invasion. Luftflotte 1 sent more than 400 aircraft and destroyed 100 Soviet aircraft on the ground, which virtually wiped out the whole of their air element in Lithuania in one fell swoop. Many of these aircraft had been based at forward airfields, which had no dispersal facilities or camouflage.

A catastrophic situation developed with terrible rapidity. Within hours, the Soviets lost some 1,200 aircraft across the whole battle front. Soviet troops were in camp, aircraft were on the ground. Many defensive units had been stationed well behind the border and were forced to make approach marches under fierce air attack. The Germans achieved tactical surprise all along the front. Soviet border fortifications were overrun almost immediately. Bizarrely, Stalin believed that it was a feint and part of some dastardly plot by Hitler to unnerve him. Given the way that Hitler had outmanoeuvred the French by attacking through the Ardennes forest, Stalin was looking for a similar stroke of subterfuge and kept his powder dry. German Army Group Centre intercepted uncoded Soviet signals 'We are being fired on. What shall we do?'[12]

Incredibly the reply came back, 'no action is to be taken against the Germans without our knowledge … Comrade Stalin has forbidden to open artillery fire against the Germans.'[13]

Four hours after the first shots were fired, when the size and ferocity of the German attack could no longer be denied, Stalin changed his mind and the Soviet High Command, somewhat optimistically and seemingly oblivious to what was happening at the border, implemented its attack policy and completely avoided defensive measures by issuing orders:

- With all their strength and means troops will attack enemy forces and liquidate them in the areas where they have violated the Soviet frontier.
- Reconnaissance and combat aviation will establish the location of the enemy aviation concentrations and the disposition of ground forces. With powerful bomber and ground attack blows aviation will destroy aircraft on enemy aerodromes and bomb the basic groupings of enemy ground forces.
- Aviation blows will be mounted to a depth of 100–150 kilometres into German territory.

The Baltics felt the full weight of German Field Marshal Wilhelm Ritter von Leeb's Army Group North as it steamrollered through Lithuania, north of Vilnius, in a north-easterly direction to establish a bridgehead across the river Dvina opening up the way to Leningrad (St Petersburg). Von Leeb's group comprised the 16th and 18th armies and the 4th Panzergruppe under Colonel General Erich Hoepner, which included the 1st, 6th and 8th Panzerdivisionen (Panzer divisions). Facing them was Colonel General Fyodor Isodorovich Kuznezov's North-West Baltic Front of the Soviet 8th, 11th and 27th armies with some 1,400 tanks all told but the border defences were held only by the 125th Rifle Division.

Lieutenant General Kurt Herzog's 291st Infanterie-Division (Infantry division) broke through at Memel but was then held up for three days by Major General Nikolai Dedaev's 67th Rifle Division. Further south, 4th Panzer Group advanced in two spearheads towards the Dvina river. They quickly advanced as far as the Dubysa river at which point Kuznetsov ordered the 3rd and 12th mechanized corps to prepare to counterattacking against the German flank.

Lieutenant General Erich Brandenberger split his 8th Panzerdivision into Kampfgruppe Crisolli, Kampfgruppe Bodenhausen and Kampfgruppe Scheller. Kampfgruppe Crisolli broke through and reached Yubarkas within hours and made rapid progress towards Seredžius, north of Kaunas, against Soviet forces that had found themselves taking heavy losses under heavy aerial bombardment and had been slow to react. Kampfgruppe Scheller ran into trouble and was slowed down in dense woodland along the border while Kampfgruppe Crisolli pressed on a further 50 kilometres to Seredžius and secured the Ariogala road bridge over the river Dubysa. The Germans moved reinforcements to back up Kampfgruppe Crisolli, which had taken up a temporary defensive posture at Ariogala while it regrouped and was resupplied.

The next day, Kuznetsov committed his tanks. Major General Alexey Kurkin's 3rd Mechanized Corps would move in from Kėdainiai and Major General N.M. Shestopalov's 12th Mechanised Corps from Šiauliai. The two tank divisions were weakly deployed, however, having been committed piecemeal without infantry support, with inadequate supplies of ammunition and fuel and with little awareness of German positions, movements or intentions. They were spotted by German aerial reconnaissance who called in Junkers Ju 88 bombers to pound them as they advanced south-west of Šiauliai. No Soviet fighters appeared and Colonel T.S. Orlenko's 23rd Tank Division sustained severe losses. Soviet forces were uncoordinated, under-resourced with fuel and ammunition, and fighting blind. With no aerial reconnaissance they didn't even know where the main German strength was.

Where engagements occurred, many Soviet tanks ran out of fuel and were abandoned. Others were outgunned and smashed by the 37mm guns of Czech-designed Pz38(t) tanks of the 10th Panzer-Regiment. There were isolated Soviet successes such as when Major General Yegor Solyankin's 2nd Tank Division with their heavy KV-1 and KV-2 tanks dispersed a force of German motorized infantry at Skaudvilė but this had little effect on the overall German advance. The Soviet 11th Army was pulled back to Kaunas on the Nemunas river and then to Jonava.

By the evening of 25 June, the Soviet 8th Army was falling back north towards Rīga and the 11th Army south towards Vilnius and Desna leaving a gaping hole in Soviet defences from Ukmergė to Daugavpils. The next day the Germans pounced. Ottenbacher's 36th Infanterie-Division (motorisiert), (motorised infantry division) had linked up with Lieutenant General Friedrich Kirchner's 1st Panzer Division who had crossed the Dubysa at Lyduvėnai. Kirchner pushed south into the rear of Solyankin's division threatening to encircle the Soviet 2nd Tank Division and 3rd Mechanised Corps who had run out of fuel. Soviet infantry had been pummelled from the air and were in no fit state to support the tanks. The commander of the 48th Rifle Division, Major General P.V. Bogdanov was taken prisoner and Solyankin was killed. The Germans prevailed but their poorly armoured Panzer II tanks had taken heavy losses. Only 44 out of 155 were still serviceable by mid-August.

Overall things had gone very much to plan as far as German Army Group North was concerned. The Dvina had been crossed at Dvinsk and Yekabpils with more than a dozen Soviet divisions having been wiped out, but in Lithuania and Latvia, the Soviets were offering strong resistance in a series of delaying actions. Overall, however, the Germans had every reason to be satisfied with their progress on the first nine days. The Luftwaffe had gained complete air supremacy despite the surprising numerical strength of the Soviet air force and the Soviets had been heavily engaged on all fronts. In view of the heavy losses suffered by the Soviet forces, the success of the German operation seemed assured.

On 29 June, Hitler instructed his forces to concentrate on Leningrad to drive the Soviets from the Baltics to secure German ore shipments from Scandinavia and enable the Finns to add their weight to the German left flank. Chief of the German Army High Command, Colonel General Alfred Jodl could see that his forces, especially the Panzers, were starting to feel the effects of prolonged warfare and didn't think his mobile armour, worn down by attrition and mechanical failures, would be able to take Leningrad and still have the strength to turn south and add weight to the drive on Moscow which was beginning to look like the main German target.

German Army Group North was to drive toward Lake Ilmen, with 4th Panzer Group in the lead, and then turn north towards Leningrad. Strong Russian resistance was to be expected. At this stage the crucial problem was maintaining contact between the motorised Panzers and the laggardly infantry divisions with their horse-drawn vehicles who were constantly delayed by mopping up and encirclement operations. To overextend the links between the armour and infantry was courting disaster but the incredible ability of the German infantry to cover ground and close up with the Panzers was demonstrated time and again even though they were denied the use of the few good roads which had been reserved for the motorised units.

Soviet forces had been driven back towards the Dvina but failed to organise a defence along its banks. German troops forced a river crossing and the way was open now for General Erich von Manstein's LVI Panzerkorps to push on towards Leningrad. A Soviet attempt to destroy the bridgehead temporarily halted Manstein's LVI Panzer Corps but by the following day the Germans were on the move again and heading towards Ostrov. The Dvina river was crossed at Rīga but the Panzers had to wait almost a week until the infantry could catch up with them. The civilian population was crowding railway stations and roads along with retreating Soviet forces but there had been no serious fighting for the city. The Soviet air force had been driven from the skies. When reconnaissance aircraft flew overhead, they were sporting the black cross of the Luftwaffe. Soviet defensive plans had made no allowance for an armoured drive on Leningrad from the south-west, but now only desperate defence could save the city.

Already Beria was gearing up his NKVD 'rear security detachments' to set up their machine guns to deter any 'unauthorised withdrawal' of front-line troops.[14] His lack of faith in Soviet fighting men was not justified, however, since, as the Chief of the German General Staff, General Franz Halder noted, despite the appalling performance of the Soviet command, they were fighting 'to the last man ... with savage determination'. Jodl added his assessment, 'the surrounded Russian armies,' he said, 'offered fanatical resistance, despite being cut off from any kind of supplies for days. Upon retreating into impenetrable forests, they would literally eat the bark and roots of trees. They were in such a state of exhaustion when captured that they were barely able to move.'[15]

There was no possibility of redeploying Soviet forces to close the gaps where the Germans were pouring through. The Red Army command at the front had all but collapsed leaving operations, communications and logistics in chaos. Lithuania was occupied within four days, and the Wehrmacht marched into Rīga on 31 June. Colonel General Georg von Küchler's 18th Army that followed the Panzer Group and covered its western flank, attacked east of the Lake Peipsi via Pskov anticipating that the Soviets would not deploy large forces to defend Estonia. Only General Albert Wodrig's XXVI Armeekorps with the 217th and 61st Infanterie-Divisionen moved up the coast crossing into Estonia at Ikla on 7 July. They met Major General I.F. Nikolaev's 10th Rifle Corps, which was part of the Leningrad forward defences along the Luga River. Some 30,000 workers were sent out of the city to build defences and on 30 June a locally drafted militia army, little more than an untrained fragmented mob with light weapons, was raised to meet the Germans. Soviet destruction battalions removed or destroyed everything that could be advantageous to the advancing Germans.

Many Estonians forced to join the Soviet forces knew that they were being ordered to take actions against the best interest of their own country and fled to join up with partisans in the forests to attack the Soviets as they retreated before the German armies. At first the partisans and German worked together against a common enemy with the Germans even supplying the partisans with modern weapons. One of the resistance groups, made up mostly of students, had formed in Tartu weeks before the Germans had attacked and now, they were armed and ready to fight. In early July the group decided to liberate their town to avoid Soviet destruction of key its infrastructure.

On 6 July German fighter aircraft attacked Raadi air base north of the river, which precipitated a rapid withdrawal of Soviet forces and NKVD. The pontoon bridge near the market hall was demolished and two days later the 150-year-old stone bridge at the north end of the City Hall Square was blown up. By now the only Soviet forces in Tartu were a destruction battalion and some of the NKVD special groups.

The Estonian resistance appointed Olev Reintalu to lead operations against these forces and liberate the town. On 10 July, the remaining Soviet forces had taken up positions close to the railway line on Rīga Street where the Germans were expected to enter the town. Another group had moved across the remaining bridge in the southern part of Tartu.

When a German reconnaissance unit entered the town, the Soviets pulled back, and partisans came out to join the German forces. The German units returned to the main force at nightfall with requests for weapons to be sent up to the partisans. During the night, the Soviets continued their demolitions by destroying the last remaining bridge, but the partisans found an unguarded weapons store that had been part of the 2nd Estonian Division and salvaged 300 rifles with ammunition. They now went hunting through the town, wearing white emblems with the crest of the Estonian Republic or an armband with the Estonian national colours for identification, looking for Soviet soldiers who had become separated from the main force.

During the night, however, Soviet artillery opened fire on the southern part of Taru and Major General M.S. Shumilov's 11th Rifle Corps advanced on the town. In response, the Germans sent units of the XXVI Armeekorps forward, but the northern part of the town had been set ablaze by the Soviets. Regular Estonian forces under Captain Karl Talpak significantly raised the morale of the partisans whose ranks had been supplemented by people coming in from the countryside. Women of the Estonian Defence League set up kitchens and makeshift medical centres for the fighters. By dawn there were some 700 of Kurg's *Miško Broliai* in the town. Buildings were systematically searched for Soviet soldiers who were peremptorily shot when found but the artillery barrage continued, and more parts of the town were set on fire by Soviet forces.

On 12 July, the stronger German forces in the form of an anti-tank platoon arrived to support the partisans but Soviet artillery spotters occupied some of the taller buildings and were able to direct accurate fire onto their positions. The Germans now retired to the further reaches of the town happy to leave the partisans to hold their positions alone and hunt down the artillery spotters one by one. The almost continuous Soviet bombardment, supplemented by sporadic air attacks was slowly reducing parts of the town to rubble and the burning of buildings continued in the northern areas. Kurg was having great difficulty in containing the aggressive Soviet forays across the Emajõgi river that split the town running north to south.

It was clear to the Germans that the Soviets, having withdrawn quickly from Latvia and Lithuania, were going to fight hard for Estonia, which they saw as the forward defences of Leningrad. There were at least two rifle corps centred on Rakvere in the north blocking their advance north of Lake Peipus. Von Küchler sent Lieutenant General Walter Behschnitt's 254th Infanterie-Division up from Viru to support the 61st Infantry Division and Lieutenant General Kurt Herzog's 291st Infanterie-Division from Kurzeme to reinforce the 217th Infanterie-Division at Pärnu.

Meanwhile, the Soviets relieved Lyubovtsev's 16th by bringing Major General Bogdanov's 48th and Major General Bogaichuk's 125th rifle divisions up to the outskirts of Tartu on a day that saw fine sunny weather break up into thunderstorms that turned roads to mud. Just to be on the safe side, von Küchler brought his 93rd Infanterie-Division out of reserve to be on hand to pile into the battle on 21 July 1941 if need be. His idea now was to drive into the rear of Sobennikov's, General Pyotr Petrovich 8th Army by taking first Põltsamaa and then Jõgeva and cutting off the main road north of Tartu but the main Soviet force withdrew before it could be isolated. Those units of the 11th Rifle Division that had been left behind as a screen tried several times to break out of the encirclement but were overcome by the German 93rd and 61st Infanterie-Divisionen who took 8,794 prisoners. The Germans were rapidly learning what was the proper size for a ring of encirclement in any given situation. It was unsound to try and envelop too much because it left potential gaps for breakout. In this case they got it right.

By the end of August, all of mainland Estonia was in German hands but in order to have complete control of the Baltics, the Germans needed to occupy the large islands of Vormsi, Saaremaa and Muhu which were occupied by the Soviet 3rd Rifle Brigade. The German 61st Infantry Division launched Operation *Beowulf* with a series of diversionary attacks codenamed *Südwind*, *Westwind* and *Nordwind*. They crossed in a fleet of some 100 barges and ferries together a number of smaller assault boats. The small island of Vormsi was taken on 9 September and a landing on Muhu followed five days later. A bridgehead was established across the causeway to Saaremaa on the following day. The Soviet troops surrendered on 5 October. None of the Soviet defenders were able to escape; their losses amounted to 4,700 killed and 19,000 captured. German casualties totalled 2,850.

The three first weeks of fighting in the north-western sector of the battlefront saw Soviet troops abandoning the Baltics and retreating 450 kilometres, leaving behind 75,000 dead servicemen, more than 1,000 tanks, 4,000 artillery cannons and mortars and more than 1,000 aircraft. Of the 170 Soviet divisions along the whole front, 28 were destroyed. By the end of 1941 almost 4 million Soviet soldiers had been taken prisoner. The liberation and defence of southern Tartu, initiated by a small group of patriotic students with no military expertise, is one of the most important achievements of the Estonian campaign and even though it did not achieve the goal of renewed Estonian independence that the students had hoped for it became an issue of national pride that sustained the Estonian people in the long dark years ahead.

Captain Jonas Sematis had been a member of the Lithuanian army but found himself a member of the 617th Artillery Regiment of the Red Army's 184th Rifle Division when the Germans attacked on 22 June. He retreated with his unit through Valkininkai when, along with a band of fellow Lithuanians, he absconded in the chaos and they all surrendered to the Germans. At a prisoner of war camp in Vilnius they were separated out from Red Army prisoners and taken to barracks on Kalvarijų Street where they were offered a chance to join Lithuanian self-defence battalions.

On the day that the Germans had launched their attack, the LAF supported them with an uprising in several Lithuanian towns and cities. In Vilnius, many LAF members had been arrested by the Soviets leaving a much-reduced capability but, nevertheless, the rebels were able to occupy the post office and radio station since there were very few Soviet troops in the city and they fled as soon as news of the German attack came through. The Germans had been happy to have the LAF on board as a thorn in the Soviet flesh but now that the Bolsheviks were being driven out they decided it was time to clamp down on all underground movements. A directive went out from Berlin on 26 June instructing von Leeb to disarm all armed Lithuanian groups and the Lithuanian police.

The arrival of German forces in the Baltics forced the Soviets to compromise if they were to have any chance of mobilising the populations to resist the occupation. Suddenly it was a case of historic unity and friendship of the peoples that had been part of the Imperial Russian Empire who now had to work together to defeat the 'fascist barbarians.' This called for the resurrection of nationalist military units, previously banned in 1938, and the acceptance of nationalist partisan units willing to cooperate with the Soviets, who had to grit their teeth and accept a brief resurgence of nationalist fervour.

Throughout the years of German occupation, the Soviets had to balance their forced identity as the 'older brother' in a family of equals who offered protection from the bully against their ambitions to recover lost ground and eventually bring the subordinate states back under the yoke of oppression, which would destroy all nationalist ambitions as its primary objective. It offered the Baltic states theoretical rights that they had no intention of allowing them to enjoy.[16]

Any thoughts the Soviets might have had about galvanising opposition to German occupation would inevitably have come up against the evidence of what was happening in the forest around the village of Rainiai just outside the town of Telšiai where Red Army troops had reacted to the German attack with panic. All political prisoners inside Lithuanian jails were supposed to be evacuated with the troops and taken back to the Soviet Union but the German attack had taken them by surprise and there was not enough time for that. The head of the investigation Department of the Lithuanian NKGB, E. Rozauska, set a precedent by saying 'As there are no possibilities to evacuating prisoners from Kaunas prison No.1, we suggest to select the most dangerous ones and shoot them to death before retreating'.[17]

On 22 June 1941, there were 162 inmates of the Telšiai prison, of whom 76 were under interrogation by the NKVD for anti-Soviet activities. Not all had been arrested for political opposition, some farmers and tradespeople had been accused of hoarding and profiteering, which under a communist regime was just as bad. All of the Soviet administration had quickly fled the town when German aircraft bombed it on 22 June, but some Red Army troops remained behind.

On the morning of Tuesday, 24 June, two lorry-loads of Red Army soldiers drove up to the prison and began making a list of prisoners according to the charges laid against them. The soldiers were desperate to withdraw from the town and did not want to be encumbered by prisoners but neither did they want to leave behind those who had been arrested for anti-Soviet activity and who would doubtless become a danger to the Soviet Union if left to join up with the Nazis. Chief of NKGB Telšiai commissariat Petras Raslanas, who was in charge of the Soviet troops in the prison later reported, 'We came to the conclusion that leaving over 70 counterrevolutionaries behind in Telšiai prison would naturally amount to an organized gang against the Red Army, and it would have constituted a crime to leave them there.'[18]

Together with Deputy Chief of Telšiai district commissariat, Security Lieutenant Ždanov, head of Telšiai district Executive Office

Domas Rocius and Deputy of NKGB Kretinga district commissariat and Second Lieutenant of Security Jermolajev, Raslanas selected forty-three but later increased it to seventy-six including two Red Army soldiers who had been arrested for unspecified crimes. While they were deliberating news came through that the Germans had broken through and were approaching the town. Some prison warders and soldiers were then sent out to the forest to start digging trenches. Republika Straße near the prison was sealed off as seventeen lorries drove into the prison yard. Each of the seventy-six prisoners was taken from their cell, had charges read out to them and each was declared guilty. Just before midnight they were taken from their cells, bound, gagged and put on the lorries, which then driven off into the forest. Their bodies would be discovered four days later.

Chapter 6

THE GERMAN OCCUPATION

On 24 August 1941, British Prime Minister Winston Churchill made a live radio broadcast in which he told the world

> [in eastern Europe] whole districts are being exterminated ... literally scores of thousands – of executions in cold blood are being perpetrated by the German Police-troops ... there has never been methodical, merciless butchery on such a scale, or approaching such a scale.

'We are in the presence,' he said, 'of a crime without a name.'[1] The destruction of whole states was creating a new sort of politics in which a technique of killing civilians was developed despite there having been no German plan for mass exterminations.

The Wannsee Conference of 20 January 1942 at which the 'Final Solution of the Jewish Problem' was discussed was still some months away. In late summer 1941, after initial successes, the Germans expected that the war against the Soviet Union would be short and there would be ample time to implement ethnic cleansing of the Jews and others when Moscow was in German hands. Despite the apparent lack of urgency in the matter, however, by the end of 1941, with von Bock's German Army Group Centre stalled at the gates of the Soviet capital, more than 1 million Jews had already been murdered and it was this, as much as anything, that convinced Reinhard Heydrich and Heinrich Himmler that it was possible to contemplate the eventual murder of all European Jewry.

The overriding objective of the first German occupying forces in the Baltics was first demolition of the nation states. Hitler's plans for the conquest of eastern Europe and the Soviet Union fundamentally included the liquidation of the indigenous communities but initially the plan was simply to remove them from their native soil and relocate them to the wastelands of Siberia. The natural economic resources of the conquered lands would then be used exclusively for the benefit of ethnic Germans and in the meantime the invading German forces would be living off the land, which would deprive the incumbents of food. The subsequent death by starvation of millions was factored into the German plans right from the start and would automatically free up the land for later occupation by German communities.

Civilian administrations would be set up as quickly as possible to remove from the Wehrmacht the burden of control of civilian populations. To facilitate this, all political leaders would be eliminated leaving the people with no discernible focus for resistance. Intellectuals who had survived Soviet persecution were targeted, as were all those administrators suspected of having collaborated with the Soviets. Thereafter what remained of the local populations would be kept at minimal cultural and educational levels sufficient for them to carry out the basic tasks allocated to them.

Hitler prevaricated over the fate to which he would condemn the Baltics but, at the last minute before invasion, decided upon annexation and 'racial cleansing'. Lithuania, Latvia and Estonia would simply cease to exist as independent states. After the spectacular early successes of *Barbarossa,* he called a high-powered meeting on 16 July 1941 that later became known as the Angerburg Conference in which, amongst other things, he reiterated his vision of extreme exploitation of the conquered territories and emphasised the need for the harshest treatment of anyone who opposed them. It was on this day that Hitler decided to appoint Alfred Rosenberg, a native Estonian, as Reich Minister for the Eastern Occupied Territories in what was now called the *Reichskommissariat Ostland* but Rosenberg, who was adequately endowed with Nazi venom but was essentially intellectually dim, was easily outmanoeuvred by SS leader Heinrich Himmler who was to become the principal police authority in the east. Within a week of the Angerburg Conference, Himmler had quadrupled the number of SS men operating behind the German front.

Rosenberg had been with Hitler since the early days of the Beerhall Putsch in 1923 and, despite, or perhaps because of, his dull mind, he appeared to be one of Hitler's favourites. Hitler valued him for his unswerving loyalty as well as his lack of threat to his leadership, which gave him a certain influence on Hitler's decision-making on lesser matters and it was Rosenberg's assessment of Baltic peoples that moulded Hitler's racial policy there. Being one himself, Rosenberg naturally saw Estonians, with high levels of Scandinavian blood, as the superior race out of the three giving them dominance over the Latvians, who were seen as having an unfortunate proclivity for Bolshevism, and the Lithuanians with such a large Polish population having no discernible virtues and coming a poor third. The last two countries would require substantial 'clearing out' of intelligencia and political leadership before being acceptable as additions to the Reich. On 13 May, the Wehrmacht High Command, in preparation for invasion of the Soviet Union, had been prevailed upon by Himmler and Heydrich to issue orders, pertaining to the populations of regions that would be occupied, authorising the shooting of all persons suspected of communist affiliation, including civilians, and gave permission for harsh reprisals to be carried out against any who resisted or posed a threat to German security.

Having drawn the Wehrmacht into his web, Heydrich knew that ordinary soldiers, not yet battle-hardened, would be reluctant to carry out the necessary actions implied in the order and so called on his *Einsatzgruppen* to show them the way but what they would ask to do next was new, even for many of them. The *Einsatzgruppen* had actually been first used by Heydrich in Austria in 1938 as an ad hoc security formation tasked with securing public buildings in the immediate aftermath of the Anschluss. Units were stationed in the Sudetenland later the same year where they were used to arrest up to 10,000 Czechs identified as being security risks to the occupying German forces.

It was there in Czechoslovakia at this time that they were first deployed to implement a program of systematic murder of persons with physical and mental disabilities, and patients of psychiatric hospitals. The man who would go on to command *Einsatzgruppe* A in the Baltics, Dr Franz Walter Stahlecker, was at this time in command of *Einsatzgruppe* Wien. There was no sense in which the *Einsatzgruppen* were, at this time before the start of the war, involved in the mass murder of Jews. When later deployed in Poland, they murdered far more Poles than Jews, for instance.

Immediately after the Anschluss, members of the Austrian *Sturmabteilung* (SA – storm troopers) had begun persecuting, humiliating, abusing and stealing from Austrian Jews. One Viennese Jew recalled that 'Austrians became antisemites all of a sudden and taught the Germans how to treat Jews'.[2] Three quarters of all Jewish businesses in Austria were in German hands by the end of 1938 and Adolf Eichmann, the head of Heydrich's *Sicherheitsdienst* (security service, SD) Jewish section, set up a Central Office for Jewish Emigration forcing some 60,000 Jews to leave the country, many of whom went to Poland. Thirty-two countries led by the US met to discuss the crisis and all but one, the Dominican Republic of Dominica, refused to take in any Jewish refugees at all.

Kristallnacht showed what could be done in Germany itself and this caused Jews to begin leaving Germany in large numbers. Then, when Germany occupied the Sudetenland, an *Einsatzgruppe* began arresting political opponents in the region but still had no orders to kill them. Again, many Jews fled. When the Germans invaded Poland in September 1939, Poles had turned on Poles and settled old scores amongst themselves after the destruction of the Polish state and the breakdown of Polish law, but it was only after the *Einsatzgruppen* arrived that the mass extermination of the Polish intelligentsia began. It was in Poland that the constraints were lifted, and the *Einsatzgruppen* first unleashed their campaign of mass murder developing their techniques and expertise as they went.

The Wehrmacht, which had its own field police, resented the interference in what they saw as their own area of responsibility of security and were hostile to any attempt by Himmler and the SS to impinge on their territory. Not only that but they had been appalled by the violence meted out by the *Einsatzgruppen* and SS in Poland. Colonel Erwin Lahousen of the Abwehr reported 'unrest' arising from 'illegal measures' taken by the *Einsatzgruppen*. 'It was annoying to the troops', he said 'that young men instead of fighting at the front were testing their courage on defenceless people'. It was a spectacularly inadequate and mealy-mouthed complaint, but it got no response and soon the Wehrmacht would be drawn into complicity in such acts when all criticism would disappear.[3]

With the disintegration of the Polish state, minorities lost much of their protection. Civil law was replaced by Nazi edict, which was aimed overwhelmingly against the Jews who were driven into ghettos. Jews suddenly disappeared from what for hundreds of years had been mixed communities. Without the protection of the law, Jewish property was looted, and Jewish women were sexually violated. The ghettos, where many died in the first few months from hunger and disease, became places where the Jews were held until arrangements could be made for their deportation but the problem for the Germans was that there was nowhere for them to go. Eichmann approached the Soviets to see if they would be willing to accept 2 million Jews from Poland but Stalin, despite his overweening and desperate efforts to retain good relations with Germany, was not interested in that at all. Hitler was not dismayed, however. He believed that this problem would find a solution after the rapid conquest of the Soviet Union when the Jews and other 'inferior' races would be deported to labour camps in the Soviet hinterlands.

Heydrich had addressed his *Einsatzgruppen* leaders in a top-secret directive of 21 September 1939 concerning 'the Jewish question in the

Occupied Territory'. As a means of achieving the 'final aim' he required 'immediate action' to concentrate the Jews in the towns.[4] Heydrich now saw his chance to roll out his own agenda beyond Poland, which he had drawn up in March 1941 by expanding the wartime judicial powers of the *Einsatzgruppen*. Hitler had approved his plans to 'pacify by eradication'.

Heydrich successfully completed negotiations with Wehrmacht Quartermaster General Georg Wagner on 26 March 1941 for cooperation between the *Einsatzgruppen* and the German army in areas of 'command and jurisdiction' to facilitate the implementation of 'special tasks' in areas behind the front lines under the control of Reich commissioners.[5] Hitler later endorsed this in a decree issued on 17 July. Under the agreement, all German army commanders were to immediately identify and register all Jews in occupied areas in the Soviet Union, and fully co-operate with the *Einsatzgruppen*. A new and unprecedented chapter in the tragic history of European Jewry was about to be written as the campaign against them was ratcheted up another notch.

While these *Einsatzgruppen* were the first German units to be called later to shoot Jews in large numbers, they were only a small minority of Germans who took part in atrocities and Jews were only one of a number of categories of victims. A detailed and nuanced work, *Die Einsatzgruppen der Sicherheitspolizei und des SD 1938–1942*, written by Helmut Krausnick and Hans-Heinrich Wilhelm was published by the Munich Institut für Zeitgeschichte in which the authors look at the structure and activities of *Einsatzgruppe* A in particular, and the nature of the relationship between them and the Wehrmacht command. Foremost in their investigations is an analysis of how the unparalleled extermination measures implemented against entire populations was made possible by the collaboration between the Wehrmacht command and the criminal regime, represented on the spot by the units of the chief of the *Sicherheitspolizei* (security police) and the SD.

Extensive *Einsatzgruppen* reports survive but reliance on these reports is problematical given that there are instances where data in these reports was manipulated to support the arguments and praise the work of the security police and SD and especially that of the *Einsatzgruppen*. This is particularly true in the Baltics where both *Einsatzgruppe A* and the Wehrmacht competed for praise in dealing with the partisans. An account of the various activities of Einsatzgruppe A that is as objective as possible, shows not only the extent of the atrocities committed in fulfilment of their orders but also that they could not have completed these criminal tasks if they had not been embedded within the German occupation and if numerous other

German offices had not cooperated.[6] The total number of *Einsatzgruppen* personnel was, in fact, far less than the numbers of German police and Wehrmacht soldiers who participated in the killings.[7]

Heydrich and Himmler had created these *Einsatzgruppen* as an organisation operating beyond German borders out of the limelight and beyond the glare of scrutiny with a free hand to carry out the most brutal acts of suppression and later to facilitate ethnic cleansing of the Jews. Whilst they were not the only ones, the *Einsatzgruppen* showed the way and led by example to an army that was becoming brutalised by war and increasingly susceptible to committing of acts of gruesome violence. In Poland, the occupying German forces had instituted and led pogroms where Jews had been subjected to violent attacks by non-Jewish civilians but it was soon clear that as a method of reducing the number of Jews it was hopelessly inefficient. However, pogroms allowed the Germans to identify those perpetrators who were the most enthusiastic tormentors and murderers of the Jews, and it was these men who were recruited to form the hard core of *Einsatzgruppen* leaders to carry out the more organised mass killings.

It was a start but a slow method of recruiting the necessary numbers to follow up the 2 million Wehrmacht forces lining up to invade the Soviet Union. Assembly of *Einsatzgruppen* for Operation *Barbarossa* began in May 1941 when the core leadership of the Kripo (criminal police), Gestapo and security police were assembled at the Frontier Police School barracks at Pretsch in Saxony. It is worth noting that many of these chosen leaders were men of high intelligence coming from legal and academic backgrounds. The enlisted men were drawn from the SS, Waffen-SS, regular police, locally recruited police, and auxiliaries recruited from Ukrainian, Lithuanian, Latvian and Estonian local volunteers and native fascist militia.[8]

There were far too few of these special units to carry out mass murder on the scale envisaged by Heydrich and Himmler and furthermore, it was clear that these much greater numbers of people that would need to be found, many of somewhat less barbaric predisposition than those already recruited, would need to be motivated to overcome a fundamental aversion to the killing of women and children. All but the very worst killers would experience emotional stress and excessive use of alcohol was not always enough for them to become fully involved in the process of extermination of whole communities. They were subjected to intense propaganda explaining why they must kill all Jews because the Jews and their communist cohorts had planned to do that very same thing to them and their families. The message was simple, as all good propaganda is. The Jews must die so that Germans may live. One of the basic tenets of Nazi propaganda was that the Bolshevik system, the greatest threat to the German people, would collapse just as soon as its Jewish collaborators were eliminated.

For their role in the Soviet war, Heydrich organised his *Einsatzgruppen* into four mobile units of specially trained SS assassins, tasked with providing security against suspected enemies of the Reich in the rear areas behind the front-line Wehrmacht forces. German historian Michael Wildt described them as 'the men who drafted the blueprints, built and operated the machinery that made murder of millions of people possible.' *Einsatzgruppe A*, tasked with operating in the Baltics and behind the Leningrad Front, was under the command of Stahlecker and comprised some 990 men, included 89 from the Gestapo, 41 from the Kripo and 340 from the Waffen-SS. Of the seventeen officers, eleven were lawyers. These were subdivided into *Einsatzkommando* units 2 and 3, each of around 120 men and *Sonderkommando* (special commands) 1a and 1b. These Sonderkommandos followed the Wehrmacht forces closely with instructions to establish early contact with local anti-Bolshevik groups and see to what extent they might be seconded to the cause.[9] They would follow German Army Group North on its drive towards Leningrad. Methods for the mass killing of Jews were developed according to no special plan but acquired a methodology devised, modified and refined with each atrocity.

Much that has been written about the activities of the *Einsatzgruppen* during Operation *Barbarossa* has come from transcripts of the International Military Tribunal at Nuremberg, especially Case No. 9, *United States v. Otto Ohlendorf, et al* and Case No. 12, *United States v. Wilhelm von Leeb, et al.* One issue of some interest is the question of when, where and from whom the *Einsatzgruppen* received the order for Judenvernichtungsbefehl (to execute all Jews), which has a significant legal bearing on the distinction between perpetrators and accomplices. At Nuremberg, SS General Otto Ohlendorf, who had been the head of *Einsatzgruppe D*, testified that the order was issued by SS Brigadeführer Bruno Streckenbach prior to the invasion of the Soviet Union but this is disputed.

A study by Alfred Streim concluded, after working through hundreds of interrogations produced in the proceedings against former members of the *Einsatzgruppen*, that the order to shoot all Jews including women and children was issued approximately between the beginning of August 1941 at the earliest and September 1941 at the latest, several weeks after the invasion of the Soviet Union. The timing is important because all relevant court decisions that found members of the *Einsatzgruppen* guilty as accomplices to murder for killing Jews immediately after the invasion of the Soviet Union would be seen to be incorrect because they were acting without a specific order. If there was no order, then they would have been perpetrators, which would have landed them with life sentences rather than light prison terms.

Streim claims that Ohlendorf made the assertion that Stahlecker gave the order before 22 June believing that he was dead, but he returned from captivity in the Soviet Union in 1955 when he denied ever having issued the order. Nor is there any strong evidence to show that Heydrich gave such an order when he attended the final preparations for deployment of the *Einsatzgruppen* on 17 June 1941. Much has been said about a verbal order but his written Operational Order No. 8 says nothing specific about killing Jews and unambiguous testimonies by several *Einsatzkommando* chiefs, including Ehrlinger in *Sonderkommando 1b*, asserted that the order was issued several weeks after the start of the Russian campaign.[10]

There has been much debate over the existence of a verbal directive of 17 June 1941 in which Heydrich is said to have instructed the *Einsatzgruppen* to liquidate Jews in all state administrative positions but his written Operational Order No. 8 of that date says nothing specific about killing Jews only that 'no obstacle' must be allowed to get in the way of the purging of Jews and Bolsheviks wherever they may be found. Nor does his telegram of 2 July to all Higher SS and Police leaders in which he wrote, 'All functionaries of the Comintern (Communist International) are to be executed', give instructions for the mass killing of Jews, only those in party and state positions. If there had been a clear instruction for mass executions of Jews, this detail would hardly have been necessary.

Of course, it must be remembered that both Heydrich and Himmler maintained a high level of secrecy over their plans for dealing with the Jews and evidence for them only comes indirectly as when Stahlecker fulminate against the civil authorities for being 'insufficiently radical' in their dealings with the Jews. In his tirade, he referred to 'fundamental orders that were not to be spelled out in writing'.[11] Only those leaders of the *Einsatzgruppen* in post in June 1941 could know who delivered the order for the mass extermination of Jewish women and children to begin. Only Ohlendorf and Rasch survived the war but Rasch was too ill to stand trial. The opening statement of his defence lawyer, however, clearly showed that the order was issued around August 1941 at Shitomor by Higher SS and Police Leader of Ostland, Friedrich Jeckeln.[12]

It was probably Himmler who made the specific order to begin the murder of Jewish women and children. In late July when he had boosted the numbers of SS troops after Hitler's Angerburg Conference, he called on SS cavalry in the Pripet Marshes to 'Drive the female Jews into the swamp.' Taking the order literally, 'Sturmbannführer Franz Magill reported back that the swamps were not deep enough to drown them.'[13] Himmler realised that he would need to be more specific. Sometime between 24 July and 1 August while the Reserve Police Battalion 45, under Major Franz, was in Shepetovka, he paid visit to Police Regiment South and gave an order that its commander Colonel Besser duly passed on to Franz. 'Shoot the Jews, women and children included,' was the clear instruction. It was well known, however, that Jeckeln had already started doing this and Chief of *Einsatzgruppe B* SS Brigadeführer Arthur Nebe hinted that it was already widely known that the mass execution of Jews had been authorised at higher levels. On 23 July 1941 he had lamented that without deportations, 'a solution' to the problem of 1.5 million Jews in Belorussia would be extremely difficult. He was clearly arguing that whatever new strategy that had replaced deportations would struggle to achieve the desired results. Clearly, he was referring to extermination. Even his mind was not willing to accept that the execution of such a vast number of people was logistically possible.[14]

Nebe's reluctance to spell out the extermination strategy on paper was reflected in a note written to Standartenführer Karl Jäger by Stahlecker to the effect that there were 'general orders from a higher authority to the security police that cannot be discussed in writing.' It had clearly been at the Angerburg Conference that Hitler himself had assumed that with victory in Russia only weeks away it was time to pursue a radical strategy towards the Jews. The speed with which it was implemented also clearly shows that plans had been laid ready but beyond a few, those who would carry out the task had not had orders to do so, and it was at this time that Himmler made a personal visit to all Einsatzgruppen commands in Russia to give that order in person.

Lithuania

In Lithuania, the liquidation of Jews began on 22 June 1941, as soon as the first German boot hit Lithuanian soil. The process would have four distinct phases:

- The pogroms and initial actions aimed at Jewish men and alleged communists between late June and early July of 1941.
- Selective killing operations from early July to mid-August

- The implementation of the 'Final Solution' in the countryside and larger Lithuanian towns from mid-August to late November 1941, followed by the ghettoization of Jews.
- The periodic selections and liquidation of the ghettos during 1942–44.

Anti-Semitism in Lithuania had been greatly fuelled by LAF propaganda, which was infiltrated into the country during the Soviet occupation from LAF printing presses in Berlin. Much of it centred on the role supposedly played by Jews as collaborators in Soviet repression. According to Povilas Šilas, a Christian Democrat deputy in the provisional government of 1941 who wrote a memoir, in 1940–41, the Jews 'sinned heavily' by being the first active collaborators of the Soviets in establishing Bolshevik power. Taking many important posts in the state institutions and administration, they effectively took control of the state security and public police. Lithuanian Jews, he claims, collaborated very actively with the Bolsheviks in compiling the lists of the thousands of Lithuanians arrested and deported.

Historian Zenonas Ivinskis says that 'Lithuanians felt deeply disappointed with and even betrayed by the Jews,' The eminent historian and writer, Liudas Truska, takes issue with this generalisation, however, and calls much of the literature on the subject 'journalistic' implying lack of rigour and he questions the reliability of 'declarative' memoirs, which, he says, are of little historical value. The historian Arvydas Anušauskas has shown that it was Russian-speaking officials sent from Moscow who were the main executors of the repressions and in general, Truska says, research conducted by historians demonstrates that the Jews had not played any special part in the 'Sovietisation of Lithuania and the repressing of its people.' LAF propaganda certainly played a major role influencing the consciousness of the Lithuanians, but Truska says that there is no evidence showing that the LAF ever called on Lithuanians to slaughter Jews, as is often asserted.

Factual evidence indicates that in 1940–41 Jews played no special role in the structures of the Soviet Government, nor its repressive institutions. The Jews, Truska says, were scapegoats for the 'deep moral crisis' of the Lithuanian nation in the late 1930s and early 1940s.[15]

Putting aside the question of the role of Jews under the Soviets, the Holocaust became a reality for them in Lithuania when Germany invaded. It was organized and controlled by the German security police assisted by Lithuanian self-defence battalions, the police department, the Lithuanian security police, and the local civilian administration.

The scale and speed of the violence can be gauged from the fact that about three quarters of the 200,000–206,000 Lithuanian Jews were murdered within the first six months of the German occupation. What Snyder calls 'the myth of [the Einsatzgruppe] total responsibility' for the massacre of Jews arose during post-war trials in the Federal Republic of Germany as a way to protect the majority of German killers and isolate the killing from German society as such.[16]

The issue of Lithuanian culpability and the extent to which Lithuanian nationals have been denigrated as the arch-perpetrators of war crimes is also hotly debated and by no means has a consensus been arrived at. Pēters Vecrumba, curator of the website *https://holocaustinlatvia.org* and acolyte of the Holocaust scholar Professor Andrievs Ezergailis published a study in 2022 in which he questioned what he called the 'systemic bias' and imposition of 'external agendas' of historians such as Kaspars Zellis, Valdis Lūmans and Dr Katrin Reichelt who seek to 'absolve Germans and blame the local population for the Holocaust.'

On the day following the German invasion of the Baltics, Leonas Prapuolenis, on behalf of the LAF, announced over the revived Kaunas radio station, 'The established Provisional and newly reborn Government of Lithuania hereby announces that it is re-establishing the free and independent state of Lithuania. Before the pure conscience of the whole world, the young state of Lithuania enthusiastically promises to contribute to the organization of Europe on a new basis. Tormented by the brutal terror of the Bolsheviks, the Lithuanian nation decides to build its future based on national unity and social justice.' Jews and communists were equally vilified. Government minister Balys Vitkus announced on the radio: 'Today, it is difficult to find a Lithuanian family in our country that has not been touched by the hand of the Jewish-Bolshevik executioner.' While the Germans were met in some quarters with 'applauding and cheering', thousands of Jews such as Dov Levin recalled that 'Although crowds of Lithuanians greeted the Germans with flowers, it was no surprise that we closed our shutters, lowered our curtains, and locked ourselves up in our homes'.[17]

On the same day, the head of Lithuania's diplomatic corps, Stasys Lozoraitis, then in Rome, having been denied an audience with the German ambassador there, sent a special congratulatory telegram to Italy's Foreign Minister Gian Galeazzo Ciano to 'express congratulations on the war against the Bolsheviks [and welcomed] the replacement of the Bolshevik occupation by the German occupation [as] a great step forward for us in the direction of the restoration of [Lithuanian] independence.' It is clear that while the policy of the remaining Western democratic world was headed in one direction, the policy of the head of Lithuanian diplomacy as well as of the provisional government in Kaunas was headed in the exactly opposite direction and goes some way towards explaining why Lithuanians abroad failed to form a government in exile during the Second World War. However, not all diplomats agreed; Dr Jurgis Šaulys even refused to attend the Rome conference because of the 'general pro-German sentiments' dominant among Lithuanian diplomats and politicians in exile.

Kaunas was taken by the German invaders on 23 June and Vilnius fell the day after. The rest of Lithuania was conquered within four or five days. The rapidity of the German advance meant that few of the almost 250,000 Jews in Lithuania had the chance to flee. Only some 15,000 made it to the Soviet Union in time. The LAF declared Lithuanian independence as the first Germans entered Lithuania. Political prisoners were freed. Retreating Soviet forces were ambushed, and Lithuanians started murdering Jews who were accused of having been complicit in Soviet crimes during their occupation. With Škirpa under house arrest in Berlin, it was left to Juozas Ambrazevičius to announce the formation of a Lithuanian provisional government in Kaunas.

Commander-in-Chief of the German army Walther von Brauchitsch reacted immediately by ordering that all Lithuanian armed groups or police units were to be disarmed and any leaders showing a propensity to resist German authority should be transported to concentration camps. It is worth noting that his directive made no mention of killing civilians, but his mood would soon change. Within days the LAF was closed down and its assets confiscated. Prapuolenis was arrested and thrown into Dachau concentration camp. Many LAF members went underground and tried to start a new anti-Nazi resistance movement, but it proved impossible to unite all the factions under one leadership.

The German administration of Lithuanian was divided into four areas centred on the cities of Kaunas, Vilnius, Shavli and Panevėžys. The police and the SS was headed up by Major General Visotski while the security police and SD was run by Jäger the head of Einsatzkommando 3 (EK3). Hauptsturmführer Heinrich Schmitz worked under Visotski and was in charge of Jewish affairs. On 1 September a civilian administration was set up under Alfred Rosenberg but a month previously, on 27 July, he had agreed with the Wehrmacht to allow Heinrich Lohse, the Reichskommissar of Ostland to begin supervising the work of the Generalkommossaire and Gebietskommissiare in the occupied areas from his headquarters in Rīga. Neither the Wehrmacht nor Rosenberg were prepared to recognise the legitimacy of local administrations.

Throughout the Soviet occupation, LAF propaganda had increasingly convinced Lithuanians that significant numbers of the

Jewish communities in the country had collaborated with the Soviet authorities. On the day after Soviet troops had entered the country in 1940, Lithuanian historian Zenonas Ivinskis had noted in his diary, 'Most of the people (at least those whom I meet) are simply craving for the Germans to come. And then the real slaughtering of the Jews would start. Fury at the Jews for their outrageous sympathies to the Bolsheviks, for their internationalism, and for their arrogance is great.'[18]

For the Jews, Soviet occupation had been a significantly better alternative to Nazi rule but for many Lithuanians the deportations and murders of Lithuanian elites by the Soviets made them yearn for the Germans to come in and rescue them from Bolshevik tyranny. Some LAF statements clearly advocated violence against the Jews and clearly gave carte blanche to activists to commit murder but others stopped short of that and simply called for expulsion and expropriation of the Lithuanian Jewish community. Evidence suggests that the calls for more extreme measures came directly from Voldemaris' man in Berlin, Stasys Puodžius.[19] In Vilnius, the 14-year-old Jew Yitskhok Rudashevski wrote in his diary, 'I think how defenceless we are, isolated from each other, exposed entirely to the mercy of the Hitlerites … Our life is a life of helpless terror. Our days have no future.'[20]

There is compelling evidence that during the first Soviet occupation, the relations between Jews and Lithuanians had been fundamentally changed. Anti-Semitic myths and stereotypes were used not only by the Germans but also by the LAF in Berlin and the anti-Soviet underground in occupied Lithuania to incite pogroms and involve Lithuanians in mass violence against their Jewish neighbours. Many private letters and diaries from that time shared the same views and depicted Jews as traitors, who betrayed Lithuania.

When the German army struck, the earliest massacres of Lithuanian Jews and communists were organized by SS Major Hans Joachim Böhme in the border area of a 25-kilometre-wide strip of land and carried out by Gestapo Tilsit, one of the components of Einsatzkommando Tilsit. A report sent to SS Brigadeführer Müller dated 1 July 1941 stated that in Gargždai, 201 people, including 1 woman, had been killed on 24 June 1941, then on the following day, 214 people were shot in Kretinga, and on 27 June 1941, 111 were murdered in Palanga. Further on in the Kaunas district, pogroms were carried out in Vilijampolė when organized groups of LAF partisans went from house to house searching for communists. A police report stated that the partisans

> Stabbed and slaughtered in the most brutal ways, men and women, old people and small children, without distinction. With terrible sadism

> they struck heads with hatchets, stabbed and shot. The partisans went into the houses and chased the people out of theirs beds into the yards, where they lined them up against a wall and shot them.[21]

In Lietūkis a large crowd of people stood and watched a brutal massacre of fifty people by assassins killing in 'blind fury'. One eye-witness account described how

> After [the Jews] were brought to the square, they were struck quite indiscriminately on the head or face until they were stunned and collapsed on the ground. Then they were struck by the convicts until there were no more signs of life. Then more Jews were brought into the square and killed in the same manner. I remained at the spot where this grim scene took place for about ten minutes. While I was watching the square, I witnessed between ten and fifteen Jews being killed.

A German officer who was called to the scene recalled that

> I had to walk away as I didn't want to see any more ... many German soldiers and also civilians continued to watch. The soldiers didn't take part in the proceedings, neither approving nor disapproving. We could hear shouts of approval and advice from the Lithuanian civilians.[22]

The LAF insurgents boosted by mutineers from the Red Army 297th Territorial Corps began a massacre of Jewish collaborators with the Soviet regime, which lasted until 28 June. During these few days, Stahlecker reported that Lithuanian partisans killed 3,800 Jews in Kaunas and 1,200 in the smaller towns. It is not possible to say what proportion of the Lithuanian population took part in or encouraged such brutality, but most would certainly have been horrified by what was going on.

Stahlecker, the head of *Einsatzgruppe A*, had arrived in Kaunas on 25 June and then Rīga on 1 July. He had been involved with virulent anti-Semitic movements since the end of the First World War and studied Law at Tübingen University before joining the Nazi Party and the SS in 1932. He became head of the Würrtemberg internal security police in 1934 where he had been spotted by Heydrich and recruited into the SD.

His report of 15 October concerned *Selbstreinigungs-aktionen* (self-cleansing actions) stated:

> It was to be expected that after liberation from [Soviet] rule, [the population of the Baltic countries] would themselves to a large extent eliminate those of the enemy left behind after the retreat of the Red Army.

> It was the task of the Security Police to set these self-cleansing movements going and to direct them into the right channels in order to achieve the aim of this cleansing as rapidly as possible. It was … important … that it was the liberated population itself which took the most severe measures, on its own initiative, against the Bolshevik and Jewish enemy, without any German instructions being evident.[23]

Efraim Zuroff, the American-born Israeli historian and director of the Simon Wiesenthal Centre in Jerusalem, has played a key role in bringing indicted Nazi and fascist war criminals to trial. With the Lithuanian journalist Rūta Vanagaitė, Zuroff places great emphasis on the role played by Lithuanian nationals in the Holocaust. In their book *Our People,* they claim that in many locations throughout provincial Lithuania, the majority of the killers of the Jews were Lithuanian volunteers, and in quite a few places, it was Lithuanians alone who carried out the murders, without any Germans or Austrians present. This was the case, for example, in Lazdijai, Telšiai, Eišiškės, Joniškis, Dubingiai, Babtai, Varėna and Vandžiogala, whereas in Onuškis, Vilkaviškis and Virbalis, the only Nazis present at the murder sites were photographing the crimes. Lithuanians physically attacked Jews in more than forty different cities, towns and villages, even before the Wehrmacht arrived, indicating again that many Lithuanians required no encouragement to harm their Jewish neighbours.

While it is true that many of the assassins were poorly educated or even illiterate, the role played by the Lithuanian elites, such as the clergy, intelligentsia and professionals was of great significance. Lithuanians not only murdered Jews in their own country. It is estimated that several thousand Lithuanian auxiliary police officers helped to carry out the systematic annihilation of Jews in Belarus. Furthermore, Lithuanian auxiliary police units murdered many thousands of foreign Jews deported to Lithuania from Germany, Austria and France.[24] While the book quickly climbed best-sellers lists, it also provoked increasing public hostility towards the author. After a short anti-Vanagaitė public campaign, led by the country's top journalists, all bookshops and publishing houses in Lithuania refused to sell anything and everything that Vanagaitė wrote.[25]

Clearly the first massacres of Lithuanian Jews were initiated by the German security police, but they were carried out mainly by Lithuanians such as Algirdas 'Jonas' Klimaitis and his group of around 600 former political prisoners and other individuals, none of whom belonged to the LAF, who had suffered under the Soviet authorities. It acted independently concentrating initially in driving the Soviets out of Kaunus but then, when the city was in their hands, they turned on the Jews and launched a pogrom burning synagogues and, according to Stahlecker, murdering as many as 5,000 Jews but this figure is seen by many as an overestimation.

Stahlecker commented on Klimatis in his report of 15 October 1941 as follows:

> Klimatis … who was the first to be recruited for this purpose, succeeded in starting a pogrom with the aid of instructions given him by a small advance detachment operating in Kovno, in such a way that no German orders or instructions could be observed by outsiders. In the course of the first pogrom during the night of June 25/26, the Lithuanian partisans eliminated more than 1,500 Jews, set fire to several synagogues or destroyed them by other means, and burned down an area consisting of about sixty houses inhabited by Jews. During the nights that followed, 2,300 Jews were eliminated in the same way. In other parts of Lithuania similar Aktionen followed the example set in Kovno, but on a smaller scale, and including some Communists who had been left behind.[26]

The report refers to the killing of 800 Jews in the suburb of Slobodka and 60 in the garage of the Lietūkis company. Thousands more were taken to Fort VII death camp and murdered there. Even before Soviet forces had fled, Jews were massacred in Shavli, Panevėžys, Plungė, Kėdainiai and Švenčionys. Mass attacks against Jews were not carried out in Vilnius, however, which was very much under control of the Poles there who were anxious not to allow chaotic violence to break out. In all, some 8,000–10,000 were killed between 23 June and 2 July.

Ambrazevičius' government discussed the ongoing assaults on the Jews in Vilijampolė and Lietūkis and declared that these actions had been carried out by the groups that had had no connection with them or the LAF but neither the government nor the Church made any statement condemning the ongoing massacres. On 2 July, *Einsatzkommando 9* (EK9) arrived in Vilnius and *Einsatzkommando 3* (EK3) in Kaunas. When *Einsatzkommando 2* (EK2) arrived in Shavli a few days later, all three commandos were split up into smaller mobile units. Jews were rounded up off the streets or from their homes and told they were being taken for forced labour. They were, in fact, taken outside the city and shot. The murder sites were Ponary near Vilnius, Fort VII and Fort IX death camps near Kaunas, the Kužiai forest outside Shavli, the Vidzgiris forest close to Alytus and the Kaiserlingas forest at Panevėžys.

When the Germans had arrived, Kaunas military commandant Jurgis Bobelis issued an order to begin forming TDA battalions (*Tautinio darbo apsauga*) which it was hoped would become the independent army of

Lithuania. Their first task, however, turned out to be the murder of Jews at Fort VII death camp. This was one of several abandoned military forts around Kaunus that had been built in the ninteenth century.

On 4 July, 416 men and 47 women were taken there and shot and then 2 days later machine guns replaced rifles when some 2,500 people were killed. According to Lithuanian Central State Archives, K-1, ap. 58, b. 47337/3, t. 1., p. 208, Pranas Matiukas, who at his trial in 1961 admitted that he 'kind of liked shooting people', was involved in the massacres and described them thus:

> Inside the fort, in the deep ravine between the slopes, about 300 to 400 people were under guard, people of Jewish ethnicity. They were there under the open sky. There were also about 100 to 150 women of Jewish ethnicity who were being guarded inside the underground fortifications of the fort itself. The shooting took place in the following manner. A group of battalion soldiers, more or less 10 people, commanded by petty officers or officers, took about 10 people from that ravine where the condemned Jewish males were being guarded. They took them about 50 to 100 metres from there, where there was a large crater caused by an explosion. Then they stood them on the edge of the pit facing the pit and shot them from several paces. After the shooting, the corpses fell into the pit. The soldiers fired from the rifles which they had, while the officers – Dagys, Norkus, Barzda – shot from pistols.
>
> The next day, as soon as it was light, we again went to the fort and surrounded the ravine where the arrested men were held. There were two or three light Bruno-type machine guns set up on the slopes. Barzda and Norkus said we would have to shoot the condemned right there, from the slope above into the ravine. Then the command was issued to begin firing. The people under fire began to run around inside the ravine, but were not able to escape anywhere, and all of them were felled by bullets. This disorderly shooting took about an hour and a half. During that time the bottom of the ravine was covered with corpses and blood.[27]

Jonas Raižys who was also tried at the same time testified that 'Because there were so many residential homes near the fort, many local residents gathered to watch the shooting'. It is believed that between 15,000 and 17,000 Jews were killed between 2 July and the end of the month.

On 27 July, Lohse instructed his Kommissars to begin 'implementation of the Final Solution of the Jewish problem in the territory of Ostland [Lithuania, Latvia, Estonia and Byelorussia]'.[28] Paragraph 4 listed actions to be taken against the Jews including a census of the Jewish population, enforcing the wearing of a yellow star, prohibition against changing residence, restrictions on movement and occupation and the seizing of Jewish property. Paragraph 5 called for the 'cleansing' of Jews from the countryside and the creation of ghettos in the towns.

On 28 July, Dr Theodor-Adrian von Renteln, Generalkommisar of Lithuania assumed control of 'the territory of the former Lithuania' on behalf of the Reich and immediately began to dissolve the Lithuanian political institutions and disarmed the partisans who had been operating under Franz Lechthaler of the German police.

On 1 August, the Lithuanian provisional government under Acting Prime Minister Ambrazevičius and Minister of Internal Affairs Jonas Šlepetys published a 'Jewish Law' placing restrictions on the Jews in accordance with Lohse's instruction of 27 July but it was not enough to save it from dissolution. Five days later, members of the government were stripped of what little authority they had and told that henceforth they would become simply 'general advisers' (*Generaleräte*). Ambrazevičius refused to recognise the instruction and resigned.

Now began the systematic destruction of the Jews en masse. On the shores of Lake Žiezdras, in the village of Pažiezdris, only 1.5 kilometres away from Linkmenys, a witness, who had been one of the partisans described rounding up Jewish families at the end of July at the village Pažiezdris, close to Linkmenys:

> In total there were about fifty Soviet citizens of Jewish ethnicity collected in the clearing … next to the lake. Adomas Lunius arrived, surveyed the gathering place and gave the command for all Jews to lie on the ground, facedown, which is what they did. Then Lunius said that we were going to shoot the Jews and that the 'partisans' must commence firing on his command, i.e., when he fires a shot from his pistol. When the Jews lying on the ground heard they would be shot they began to yell and cry. Standing next to the shooting site, I clearly saw that Adomas Lunius shot from his pistol, although I did not see where he shot, whether into the air or at the Jews lying prone. After he fired, this was at about eleven or twelve o'clock in the day, all the 'partisans' (insurgents) who had weapons began to shoot the Jews lying on the ground. The shooting of the Soviet citizens of Jewish ethnicity lasted about fifteen minutes.[29]

On 7 October, a truck-load of about thirty partisans in military uniform of the former Lithuanian army arrived in Švenčionėliai from Kaunas accompanied by a German officer. Over the course of 2 days, they murdered 3,476 Jews from the area.

A witness, Juodis-Černiauskas recalls that when he passed them in the street, they appeared to be very drunk and were making a lot of noise. At the end of July, 789 prisoners, at least 500 of whom were Jews, were held in the 37 cells of the Ukmergė prison. By 6 September, there were only eleven remaining. Standartenführer Karl Jäger's report of 1 December noted that:

> It was only possible to achieve the goal of cleansing Lithuania of Jews because of the Rollkommando consisting of select men under the command of Obersturmführer Hamann, who understood my goals implicitly and was able to ensure cooperation by the Lithuanian partisans and the appropriate structures … [the German officers] often came in a passenger car, while the main forces came in one or two trucks, or sometimes on a Lietūkis bus. Local police and activists often collaborated with the Hamann group in the countryside.[30]

At the town of Šeduva, the Jews constituted slightly more than half of the 5,000 or so population. Witnesses recall that it was young men wearing white armbands who rounded up the Jews. There were no Germans in the town at that time but they arrived before the shootings began. 'It was a horrible time,' one resident of the town said, 'I don't remember whether anyone tried to rescue or hide Jews, because everyone knew: if you were caught rescuing them, you would be shot.'[31] Many small Jewish settlements in the countryside were wiped out by mobile killing units in a single day whilst larger ones such as at Panevežys, Rokiškis, Ukmergė and Utena it took two or three days to complete the exterminations.

On 25 June, Red Army soldiers had taken seventy-six 'political' prisoners out of the Telšiai Prison brutally tortured, murdered and buried them in the nearby forest. The burial site of four pits was discovered on 28 June when locals, who clearly associated Jews with the crimes of the Soviets brought Jews from the town to the burial site where they were beaten and forced to dig up the bodies with their bare hands. These same Jews would be part of a group of eighty murdered on the same site on 14–15 July.

Medical examination of the Telšiai Prison corpses showed that only ten prisoners had been shot while forty-six corpses could not be identified due to the appalling nature of the injuries inflicted on the victims before being shot. Evidence shows that the exhumed bodies exhibited wounds and deformations that had been inflicted with bestial cruelty. It remains unclear why the Soviet soldiers were driven to inflict such wanton punishment before carrying out the executions.

When Jäger's EK3 had arrived in Kaunus, he was appalled to find 'Jews were still walking freely in the main streets' and immediately set about creating a ghetto in the poor Vilijampolė section of the city.[32] Some 30,000 Jews were driven into the Kaunas ghetto on 15 August which was divided between the 'large ghetto' and the 'small ghetto'.

These were separated by wooden footbridge over Panerių Gatvė. 'Trakia' and 'Caucasus' ghettos at Shanli, saw 5,000 sealed in at the end of the month and in early September 40,000 Jews were in the Vilnius Ghetto No. 1 and Ghetto No. 2. The idea of two ghettos in each town was to separate those deemed useful for work from the remainder.

The rationale for the establishment of ghettos was laid out by Stahlecker in his 15 October report. A large part of the skilled trades, he said, was in Jewish hands. Many trades were manned entirely by Jews and they were 'indispensable at present for the repair of essential installations, for the reconstruction of destroyed cities, and for work of military importance'. He also drew attention to the 'considerable resistance by officers of the civil administration against large-scale executions' and the fact that violent pogroms against the Jews by locals was causing far too much disruption. The answer was to seal off the Viliampole Quarter in a triangle between the Nemunas and Neris rivers and one of its branches, an area that was connected to Kaunas by a single bridge and move all the Jews there.

Police collaboration is clear from a letter marked 'top-secret' and dated 16 August 1941 in which the Director of the Kaunas Police Department, Vytautus Reivytis writes,

> Immediately detain all men of Jewish nationality from 15 years of age and those women who had become notorious in their Bolshevik activity, or who even now distinguish themselves by the same activity or insolence. The detained persons are to be gathered at the main highways, and detained ... until they are taken and transported to the camp.[33]

In addition, around 5,000 Jews who had been deported from Germany and Austria were murdered at Kaunas in November. About 80 per cent of all Lithuanian Jews had been killed during the first four and a half months of the German occupation. The number of *Einsatzgruppe A* personnel was in the low hundreds and, whilst they were certainly in charge giving the orders, the round up and murder of Jews on this scale could not have been conducted without the assistance of thousands of Lithuanian volunteers. Stahlecker wrote on 15 October: 'The goal to clear Lithuania of Jews could be achieved only thanks to ... the cooperation of Lithuanian partisans and the respective civil offices.'[34]

Altogether 173,000–177,000 Lithuanian Jews were murdered; 111,000 Jews by EK3 and around 46,000 by EK2 while another 2,000–3,000 were killed by local Lithuanian police and irregular forces. By the end of November only 20,000 Jews remained in the Vilnius ghetto, 17,500 in Kaunas, 5,000 in Shavli and 500 in Svencian.

Something needs to be said about the Jews reaction to what was going on. Stahlecker reported that

> Particularly strong and comprehensive measures had to be taken in ... Kovno where the Jews have armed and fought actively in guerilla warfare and caused many fires ... In Latvia, as well, Jews participated in acts of sabotage and arson ... In Dvinsk so many fires were started by the Jews that a large part of the town was lost.[35]

Ohlendorf expressed admiration for the way that Jews facing the firing squads 'went to their deaths singing the Internationale'. Blobel's twisted, depraved mentality saw the victims as

> Resigned to their fate [because] human life was not so valuable to them [the Jews] as it was with us. They did not care so much. They did not know their own human value ... I must say that our men who took part in these executions suffered more from nervous exhaustion than those who had to be shot.

One German businessman who witnessed executions described them as follows:

> The people who had got off the trucks, men, women, and children of all ages had to undress upon the orders of an SS man, who carried a riding or dog whip ... Without screaming or weeping these people undressed, stood around in family groups, kissed each other, said farewells and waited for a sign from another SS man, who stood near the pit, also with a whip in his hand. During the 15 minutes that I stood near the pit I heard no complaint or plea for mercy.
>
> I watched a family of about eight persons, a man and woman, both about 50, with their children of about one, eight and ten, and two grown-up daughters of about 20–24 years. An old woman with snow-white hair was holding the one-year old child in her arms and singing to it, and tickling it. The child was cooing with delight. The couple were looking on with tears in their eyes. The father was holding the hand of a ten years old and speaking to him softly; the boy was fighting his tears. The father pointed towards heaven, stroked his head, and seemed to explain something to him. At that moment the SS man at the pit shouted to his comrade. The latter counted off about 20 persons and ordered them to go behind the earth mound. Among them was the family which I have mentioned ... The pit was already two-thirds full. I estimated that it already contained about a thousand people. I looked for the man who did the shooting. He was an SS man who sat at the edge of the narrow end of the pit, his feet dangling into the pit. He had a tommy gun on his knees and was smoking a cigarette.[36]

What was in the minds of those doing the actual killing, men who were by no means restricted to only the rank and file. Some of the most savage executioners were to be found among the leaders and commanders of units, who personally supervised the murders with apparent pride in a duty well performed.

Lieutenant General Erich von dem Bach-Zelews was not part of *Einsatzgruppe A* but his attitude to massacres was common to many who were. 'I am of the opinion,' he said, 'that when for years, for decades, the doctrine is preached that the Slav is an inferior race and the Jew not even human, then such an outcome is inevitable.'[37] Brigadeführer Odilo Globocnik believed that

> If after us such a cowardly and rotten generation should arise which would fail to understand the nature of our work which is so good and so necessary, then all our National Socialism would have been in vain. On the contrary, bronze plaques should be put up with the inscription that it was we, we who had the courage to achieve the gigantic task.[38]

Ohlendorf was clear that the Supreme Command of the Wehrmacht had given the campaign of slaughter not only information but also directives to support the execution of these measures. Some of the Wehrmacht commanders complained that the Einsatzkommandos were too slow in killing Jews and threatened to take matters into their own hands.[39]

The killings ceased at this time because there was a dispute within the German administration over whether all the remaining Jews should be killed or those working in factories should be spared. Von Renteln argued that, 'Jews ... are needed as skilled workers ... It is impossible to carry on work without Jews ... in the leather-tanning industry. Every single artisan in this industry is Jewish.' Lohse saw it differently but searched in vain for a copy of regulations authorising the killing of skilled Jewish workers. The authorities in Berlin seemed to come down on Lohse's side but clearly tried to keep out of the matter by replying on 14 December saying that verbal instructions had been delivered to the effect that 'Economic considerations should fundamentally remain unconsidered in the settlement of the [Jewish] problem,' but that all decisions concerning the issue should be made by the local administration.[40]

The head of the political department in Rīga weighed in with his demand for 'the prevention by all means of the removal of the Jewish labour force from the supervision of the Wehrmacht.' Berlin eventually was forced to make a decision and resolved the problem by stating that 'the liquidation of Jews employed as skilled workers in armament factories and workshops of the Wehrmacht [must] be stopped as there is no possibility of replacing them.' Jäger was not best pleased by this. He was compelled to comply with the directive but in his December report he vented his spleen by complaining that he 'had intended to kill off these working Jews and their families [but had] met with the strongest protest from the civil administration.'[41]

The period December 1941 to July 1943 was characterised by exploitation of the surviving Jews in the armaments industry and elsewhere. Despite Göring's order 'Utilisation of Manpower in the Occupied Territories in the East and Despatch of Workers from these Territories for Employment in Germany' and Rosenberg's subsequent order of 19 December making employment compulsory for all persons aged 18–25, nothing was done to train non-Jews to take their place. The rulings did have the effect of antagonising the Lithuanians who saw thousands of family members shipped off to work in factories in Germany and many others forced into manual labour at home.

The earliest mention of the use of foreign labour to fill unemployment gaps had been at a meeting on 23 May 1939, between Adolf Hitler, Hermann Göring, Erich Raeder, Wilhelm Keitel and representatives of the Wehrmacht. According to the minutes of the meeting, Hitler stated that 'the population of the non-German areas will perform no military service and will be available as a source of labour.' Once eastern provinces were occupied, Nazi labour authorities quickly laid out plans to utilize eastern European labour based on the strategies applied in Poland.

Initially it involved only political prisoners, prisoners of war, and the Jewish population but soon all inhabitants between the ages of 16 and 60 in German-occupied territories in eastern Europe had to register with the *Deutsche Arbeitsfront* (German Labour Front, DAF). By November 1941, the DAF had created a volunteer work program promising high wages, additional food rations, and better housing in exchange for a six-month stay working in Germany. It was soon clear, however, that these were empty promises and when word got back from the work areas about condition the number of volunteers declined and the need for foreign labour increased. This coincided with the appointment of Fritz Sauckel as *Generalbevollmächtigter für den Arbeitseinsatz* (Plenipotentiary General for the Utilization of Labor, GBA) in late March 1942. He brought in a new labour policy that relied on compulsory labour conscription for all the eastern occupied territories and completely overhauled and radicalized the entire Nazi labour system. Sauckel's forced labour policy demanded quotas of workers from each district and city. Labour officers who were assigned the military rank of Sonderführer to facilitate coordination for rounding up civilians with the Wehrmacht.

In August 1942, Sauckel and Rosenberg approved the use of force by the Wehrmacht during recruitment campaigns if people refused to comply. Although, it is difficult to identify an exact point when Nazi authorities began to rely on the use of force to fulfil labour quotas but after the German surrender at Stalingrad and there were severe German losses on the Eastern Front more brutal tactics were introduced. It was now common for the Nazi authorities to take people off the streets or pull them from their homes. In some instances, young adults were taken during school or church services. Police also threatened to punish relatives in order to coerce people to comply with labour conscription orders. By the beginning of 1943, failure to enlist resulted in severe beatings and, occasionally, death.

While Jews, Roma and communists suffered grievously under the Nazis, other civilians found that their lives were dramatically altered also as they were subjected to total labour and economic exploitation. Jews who were not killed had been subjected to forced labour (*Zwangsarbeit)* while non-Jews were expected to perform labour duty (*Arbeitspflicht*). This meant that they had to perform occasional tasks on demand in addition to their normal work. The unemployed were soon shipped out as slave labour to Germany. All captive peoples were also forced to contribute economically to the Nazi war effort through high taxes and periodic confiscation of cash, jewellery and other valuables.

Widespread dissatisfaction translated into both organized and spontaneous grassroots resistance but the Balts, in general, limited themselves almost exclusively to non-violent political and cultural resistance unlike the Polish underground 'Home Army' who conducted precision strikes on crucial military, industrial, transportation and communications targets, as well as individual assassinations of police and military personnel.[42]

The employment of Jews became of paramount importance given that employers had to pay the local administration only a third of what a non-Jew would cost. The age limit was reduced and children as young as 13 were put to work. The killing of Jews continued, however. Minor misdemeanours were punished by death. The buying and selling of food, failure to wear the yellow star, women who co-habited with employers would all see their perpetrators executed along with those who became too sick to work.

Soviet partisan activity increased in the eastern regions of Lithuania during the early part of 1943. This together with the devastating German defeat at Stalingrad and the increasingly oppressive German administration encouraged Lithuanians to believe that it was possible to conceive of an end to German occupation. When ex-officers of the

Lithuanian army were invited to join the German forces, they refused and prepared to flee into the forests if compelled. The Germans clamped down on dissent by closing the universities in Vilnius and Kaunas. Demonstrations against the closing of many schools were brutally put down by the Germans. Mass arrests were made, which began to create an atmosphere of terror in the cities.

The Germans were unwilling and unable to defend the civilian population from attack by Soviet partisans, but they were forced to allow locals to set up self-defence groups. Where villages were suspected of harbouring or abetting partisans' brutal collective punishment was meted out but otherwise the Nazis left the population outside the towns and cities largely to its own devices.

When part of Byelorussia was annexed to Lithuania in March 1942, Jews living there also came under the control of Gebietskommissar Horst Wulff in Vilnius. Where Soviet infiltration had been suspected, whole communities were deported en masse to Germany. In Byelorussia, the Jews had initially been less brutally handled than the Lithuanians but now found themselves concentrated in the ghettos of Ašmena, Švenčionys, Mikališkės and Salos where many of the sick and elderly were liquidated. More and more young men, Jews and non-Jews, were fleeing to join the partisans and where their absence was uncovered, other ghetto inmates were executed in reprisal. At Baltoji-Volkė, sixty-seven were shot because six of their camp had fled into the forest. At Kena the whole camp was liquidated, and 240 Jews murdered while at Bezdonys another 350 were executed on the spot as that camp was closed down also. It was not only Jews who were now being persecuted. Lithuanians who were insufficiently compliant with German regulations were punished with, in some cases, whole villages destroyed. German terror tactics were intensified. The Germans became increasingly concerned about poor security around the ghettos with numbers of Jews absconding to join the partisans so many of the smaller ghettos were closed down and the populations transferred to Vilnius and Kaunas.

It was the escalation of the killing to include women and children that was the turning point as persecution of the Jews transitioned into genocide. There is very limited documentary evidence to indicate at what point the orders for this escalation were issued and who it was precisely that issued them and to whom. It is known that the entire Jewish population of Auce, amounting to around 100 men, women and children, on the Latvia-Lithuania border was murdered on 11 July. The method of execution here followed an established pattern whereby local Latvian self-defence personnel or auxiliary police units 'collected' the

Jews in one place and waited for an SD auxiliary Latvian unit, or an ad hoc unit specially set up for execution, to arrive and carry out the murders.

At Auce, the Jews were herded into a brick shed near the Vecauce Castle on the outskirts of the town by locals on 5–6 July. German SD units under Rudolf Batz and Alfred Becu arrived five days later from Jelgava with Latvian auxiliaries led by Mārtiņš Vagulāns. They conducted mass shooting of the imprisoned Jews in the Putnu Forest. This unit of *Einsatzgruppe* had entered Jelgava on 29 June and already murdered all Jews there on the shooting range of the former 3rd Jelgava Infantry Regiment of the Latvian army.

The train station at Ponary, just outside Vilnius, had been chosen by the Soviets during their occupation as an oil storage depot. They had dug huge pits in preparation for the underground storage tanks but fled in June 1941 before they could start constructing the buildings. When EK9, under SS Obersturmbannführer Dr Albert Filbert, arrived to replace EK7 on 2 July they soon worked out exactly what these deep, open pits would be used for. At his trial in June 1962, testimony was given against Filbert by his deputy in 1941, Wilhelm Greiffenberger, showing that Filbert received an order to include Jewish women and children in the massacres at the end of July 1941 and immediately carried it out. A month earlier at the end of June in Treuburg, Filbert had informed his entire command that they would be called upon to shoot Soviet Jews and other 'subversive elements but at that time he implied that the order referred only to Jewish men.[43] Clearly nobody in the higher command structure of the SS was confident that large-scale massacres of civilians would be condoned by the Wehrmacht whose cooperation would be required so the wording of the orders were specifically designed to disguise the extent of slaughter envisaged by Heydrich and Himmler while allowing wide discretionary powers to commanders in the field over how they implemented them. Men like Filbert would be well able to read between the lines of Heydrich's orders.

On the day that Hitler had given his approval for *Einsatzgruppen* actions, Heydrich issued Operational Order No. 8, which included new guidelines concerning the treatment of prisoners of war. These stipulated that Jews, combatants and civilians in prison and transit camps in occupied ex-Soviet territories were to be separated according to 'racial origin' but there was nothing in the order that specifically called for the murder of Jews.[44] Much would be understood and taken as read without words on paper, however. Neither did Chief of *Einsatzgruppe B* Nebe require specific orders to know what was required of him. Heydrich already knew from reports coming in from him that 'large-scale liquidations and complete capture of functionaries, political commissars, saboteurs, agitators, snipers, etc' had been undertaken. The 'etc.' in Nebe's report would have been readily understood to mean Jews.

The *Einsatzgruppen* were not only methodical exterminators but also meticulous record keepers. Each commando sent regular reports to their *Einsatzgruppe,* which were forwarded to the *Reichssicherheitshauptamt* (RSHA – Reich Main Security Office) Subdivision IV A-1-Office for Communism, War Crimes and Enemy Propaganda in Berlin. Almost 200 of these reports arrived daily between July 1941 and April 1942. They were then summarised, sifted and edited by SS Colonel Kurt Lindow and given out periodically as Operational Situation Report USSR to a selected list of offices. To show just how detailed the records were, Stahlecker noted in one report that a total of 229,052 people had been executed under the 'guidance' of *Einsatzgruppe A*.[45]

It was EK9, of *Einsatzgruppe B,* who had already been shooting Jews of military age in the street in significant numbers. By 8 July 1941, 90 had been shot in Lida and 321 in Vilnius. A week later another 627 had followed. In total by the time EK9 left Vilnius on 20 July, they had killed around 5,000 Jews and 'the conduct of EK9 during the first five weeks of the campaign was not exceptional.' Clearly, unofficial verbal orders under which these actions were conducted had been interpreted as including widespread murder of male Jews of military age.[46] Some Latvian doctors took part in the sterilization of Jews that began in Bauska in the first days of July 1941. On 11 November 1941, the German occupation authorities issued an order to allow sterilization by local doctors in the hospitals of Daugavpils, Rēzekne, Ludza, Liepāja, Venstspils, Jelgava and Jēkabpils.

During the first few weeks of the occupation, the response of the Wehrmacht to atrocities was very much on Heydrich's mind. During and immediately after the German attack against Poland there had been a great deal of outrage expressed by Wehrmacht commanders over the activities of the SS and *Einsatzgruppen* as many thousands of Polish civilians were executed and it could not be taken for granted that they would turn a blind eye to what was happening in the Baltics and elsewhere in the east. It was, therefore, some relief to receive reports such as the one dated 6 July saying that the army was showing 'gratifyingly good attitude towards the Jews' and two weeks later one from the same source indicating their 'complete agreement regarding our further activity.'

Another unit reported that EK8 had collaborated 'particularly successfully with the relevant departments of the Wehrmacht.' Nebe wrote delightedly that

> The activity of my *Einsatzgruppe* is acknowledged and promoted by all Wehrmacht departments in every way. [My] measures [had been met with] the most complete understanding by the leadership of Army Group Centre. The Secret Field Police had even provided troops to support the liquidations.[47]

Within five weeks of the German attack, the SS leadership felt confident enough about Wehrmacht cooperation that they were ready to expand the slaughter to include Jewish women and children.

Meanwhile von Leeb's German Group North was experiencing a high level of combat losses as the German advance stuttered. Nazi Propaganda Minister Joseph Goebbels noted that 'the mood in the Reich has become somewhat graver. It is gradually becoming clear that the eastern campaign is no stroll to Moscow.' Security in the occupied areas was also a worry as Chief of the Oberkommando der Wehrmacht (OKW – High Command of the German armed forces) Wilhelm Keitel wrote to the commander of his reserve units in the east, General Fritz Fromm, 'The war waged behind the front by gangs and snipers is a very considerable strain on the lines at the rear and for the pacification of the conquered territory … very brutal measures must be taken.' The German army Commander-in-Chief, von Brauchitsch directed his 'troops available for securing the conquered eastern territories' to 'spread that terror which alone is capable of eliminating any appetite for defiance on the part of the population.'[48]

This time, his language was much more bitter, no doubt, due to the German casualty figures that landed on his desk every day. He drew attention to 'partisan sections in our own rear area' who were to be 'ruthlessly put down by force of arms to the point of annihilating the enemy.' If necessary, collective violent measures were to be carried out immediately against towns and villages. Hitler's decree of 17 July made it clear that 'any and all 'policing measures' in the occupied east were 'a matter for [Himmler].'[49]

By the end of July, the *Einsatzgruppen* in the east were reinforced by 6,000 members of the *Ordnungspolizei* (order police) and 11,000 SS men. The escalation in killing could not have happened without this huge increase in numbers. The plan now was to accomplish the task of eliminating Jews and Bolsheviks in the occupied areas by the end of the year when it was still, despite the setbacks, envisaged that the war would be won.

The frustration felt by Heydrich at what he clearly saw as the totally inadequate rate of killings was felt most acutely by Filbert when he was given a dressing down by his boss. He responded by calling together his officers at Viyelka and, in an 'agitated, bitter, and very serious' mood, explicitly ordered them to shoot Jewish men and women, saying 'You start tomorrow!' A few days later the order was amended to include children.[50] He demanded that all his SS leaders had to personally take part in the shootings and ordered that anyone who suffered mental breakdowns as a result of shooting women and children was to be sent home immediately as being unfit for duty.

On 30 July, the first known shooting of women took place in Vileyka and days later the first children were murdered in that place. EK9 reported that 'in Vileyka, the entire Jewish community [of 500 people] had to be liquidated.' Very soon afterwards, some seventy men and thirty women were shot in the nearby town of Maladzyechna. Two weeks later, the killings gathered pace in Vibetsk and, on 12 August, at Surazh with Jewish men, women and children of all ages murdered.

Historian Alex J. Kay attributes the pause between the first shooting by EK9 of women at Viyelka and the Surazh massacre, when the entire Jewish population was wiped out, to 'a brief period of acclimatization within the commando'[51] that had never killed women and children in large numbers before. It must, says Kay, have taken some getting used to. Such documentary and anecdotal evidence that exists shows that EK9 was the first German unit to deliberately conduct mass executions of Jewish women and children making Filbert the conduit through which the Holocaust was supercharged towards its grotesque conclusion. During the final dissolution of the Vitebsk ghetto, EK9 shot all the 4,000–8,000 Jews.

Filbert was replaced as commander of EK9 on 20 October, when he returned to Berlin to face charges of embezzlement and bribery. Before the war he had qualified as a lawyer specialising in bankruptcy law and had been appointed as a full-time employee in the SD main office in Berlin on 1 March 1935. By 1939, he was deputy head of office VI (SD overseas), but his career hit a brick wall when his brother Otto was arrested in Magdeburg charged with 'malice' towards the state and sentenced to four years imprisonment in Dessau. With no promotion in prospect, he volunteered to join the *Einsatzgruppen* in early 1941 and was appointed to lead EK9. The charges brought against him in 1941 led to a two-year house arrest after which all charges were dropped and he was rehabilitated to head up the new economic crime section in the criminal police. He had probably been charged initially for his close association with Werner Best and Heinz Jost both of whom had fallen foul of Heydrich but Heydrich was dead and it was Himmler who had brought him back in from the cold.

After the war, he changed his name to Albert Selbert and became the manager of the Berlin branch of the Braunschweig-Hannoverschen

Hypothekenbank but his cover was blown in 1959 when he was arrested at his apartment, No. 49 Bamberger Straße in Berlin-Schöneberg, and put on trial charged with the murder of an unknown number of people. The court found that he had acted 'from base motives and with forethought' and furthermore that he had 'striven to have shot all Jews he could possibly get hold of and that he acted inhumanely towards the Jews'. He was sentenced to life imprisonment.[52]

On 9 April 1963, the West German Federal Supreme Court rejected Filbert's appeal and thus confirmed the verdict against him as legally binding. Thirteen years later he was recommended for release since he was almost blind and on 5 June 1975, he was released from Berlin's Tegel Prison. In 1978 at the age of 78, Filbert took part in a feature film *Gun Wound: Execution for Four Voices* playing the part of a mass murderer. The film was premiered at the Venice International Film Festival in August 1984. Filbert died on 1 August 1990 still claiming that he had been a victim, shaped by the incarceration and death of his brother in Buchenwald concentration camp. Faced with a hopeless situation with no way out, he said he had been forced to commit terrible deeds.

By 1942, it was clear to Himmler that the shooting of women and children was having a serious effect on the mental stability of the commandos so he directed that they should, instead, be murdered by gassing. Special vans were constructed by the Saurer firm in Berlin and shipped out to the occupied territories. These were closed, air-tight trucks, like a box car, with a heavy door in the back and no windows and with the capacity for holding fifteen to thirty persons.

The killing, by monoxide gas produced by the engine was supposed to take ten minutes, but often, due to mechanical defect, the crowded victims suffocated without being gassed. These gas vans were not popular with the men, some of whom had wives and children at home. They complained at having to unload the dead bodies and suffered deep psychological injury as a consequence. The vans were soon discarded as impractical but larger versions would later be used in the Chelmno extermination camp in Poland, where over 300,000 people were executed in them.

At Ponary, with the help of Lithuanian volunteer (*Ypatingasis būrys*), the Special Squad of the German Security Police and SD, filled the huge oil storage excavation pits with the bodies of Jews whom they shot on site all through the summer and autumn months. Estimates of the numbers murdered vary from 21,700 (Snyder) to 33,500 (Arad).[53] The pits were so extensive that Ponary became an end point for many trainloads of victim. In one day, 4 April 1943, 2,000 Jews were offloaded and shot. Another trainload arrived while this was taking place and a mass breakout occurred during which another 1,000 were killed, the others manging to flee to the Vilnius ghetto. These murders were apparently a premeditated action since, in a report of April 1943, the chief of the security police stated that 'some 4,000 underwent special treatment at Ponary.' It had been planned to take place sooner but so many of the security forces had been occupied taking punitive action against farmers who had refused to surrender their crops.[54]

On 21 June 1943, after the Warsaw Ghetto Uprising and the lifting of the siege at Leningrad, Himmler decided to liquidate all the ghettos in Ostland and set up concentration camps instead where the prisoners would be subject to much stricter supervision. The civil administration objected to having its Jewish workforce handed over to the SS but the SS prevailed. The Vilna and Swieciany ghettos were liquidated and the ghettos in Kovno and Siauliai were converted to concentration camps. A few months later approximately 1,200 babies, children and elderly inmates were murdered in the Kovno ghetto, and many children were sent from the ghetto to labour camps in Estonia.

Some of the population of the Vilnius Ghetto was deported to Estonia and Latvia in September while 3,500 women and children were sent to extermination camps leaving the old and sick to be taken and murdered at Ponary. About 1,500 hid in cellars or fled into the forest. Vilnius was emptied partly to provide manpower in Estonia and Latvia and partly because it had become a centre of resistance and a recruitment centre for partisans. Kovno and Shavli were turned into concentration camps and handed over to the SS.

Hauptsturmführers Forster and Schlaff were in charge at Shavli where the able bodied worked on airfield construction at Linkaičinia, Daugeliai, Pavenčiai and Akmenė. On 5 November 1943, 575 children and 191 elderly from Kaunas were transported to concentration camps in Poland leaving about 2,000, another 1,000 of which, mainly children, suffered a similar fate on 27 March 1944. The next day 300 children plus some elderly were taken to Fort IX death camp and murdered. When Jewish camp police officers refused to cooperate with the authorities by searching for Jews hiding in the ghetto, thirty-seven of them were killed along with their commander and the *Judenrat* (administration body) in Kaunas was disbanded.

During the German evacuation of Lithuania, Jewish prisoners were the responsibility of the SS. On 2 July, 2,000 were taken from Vilnius and murdered at Ponary. Kaunas was liberated on 1 August 1944 when several hundred Jews were found to have been hiding outside the ghettos.

When it was clear that the Soviets were going to occupy the Baltic region again, the Germans created a special Kommando 1005

(Sonderaktion 1005 or Enterdungsaktion) unit under Standartenführer Paul Blobel whose purpose was to eradicate all evidence of the mass murders that had been carried out at Ponary and Fort IX death camp. In an affidavit signed at Nuremberg by Blobel on 18 June 1947 he said,

> In June 1942 I was entrusted by *Gruppenfuehrer* Mueller with the task of obliterating the traces of executions carried out by the *Einsatzgruppen* in the East ... his order was top secret and *Gruppenfuehrer* Mueller had given orders that owing to the need for strictest secrecy there was to be no correspondence in connection with this task ... The burning of the bodies [in Rīga and Reval] began only in May or June 1944 ... According to my orders I should have extended my duties over the entire area occupied by the *Einsatzgruppen*, but owing to the retreat from Russia I could not carry out my orders completely.

Jews were brought in to dig up the bodies and burn them. Blobel boasted of the special incinerators he had designed to carry out the work, but the Soviets overran the areas before the work could be completed. Some of the Jews who had done the digging fled to survive and bring the story to the world, but those who remained were shot by the SS before the Soviets arrived.

On Monday, 18 June 1951, in the floodlit yard of Landsberg Prison in Bavaria, Blobel was led to the scaffold and given a brief moment for his last words. 'I die in the faith of my people,' he said. 'May the German people be aware of its enemies.'[55]

Ever since the German attack in 1941, Soviet fighters, mainly groups organized by the NKGB or NKVD had been infiltrated into Lithuania to carry out 'special tasks' of sabotage and intelligence gathering. They maintained a low profile and rarely moved beyond their remit but in early 1942, the activities of what they believed were organised underground groups and partisans came to the attention of the Supreme Reich Security Board in Berlin. These were not the Soviet special units but were, in fact, little more than tiny partisan groups that include Soviet soldiers who had got separated from the Red Army as it retreated and Soviet prisoners of war who has escaped.

These groups were not ideologically driven and neither did they get support or guidance from Moscow. They were largely ineffective and soon realised that if they did not arm themselves, they would soon be destroyed by the German military forces. In what was essentially a move towards self-preservation rather than an organised movement, these disparate fugitives began to join up into armed groups. Gangs of armed individuals began visiting farms demanding food and clothing.

Occasionally deaths were reported if help was not forthcoming from the hapless farmers.

Local police, who were very poorly armed compared to the partisans, feared that individuals and small gangs might form into larger units and start terrorising bigger communities. Officers at the Anykščiai police station demanded that if they did not receive modern weapons and at least 100 rounds of ammunition for each police officer, they could not be held responsible for any trouble breaking out.

Further east, however, in Švenčionys is a village in the Švenčioni district county, the police faced graver threats from specially prepared groups of saboteurs from Belarus led by the former deputy chairman of the Executive Committee of Švenčionys county, F. Markovas. It was not by chance that these partisan groups were mostly gathered in the counties of Šiauliai, Kėdainiai, Panevėžys, Alytus and the greater part of the Vilnius region, where the majority of the population were Russians and Poles, those people most feared and distrusted by the German occupiers. Many acts of sabotage were carried out mainly against the railways. On 5 February a locomotive and six wagons were derailed at Švenčionėliai-Ignalina and tracks were repeatedly blown up.

During the war, the history of the Lithuanian partisan movement inspired by Moscow was divided into three periods of the German-Soviet war whose transition points coincides with leadership changes of the Soviet partisan movement in Lithuania. Between 22 June 1941 and 18 December 1942, Bolshevik activity was conducted under the leadership of the Central Committee of the Communist Party of Lithuania (LKP(b)) and is characterised by the fact that partisan units were essentially made up of Soviet activists who had remained in the country or who were specially sent by Moscow to carry out specific tasks such as disorganising movement on roads and railways, purchasing weapons and ammunition, destroying telephone and telegraph lines, destroying weapons, ammunition and fuel warehouses, disrupting industrial production and establishing contact between partisan organizations.

It was a time which the ideological, political and anti-fascist struggle in Lithuania began. One group of Red Army officers was operating in Raseiniai county and a mixed group of Soviets and Lithuanians in Rokiškis county. Fearful of reprisals, there was no great enthusiasm within the population for any sort of organised resistance at this stage and these partisans were not able to count on its support. Evidence preserved in the LPJŠ files shows that in July and August of 1941 at least six NKGB agents, V. Vildžiūnas, A. Milvydas, V. Šiupinis, K. Macevičiaus, K. Petrikos and A. Godliauskas were sent to Lithuania to assess the situation, seek out potential resistance fighters and attempt to bind them into an organised force. Altogether, some eighty NKVD employees were sent over the next months with another forty from Mozyria in Belarus.

The partisan threat was growing. At the beginning of May 1942, the residents of the town of Švenčioni were presented with a decree that threatened people who disobeyed the orders of the German military and civil authorities would be sent to join the German army on the Soviet front and a notice made clear that for every German officer shot, 200 local residents would be arrested and killed. It's likely that Soviet partisans paid little heed to these threats, which made them a threat both to the Germans and the local Lithuanians. In the spring, after the Soviet winter had blunted the German advance on Moscow, two operational groups of the Central Committee of the LKP(b) were sent to Lithuania to establish contact with groups already there and report back to Moscow.

Unfortunately for them, it was not long before they were caught and executed. This prompted Moscow to improve survival chances of their infiltrators with more rigorous selection from the 16th Lithuanian Rifle Division who were given special training. Records show that altogether about 500 people graduated from special training schools, but Moscow was constantly getting requests from groups inside Lithuania to send more support. At this stage the great bulk of partisan activity was by Red Army personnel. There was little support from the local population.

On 13 May, 100 Lithuanians who had fled from the Germans and 200 officers of the 16th Lithuanian Rifle Division, which included former Lithuanian soldiers were selected for special training. Several partisan groups, including Arlauskas (Petrov), Petro (A. Afonino), Miškos (Mažūnas), Dūdas (Bakučis), Pran (L. Solomin) and Alksnis (Kunigėnas), were formed in Moscow and sent into Lithuania but only three small groups saw action. On 7 July, the Petro group of seven people were sent to Trakai county. On 17 July, Alksnis group of seven people to went to Vilnius, and on 29 July, Dūdas group of seven people to Šiauliai county.

On 19 May partisans from Belarus attacked a Wehrmacht car and killed the German senior lieutenant, District Commissioner Beck and two Zonderführers. On another occasion, Deputy District Commissioner Grulys and Lieutenant Šmitas were killed when they stopped for a pregnant woman who appeared to be in distress on the road. For this act, the Germans took retribution by rounding up a number of civilians and taking them to the Jewish cemetery Švenčioni where they dug their own graves before being shot and dumped in them.

In the second stage from December 1942 until the end of 1943, the Soviet State Defence Committee founded the Lithuanian Partisan Movement (LPJŠ) with Sniečkus in charge. In Lithuania, recruitment into partisan ranks started up in urban areas in an attempt to create a resistance movement from within. In August 1942, he had received augmented instructions for partisan activity. For the first time he was to collect military intelligence and carry out acts against those in the local community suspected of treasonous collaboration with the Germans. The result was a strengthening of the partisan and anti-fascist struggle. In late November 1943, groups of saboteurs and Red Army intelligence officers were sent in to establish contact with others previously deployed to try and coordinate actions. These groups were named after Lithuanian folk heroes such as Perkūnas, Margiris, Birutė, Kėstutis, Žalgiris, A. Mickevičius, K. Kalinauskas, Žemaitė, etc. but were composed mainly of Red Army personnel.

Partisan units became increasingly made up of ex-soldiers of the Lithuanian army. German reports of the time, however, make much of the Red Army involvement both from Russian stragglers and escaped PoWs who were hiding out in the forests as well as others coming across the border. Soviet archives speak of Aleksandrovich's squad in Raseiniai county made up of former Red Army officers and ordinary soldiers, and Djakov's squad made up of prisoners of war and residents. Some researcher suggests that only about 22 per cent of all Lithuanian partisans were Russian, but it was these who were the warfare specialists who organised military operations, led them, trained recruits in weapons and tactics and instilled discipline.

It was during 1943 that partisan groups were swelled by Jewish recruits who had fled from the ghettos, but they were not particularly welcomed by the non-Jewish members. Sniečkus warned his men to 'be careful when using people of Jewish nationality'.

The Soviets, however, were anxious to avoid ethnic strife. They did not want to lose Jewish support for their underground activities. The most ardent anti-Semites were forced to show restraint or face Soviet justice which would have been a bullet.

Then at the beginning of 1944 all partisan activity was coordinated by the underground committees of the northern and southern regions of the LKP(b). The number of partisans increased, the organization improved, and combat actions became more effective and partisan activity evolved into what might now be called a movement. The LPJŠ had a great deal of difficulty contacting other groups already deployed and could not easily maintain communications with Moscow so operational groups were formed under the auspices of M. Šumauskas-Kazimieras of LPJŠ. These special groups would be given authority to take control on the ground to recruit Lithuanian partisans, appoint leaders, distribute weapons, medicines and documentation.

An operational group with subordinate groups was sent to the forests of Begomli on 20 April 1944 to establish bases in the village of Losinai in the forests of Adutiškis, another near the Ponomoriovo Brigade in the forests of Kazėnai near the village of Jakšti and a third one in the Ušačiai district, in the village of Lesina. The men were landed by glider but two craft crashed killing fifteen and injuring several others. Forty-six made it into the country and were able to begin organising a proper partisan movement in Kaunas Vilnius, Šiauliai region and Suvalkija.

Many Lithuanians did not look upon a return of the Soviets with equanimity but after German military setbacks on the Volga and at Kursk it was becoming an increasingly likely outcome. The message coming from Moscow was 'the Soviet authorities can give you and your families gifts if you start serving the Soviet people honestly ... Lithuanians, serving the Germans [will be] brought to justice and will receive a heavy punishment.'[56]

Sniečkus wanted to increase propaganda and agitation to attract more people from the rural communities whom he believed were the basis of the entire Soviet partisan movement. German reports suggest that the increase in partisan activity increased the general mood of anxiety since it clouded the issue of the extent to which resistance was growing. Sniečkus made it even more difficult for the Germans to gauge the strength of partisan groups. No longer would recruits have to run off into the forest, he said, they can remain on their farms and do not even have to think of themselves as partisans; the idea of carrying the burden of such a name with all its connotations of danger had often prevented people from joining the movement. Recruitment continued to be a problem, but Sniečkus was upbeat in his reports to Moscow about the numbers of local volunteers and often exaggerated them. Early in 1944, he instructed his staff to always emphasise the leadership role the Lithuanians were playing in the partisan movement to give the impression of greater involvement of locals.

With the tide now turned inexorably against the German armies in the east, the Soviets became increasingly concerned about the attitude of the Lithuanian people to a future Soviet occupation. They were not pleased to discover that in places there was little enthusiasm to see them back and many Poles around Vilnius wanted to be reconnected to their own country. Most Lithuanians were obviously anxious to see the return of a liberated independent Lithuania, but few expected to see it. In the countryside the prospect of Soviet reoccupation was particularly unwelcome by farmers who had seen what Soviet policies of collectivisation had done to their livelihoods. Persuasion was not seen as a productive strategy so in order to force the rural population to oppose the German occupation, Soviet partisans would regularly visit farms and villages and mete out violence to those who refused to cooperate. LPJŠ did not object to these partisans thieving food, weapons and clothing from the local population but they would not countenance the theft of money and personal possessions. It cannot have been easy for Lithuanian partisans to turn a blind eye to activities of the most violent Soviet bands such as those operating in the Rūdninkai forest region who would think nothing of killing residents which they did in Delhi when they stole the last cow in the village. This group was particularly ill-disciplined and contained many criminals. The partisans of Mickevičius's group had got drunk in the village of Pakrempiai on 31 May and began stealing clothes from the residents. One of them, S. Urbelis, killed a mother and her child in the village of Potolčiai for suspecting that she had connections with Belarusians.

Sometimes they laid waste to entire villages such as at Kaniūki on 29 January 1944 which was burned to the ground and all the animals slaughtered because the residents were suspected of anti-Soviet sentiments. In the village of Kaniūki, auxiliary police officers found the village burned, people and slaughtered animals.

The acts of sabotage and Soviet violence towards the Germans, which resulted in retribution massacres of civilians, was perpetrated with impunity regardless of the consequences. Partisans operating in Raseiniai county killed Gestapo Captain Lionga, the chief of police in Kuršėnai, and German General von Bezechė was ambushed in his car on the Skaudvilė-Kelmė road. Chief of Utena county Žukas, Biržai mayor, Rokiškis and Police Chief Žukauskas were assassinated also.

The partisans were not content with fighting the Germans, they wanted to fight each other as well. There were fierce battles for territorial supremacy between Soviet partisans and Byelorussian partisans in eastern and southeastern Lithuania. One battle was reported on by Field Marshal Ragauskas at the Poliani Manor who stated that on 31 January 1944, 60 Bolsheviks and 500 Belarusians squared up to each other and then in March a large force of Polish partisans gathered in the southern and northern parts of the Rūdninkai forest ready to fight with the Soviets. Sniečkus didn't see how he could work with the Poles who were siding with the Byelorussian partisans against the Soviets. Others made a great effort to divert the Poles towards fighting the Germans and slowly the groups began working in a common cause.

The more active they became, however, the more their resources were stretched. They were always short of ammunition and avoided direct confrontation with the Germans where possible. Therefore, they looked for other effective ways of taking action. One of the easier targets were sawmills, which were quite easy to set on fire and often located in forests where the partisans were strong. Most of the timber from the forests went into the German war machine but the partisans had to be careful not to damage the local economy.

The campaign to recruit local sympathisers to the German cause in Lithuania was not particularly successful and commanders there were forced to explain why. The Generalkommissar of Lithuania, Theodor von Renteln, reported to the Ministry for Ostland, listing a total of fifteen reasons why Lithuanians had been so unresponsive and why so few had resisted joining the SS Legion. The main cause, he said, was that the Lithuanians mentality made then unfit for fighting which was not helped by the negative attitude towards the Nazis shown by the Catholic clergy in a strongly religious country. These same clergy cannot have been any better disposed to the Soviets, but that country had suffered less persecutions than other Baltic states during the Soviet occupation of 1940–41 and the Bolshevik threat seemed rather less acute.

Latvia

The Germans first struck at Latvia from the air with the bombing of Rīga and Soviet troop concentrations around the naval base and commercial port of Liepāja. A flotilla of Soviet ships headed by the *Kirov* fled Rīga loaded with looted hardware, but several were sunk by German aircraft. The Soviet 24th Corps Aviation Quadrille was destroyed on the ground and in the air. German armoured columns raced towards Daugavpils and Jekabpils while Soviet forces retreated in disarray. The Latvian 24th Territorial Strelnieki Corps, already emasculated and demoralised by Soviet purges saw mass desertions often to the German side.

Liepāja, which would become one of the places notorious for being the scene of some of the most horrific massacres of Jews, was of significant strategic importance to the advancing Germans who had planned to capture it on the first day of their invasion. Lieutenant General Kurt Herzog's 291st Infantry Division met stiff resistance, however, from Major General Nikolai Dedaev's 67th Rifle Division. Hard fighting took place over several days as the town suffered heavy damage from shelling and fires. Herzog finally broke through the Soviet defences and took the town on 29 June.

Liepāja now came under the command of Korvettenkapitan Stein of the German navy. His first act was to issue an order for ten hostages be shot for every act of sabotage against the occupying forces. He then turned his attention to the Jewish population and, on 5 July published the following set of anti-Jewish regulations in a local newspaper:

- All Jews must wear the yellow star on the front and back of their clothing.
- Shopping hours for Jews were restricted to 10:00 a.m. to 12:00 noon. Jews were only allowed out of their residences for these hours and from 3:00 p.m. to 5:00 p.m.
- Jews were barred from public events and transportation and were not to walk on the beach.
- Jews were required to leave the sidewalk if they encountered a German in uniform.
- Jewish shops were required to display the sign 'A Jewish-owned business' in the window.
- Jews were to surrender all radios, typewriters, uniforms, arms, and means of transportation.

The response of Latvia's population to German occupation was, to a great extent influenced by their experience of the previous Soviet occupation and their ambitions to recover national independence. The Soviets abandoned Rīga before the Germans arrived and locals swarmed into the streets waving national flags. The radio station played the national anthem. Crowds flocked to the Freedom monument. When the first Germans arrived, they initially allowed this outburst of nationalistic fervour to continue but soon it was apparent that several thousand people who had gone into hiding from the Soviets to create a resistance movement would now pose a serious threat to the German forces.

Several small bands emerged under the control of men such as Lieutenant Voldemars Veiss, Lieutenant Colonel Roberts Osis and Karlis Aparats who harassed retreating Soviet forces. This had been a boon to the Germans but when theses partisans took it upon themselves to exact revenge by going on rampages killing those they suspected of having been responsible for the deaths of Latvians under the Soviet occupation, such a measure of chaotic violence, which was essentially outside their control, was way beyond what the Germans were prepared to tolerate. In Rīga, Veiss, who controlled a sizeable force of some 400 men, tried to amalgamate the many small bands of rebels into a cohesive unit that could work alongside the German occupiers, but the Germans were not going to allow armed civilians to remain at large once the Soviets had gone.

On 8 July, the partisans were forced to disarm and many of their ranks were recruited into auxiliary police units under direct German control. Veiss, however, continued to play a role for the Germans when Stahlecker gave him the job of organising self-defence forces around Rīga *Ordnungspolizei* (order police)-*Hilfspolizei* (auxiliary police) but strictly under SS control. There is no evidence to suggest that these units took any part in any atrocities.

In these first few heady days, the Latvians even attempted to form a government under Colonel Ernests Kreismanis and Bernhards Einberg with Colonel Alexandrs Plesners in charge of military matters. Gustavs Celmiņš had refused to allow his Pērkonkrusts to join, expecting that he would get preferential treatment from the Germans. The fascist group *Ugunskrusts* (Fire Cross) had been founded in Latvia in 1932 by Celmiņš but reformed itself as Pērkonkrusts two years later. Pērkonkrusts was a fiercely anti-Semitic organisation but did not have particularly strong affiliation to the Nazis. The movement was actually outlawed in Latvia when Celmiņš was arrested and imprisoned along with other members of the group after Ulmanis' coup in 1934. After his release, he was exiled to Helsinki, his wife was Finnish, where he formed alliances with other far-right groups in Europe.

When the Soviets occupied Latvia in 1940, most Pērkonkrusts prisoners remained firmly behind bars but others were deported to Siberia. Meanwhile German propagandists called on *Pērkonkrusts* sympathisers in Latvia to join Viktors Arājs *Sonderkommando* fascist group (official name: Latvian Auxiliary Security Police, later known as Latvian Security Division of Security Police and Security Service). A number of prominent members of the Arājs Sonderkommando, such as Herberts Cukurs, Kārlis Ozols and Konrāds Kalējs, had been active in the Pērkonkrusts, which tended to suggest that there was a greater migration of members from one to the other than there actually was. The sketchy picture given by KGB files is derived mostly from trial transcripts of a number of Arājs' men that are not always helpful in the search for the truth.

Celmiņš had returned to Latvia with the invading German army as a Wehrmacht Sonderführer and his Pērkonkrusts along with the LKNS (National Federation of Latvian Fighters, *Latviju Kareivju Nacionālā Savienība*) were put to work. Stahlecker had refused to officially recognise either of these outfits but arranged for them to operate under the aegis of his *Einsatzgruppe A*. Despite suffering injuries when his vehicle ran over a landmine near Liepāja, Celmiņš went on to head a recruitment drive for volunteers to join the Latvian Auxiliary police battalions (*Schuma*) who were complicit in several massacres of Latvian Jews.

Ezergailis claims that, after Pērkonkrusts was banned on 17 August 1941 Celmiņš 'was actively opposed to the Nazis' through a group he formed calling itself 'Free Latvia' but there is no evidence about any resistance activities on his part, except for the dissemination of a few leaflets.[57] Celmiņš's anti-Nazi sentiments, however, did lead him to forge strong ties with Finnish Intelligence and publish an underground newspaper *Brīvā Latvija*. It was this that finally saw him incarcerated in Flossenbürg concentration camp in 1944.

When Einbergs had a meeting with Stahlecker, he came away with an unequivocal understanding that anything approaching a provisional government of Latvia was quite out of the question so he changed tactics and offered the services of his followers as a sort of liaison between the Germans and the Latvian people. Stahlecker didn't mind that, preferring to deal with Einbergs rather than with Celmiņš but made it clear that Einbergs would be nothing more than a mouthpiece for the German administration.

This arrangement allowed the former Latvian Finance Minister Alfred Valdmanis, together with Plesners and Lieutenant Colonel Viktors Deglavs to set up a kind of shadow administration, which they hoped might acquire some powers of its own in the fulness of time. There is evidence to suggest that Valdmanis had been preselected in Berlin for a role in administering the Latvian economy after occupation. The Latvian Professor of History, Haralds Biezais, described Valdmanis as having been 'a genuine and staunch supporter of German policies' and called him 'the most striking collaborator', but documentary evidence suggests that he rapidly fell out of favour with Rosenberg.[58] He had, however, acquired the 'confidence of the highest military authority' for his economic expertise while Deglavs and Plesners were there to assist with political and military matters.[59]

It soon became clear, however, that Valdmanis was manoeuvring to gain advantage, as Stahlecker's military administration was giving way to a civil one set up by Rosenberg, by planning to take his team to Berlin for a personal audience with Hitler in an open challenge to German occupation policy for Latvia. Their ambitions were squashed, however, when Deglavs was found with a bullet in his head on 18 July on the steps of Plesners' apartment, apparently a suicide. In their book *the Waffen-SS: A European History*, Jochen Böhler and Robert Gerwarth claim that Deglavs was assassinated, and his close associates removed from any position of responsibility.

Much debate centres on the 'interregnum' between the evacuation of Soviet forces and the arrival of German ones in the towns and cities. Ezergailis asserts that this was too short to have allowed Latvians to be executed without the Germans having knowledge of it and as soon as the Germans arrived, they exercised 'iron control', but others draw attention to the German civilian administration as a 'weak institution'.[60] In his book, *Latvia in World War II*, Valdis Lūmans cites evidence that there was spontaneous harassment and murder of Jews, especially in the countryside, in the first few days after the Soviets had left but, he says, there were others who testified that the persecutions did not start until they were instigated by the Germans.[61]

The murder of Jews had already started in Latvia during the first days after the German attack although the mass killings only started a couple of weeks later. The first phase of the executions was carried out by the German security police and their associated *Einsatzgruppen* before the ghetto phase that culminated in the Rumbula massacres of late November and early December. The sociologist Zygmunt Bauman has maintained that by characterising these crimes as 'Germanic' some commentators have tried to deflect blame from the local population and distance them from the criminals who were a 'disease of civilisation' rather than 'its legitimate creation'. Debate rages as to the extent to which culpability for the murder of the Jews in Latvia can be apportioned between the occupiers and the occupied.[62]

The extermination of Jews began in Grobiņa, near Liepāja on 23 June 1941 when SS Obersturmbannührer Reichert's *Einsatzkommando 1a* of *Einsatzgruppe A* killed 6 Jews. On 3 July Erhard Grauel's *Teilkommando 2* started to kill Jews in the town and within the next few days the executions of Jews began also in Durbe, Priekule, Asīte and Rīga. In the late afternoon of 29 June in Liepāja seven Jews and twenty-two Latvians were shot and thrown into a bomb crater in the middle of Ulicha Street and a few hours later, Walter Hahn, a Viennese musician was shot on Hika Street.

On the next day, soldiers went to the city hospital, and murdered several Jewish doctors and patients, including the 10-year-old Masha Blumenau.[63] A detachment of *Einsatzkommando 1a* killed, another musician Aron Fränkel, at the Hotel St Petersburg and then rounded up several hundred Jews and took them to Raiņa Park where the Soviets had dug defensive trenches. The Jews were shot and pushed into the trenches. Much of the evidence for murders at Liepaja was provided by survivors D.F. Ziovtson, M.N. Libaur, A.Sh. Vesterman, I.A. Melidenshtam and M.D. Siutelsons.

In the case of the Latgale killings, some researchers have stressed the much more active role played by locals, but it has been difficult to discover exactly what happened at Rēzekne. It is known that on 4 July, before any *Einsatzgruppe* units had arrived, around 400 men were rounded up into the marketplace when 10 of them were shot as a warning to others. The survivors were thrown in prison. The *Sonderkommando 1b* only left Daugavpits on 7 July and arrived two days later to be met by a group of locals under the command of Aleksandrs Macs. According to a *Sonderkommando 1b* report of 18 July written by SS commander Erich Ehrtinger, exhumation of bodies buried in Rēzekne prison was started by Jewish forced labour under the supervision of German special units.

A priest of St Andrew's Church in Rēzekne, Jezups Grisans, claims that a number of cellars were opened in some houses with grizzly evidence of communist tortures. The former Aizsargi leader, Alfreds Berzins wrote a memoir in which he reiterates the claims and says that the people of the town were invited to see inside the cellars for themselves. Grisans says the Jews who had dug out the decomposing corpses with their bare hands were set upon and beaten.[64]

Latvia was under strict military rule in the first weeks of occupation but some Wehrmacht officers were less than happy with what they witnessed. General Franz von Roques, commander of the Wehrmacht Rear Area was an 'old-style' *Junker* (German aristocrat) who had little time for the Nazis. He was tasked with maintaining order and regulating civilian life in those territories won by the front-line forces, but he had been allocated insufficient resources and was forced to coopt local support. He complained to von Leeb about the violence meted out to the Jews but was told to 'keep out of it'. He refused to keep quiet, however, arguing that extreme violence made his job more difficult. It was Stahlecker's *Einsatzgruppen units* that caused him the most problems, but he needed them to perform security duties and was loathe to openly confront Stahlecker over the issue. He did, however, disband the Pērkonkrusts, which enraged Rosenberg and doubtless expedited the introduction of a civilian administration on 25 July after which Latvia became a major supply and logistical base for German front-line forces in the Soviet Union and a place of rest and recuperation for wounded.

Many other Latvian soldiers left with the Soviets and took part in the defence of Moscow later in the year. Up to 70,000 civilians, including 20,000 Jews, fled east ahead of the German Panzers but many were inevitably cut off and others were prevented by Soviets from crossing the border. The Germans made much propaganda use of the often-mutilated bodies of some 1,300 political prisoners who had been murdered by the Soviets in Latvian prisons and were quick to associate the Jews with these Soviet crimes. This proved to be a perfect opportunity for erstwhile communist collaborators to turn their coats

General Pavel Bermondt-Avalov

A column of Red Army troops in Vilnius. September 1939

Lithuanian troops enter Vilnius on 29 October 1939

Red Army units marching in the town of Eišiškės on 15 June 1940

The Red Army entering Kaunus on 15 June 1940

Estonians being deported to Siberia in Soviet cattle wagons.

Children being deported to the Soviet Union in June 1941

Lithuanian rebels leading disarmed Red Army soldiers in Kaunas in 1941

Leonas Prapuolenis, leader of the June Uprising on 23 June 1941

The Great Synagogue of Riga

Still from the newsreel of the burning of the Great Synagogue

Still from the newsreel of the burning of the Great Synagogue

Liepaja, Latvia, Local collaborators gathering Jewish children before their execution

Jews at Liepāja December 1941 just before being murdered

Murdered Jews at Liepāja December 1941

Jewish women before their execution in Skede, Latvia, December 15-17, 1941

Deportation of Jews from Bielefeld in Germany to Riga in Latvia. Bielefeld, Germany, December 13, 1941.

Deportation of Jews from Bielefeld, Germany, to the Riga Ghetto, Latvia, 13 December 1941

The Kiviõli labour camp of the Vaivara concentration camp in 1944.

Kovno, Lithuania, 26.10.1943, deportation of Jews from the ghetto to the Auschwitz and Klooga camps

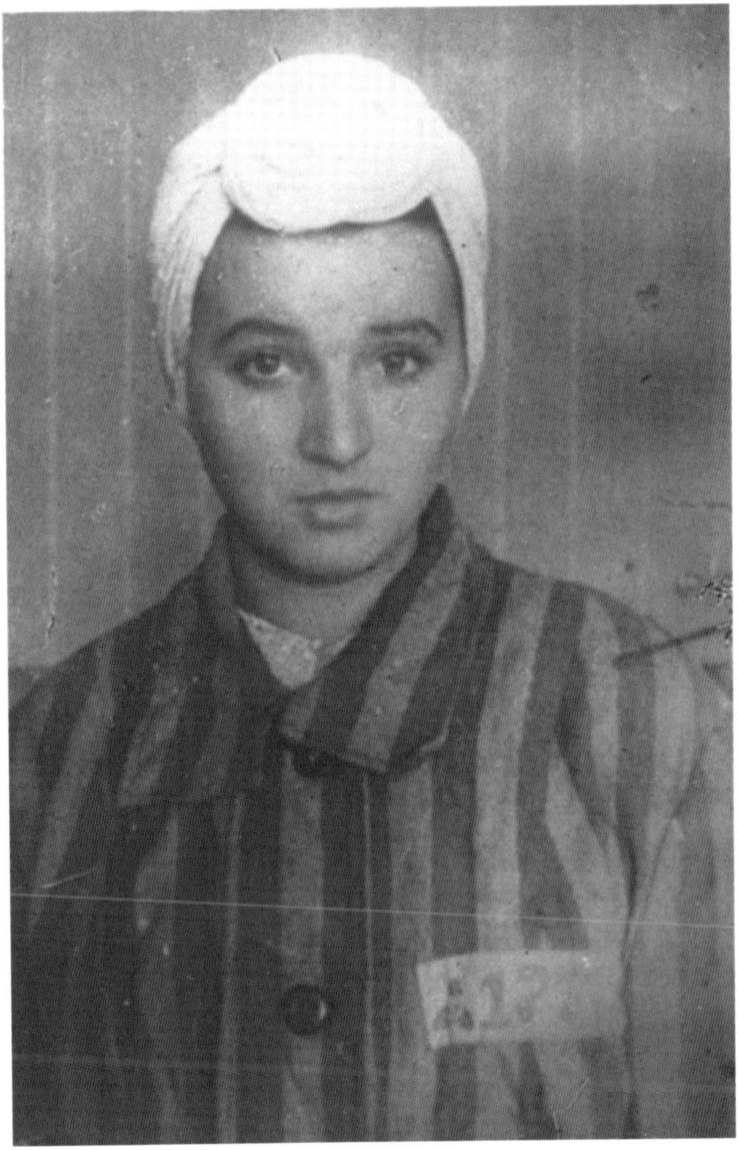

4-year-old Sara Bialovadska, imprisoned in the
Kaiserwald concentration camp near Riga. Latvia, 1943

Riga, Latvia, 1942-1943, Jews on their way to forced labour

Latvian partisans

Latvian partisans

Lithuanian forest brothers

The family of Janis Lipke, the Riga dockworkers who saved the lives of Jews

Martin Sandberger, defendant during the Einsatzgruppen trial in Nuremberg, March 1st, 1948

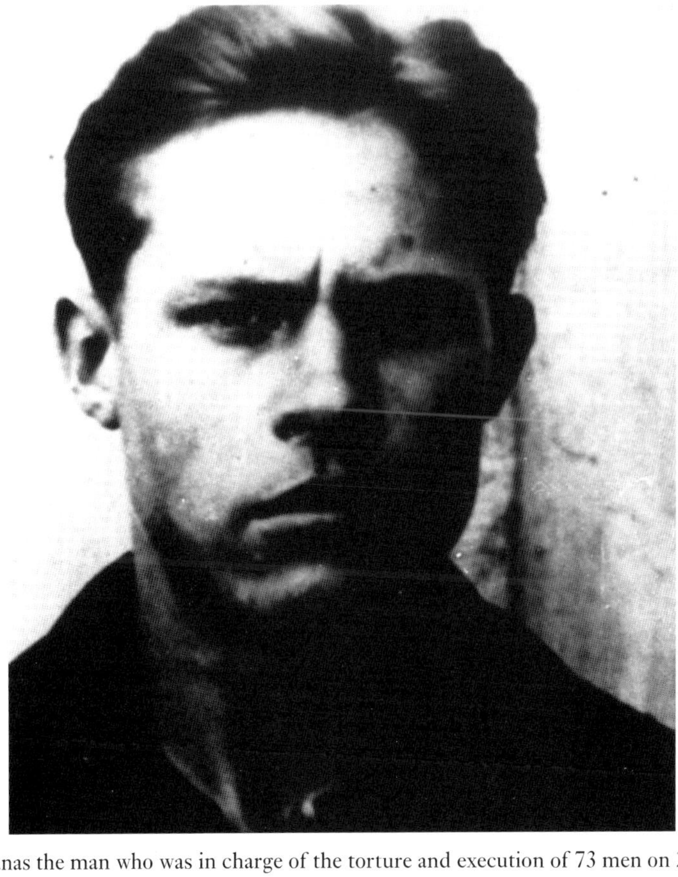

Petras Raslanas the man who was in charge of the torture and execution of 73 men on 25 June 1941

Pertras Raslanas at home in Moscow in 1977

Friedrich Jeckeln (standing, at left) SS war criminal and murderer, on trial in 1946 in Riga. Other defendants from left to right : 2. Generalmajor Hans Paul Kupper, 3. Generalleutnant Siegfried Ruff, 4. SA-Standartenführer Alexander Bocking, 5. Generalleutnant Wolfgang von Ditfurth, 6. Generalleutnant Albrecht Baron Digeon von Monteton, 7. Generalmajor Bronislav Pavel.

and demonstrate fealty to the Nazis by becoming Jew-hunters and Jew-killers and deflect suspicion from themselves.

In the countries of the former Soviet Union, the difficult issues of the Holocaust were suppressed and made taboo for decades. This made study of the role of the Latvian population in the persecution of Jews somewhat problematical. Three main areas of contention in particular are the extent of active participation in the crimes, the passivity or indifference to them and the level of opposition to them. In her lecture to the Topography of Terror Foundation in Berlin on 15 November 2011 and book, *Lettland unter deutscher Besatzung 1941–1944, Der lettische Anteil am Holocaust,* Katrin Reichelt described her attempts to analyse the evidence of how the overall population collaborated under the German occupation.[65]

The main problem she encountered when carrying out her research was that while the Baltics were under Soviet control up until 1989, 'issues of the Holocaust were supressed and made taboo for decades' and since that time, historians of the Baltic occupations have 'enriched it with their own perspective.'[66] She emphasises Heydrich's entreaties to his *Einsatzgruppen* to intensify 'self-purification' efforts by exploiting 'the mood of the population' after its traumas of the Soviet occupation. The strategy was to emphasise the role of Jews in the implementation of Soviet policy and to take advantage of 'pre-existing patterns of Latvian anti-Semitism.'

This idea of deep-rooted antagonism towards the Jews was, according to the eminent historian Sir Martin Gilbert, attributed to the pervasive residual influence of Martin Luther's 'brand of virulent anti-Semitism.' 'The Germans', he wrote, 'had confidence that the Lithuanian and Ukrainian ... murder gangs ... could be turned easily to mass murder'.[67] Reichelt says it was Latvian 'so-called volunteers, activists and vigilantes' who took advantage of the Soviet retreat to 'proceed with massive violence against Jews and alleged communists.'[68]

Her conclusions, however, have been vehemently opposed by Professor Emeritus of History at Ithaca College, Andrew Ezergailis, until his death in 2022, who described Reichelt's contention that 'Latvians did not need Germans to molest and kill their Jews' as a 'swing between righteousness, denial, and revenge'. He identifies Reichelt as one more 'fire-breathing' German writer and historian in the mould of Anatol von Lieven whose 'understanding of the Nazi occupation stands in stark opposition to [that of the] Latvians' and who seeks to deflect at least some blame for the Holocaust onto the local populations of occupied regions.[69]

Specifically, he challenges the Luther theory of anti-Semitism and says that rather than being 'isolated and cursed, Latvian Jews were 'societally engaged and politically active'.[70] Much misinformation, Ezergailis claims, stems from an overreliance on the Soviet propaganda booklet *Daugavas Vanagi,* which Jukka Rislakki says was aimed at discrediting exiled Latvian leaders in 1962.[71]

Rīga had been founded by German Christians as a city state and became a major trading port ruled by German 'Baltic barons'. Despite becoming part of Imperial Russia in 1710, there were still 62,000 Baltic Germans living in Latvia in 1939 and had, up to that time, been the elite of society; wealthy, educated and socially active. This had caused great resentment towards them and many Latvians viewed their German population as oppressors. These German-Balts were particularly well disposed towards Germany, especially in its Nazi colours but had not made a fuss when Latvian Riflemen had fought on the side of Russia against Germany during the First World War.

After a year of Soviet terror, in 1941, they, like most Latvians, were pleased to see the Germans drive the Red Army out of their country. Whether, as some insist, the Latvians thought it presaged a return to independence, however, must be questioned by the evidence of murderous judgements the German had meted out to the Poles and neither would it have escaped their attention that the Soviet occupation they had just suffered was a direct result of German-Soviet collaboration. Whether or not the replacement of one draconian administration by another would prove to be advantageous would soon be put to the test.

For Baltic Jews, Heydrich's verbal instructions of 17 July 1941 would show that any vague optimism was entirely misplaced. Their fate had been decided when he instructed the *Einsatzgruppen* to liquidate Jews in party and state positions as a first step in the eradication of 'racially undesirable elements' to open up *lebensraum* (expansionism) into which Germanic peoples could expand. The Germans, Reichelt says, were confident that they could exploit a society traumatised by a year of Soviet occupation and encourage within it a belief that Jews had played a major role in their misery by collaborating with the Soviets in their reign of terror during which the young especially had been 'brutalised and criminalised'.

Ezergailis agrees with her when she says that she believes the Latvians would have welcomed the Germans as saviours who evicted the Bolshevists but, in the most scathing manner, completely rejects assertions that the Latvians were willing collaborators in the atrocities that followed. The very presence of the German military, he says, with their one-sided imposition of rules, gave them all the power they needed to carry out their ethnic cleansing. Reichelt, he says, uses the argument of Latvian complicity as an attempt by 'the heirs of Nazism' to 'polish their wounded ego.'

Reichelt, however, expands upon her theme by asserting that the 'role of native populations as stooges' was an essential part of the Nazi plans and had been 'firmly calculated in advance' as indicated by Heydrich's instructions of 29 June 1941 to the *Einsatzgruppen* to apply 'self-purification' of occupied societies using anti-communist and anti-Jewish elements, which he estimated to constitute a 'large section of the population.' These were to be 'triggered [and] intensified where necessary' in such as way as to leave no evidence of the role of the Germans and to give the local perpetrators no 'political assurances' of reward for their actions. Reichelt further explains the absence of documentary evidence as an understandable German wish to distance themselves from some of the responsibility for carrying out the orders.

On the other hand, Ezergailis believes that the Germans, following Heydrich's instructions to inspire pogroms, 'induced' the local population to seek vengeance by creating 'self-defence' forces, known in Poland as *Selbstschutz*. During the first hours of occupation, the Germans created military command structures (*comandantures)* that recruited local volunteer units. These units, based on the pre-war *Aizsargi* wore armbands in Latvian colours and were extensively used by the Germans for about the first six weeks of the occupation after which they were peremptorily disbanded. Eizergailis challenges the 'broad coalition of opinion' that these *Aizsargi* units existed in Latvia and were active before the imposition of control by the *comandantures*. While there were Latvians who volunteered to join up as soon as the Germans arrived, Eizergalis says that these were few in number and the vast majority of 'self-defence' units were created through a draft that focused on bringing in men whose families had been persecuted by the Soviets.

The difficulty the Germans had in recruiting local agents to attack the Jews was clearly shown by Stahlecker's report of 15 October 1941. It also highlighted the German policy of blaming locals for the mass violence:

> It proved to be considerably more difficult to set in motion similar cleansing Aktionen [to those in Lithuania] and pogroms in Latvia. The main reason was that the entire national leadership, especially in Rīga, had been killed or deported by the Soviets. Even in Rīga it proved possible by means of appropriate suggestions to the Latvian auxiliary

> police to get an anti-Jewish pogrom going, in the course of which all the synagogues were destroyed and about 400 Jews killed. As the population on the whole quietened down very quickly in Rīga, it was not possible to arrange further pogroms.
>
> Both in Kovno and in Rīga evidence was taken on film and by photographs to establish, as far as possible, that the first spontaneous executions of Jews and Communists were carried out by Lithuanians and Latvians.[72]

Reichelt agrees that Latvian 'self-defence' forces were initiated by the presence of both the Wehrmacht and *Einsatzgruppe A* and did not predate their arrival. She calls them a 'wild and mottled bunch' whom the Germans 'succeeded in restructuring … into a functioning Latvian auxiliary police force' able to be deployed on a longer-term basis. Stahlecker utilised these auxiliaries right from the start to perform not only routine police duties but also the 'most extreme' activities including murders but only under the strict control of the German security forces. It is Reichelt's contention that, under Lange, the murder of Jews was carried out with 'orderly and systematic' cooperation between the Einsatgruppe and the Latvian police. The way in which the character of the eastern European Holocaust differed from that in western Europe, was the way in which killing took place in almost every Latvian town. There are more than 230 mass graves from the German occupation. Everyone knew what was happening to their Jewish neighbours.

Ezergailis takes to task those, such as Efraim Zuroff, who claim that there was 'active and often fanatical assistance' provided by a 'considerable part of the population' with widespread collaboration between the German occupiers and the Latvian population. Ezergailis suggests that the Germans would have regarded any such offer of assistance by the Latvians on such a scale as risible. As far as Stahlecker was concerned, the Latvians would do exactly what they were told to do or face the consequences and they were left in no doubt as to what they would be.

Once the larger cities of Daugavpils, Rīga and Liepaja, were under German control *Einsatzgruppe A* immediately endeavoured to secure Latvian assistance to implement their policies. Improvised controls soon became institutionalised. Reichelt assertion that the Nazi occupiers exploited the deep-rooted anti-Semitism, which resulted in the ex-judicial murder of 'unknown numbers of Jews in anticipation of the German invasion' is challenged by Ezergailis. It is true, however, that after a year of Soviet brutality, in which many Latvians had been murdered, others deported and many more suffered trauma, much of the population saw German occupation as a liberation and their anger was easily and conveniently diverted towards the Jews whose vibrant communities had been engaged widely both economically and politically in Latvian society. Evidence of widespread anti-Semitic prejudice, over and above that experienced in all eastern European countries at the time, in either the social or political realm is hard to find. Ezergailis refutes the case of virulent anti-Semitism against the Latvians as an example of a 'public relations campaign designed to … paint the murder of Jews as the spontaneous work of locals'.[73]

One of the central dilemmas facing resistance movements in all three Baltic countries was the knowledge that a successful outcome of the struggle against one occupation army did not lead directly to the restoration of sovereignty but threatened only to pave the way for occupation by another. The foundations of Latvian resistance movements were laid down during the Soviet occupation, which began in 1940 and certainly did not end with the retreat of the Nazi forces in 1944.

Latvian resistance under German occupation was initially muted and concerned itself with such things as working within the education system to maintain high academic standards and preserve a national Latvian spirit amongst young people refusing to allow them to become cowed by the oppressors. The internal justice system and other government organisations likewise worked to preserve Latvian values as much as possible. There were certainly communist partisans who dearly wanted to drive out the Nazis, but many were motivated only by a desire to preserve the interests of the people and fight for the restoration of a free and independent Latvia. The one-time Latvian ambassador to the United States wrote '[the] underground movement, however, is by no means communistic, but is strictly national-patriotic. If there is a communist or so, they are very few in number and they are firmly acted against by the patriotic organizations.'[74]

A number of resistance groups were formed including the Latvian Nationalist Union (*Latviešu Nacionālistu savienība*), Latvian Hawks (*Latvijas Vanagu organizācija*) and Latvian Guards (*Latvijas Sargi*) who published underground newspapers People's Voice (*Tautas Balss*) and Latvian Way (*Latviešu Ceļš*).[75] It was not really until 1943, however, by which time the Wehrmacht had suffered the crushing defeat at Stalingrad, that the Latvian resistance movement became more active and began looking to the west for salvation.

Most of the Jews had been rounded up by the end of August and there remained only the registration and confiscation of Jewish property. By mid-July, *Einsatzkommando 1a* alone had shot 1,150 male

Jews in Daugavpils and German security police together with an active and self-initiated supporting group under the control of Viktors Bernhard Arājs, whose name translates into English as 'ploughman'. Arājs had been born in Imperial Russia and brought up by a divorced mother of Baltic-German descent and, like Stahlecker, had trained as a lawyer. Although he had studied Soviet law, he was not a communist sympathiser and nor is there any evidence that he had pro-Nazi sympathies but he served both sides equally well. Having moved to Rīga, rapidly becoming a modern highly developed city, he joined the Latvian police force, where he soon gained a reputation for being ambitious, ruthless and extremely bigoted, but he left in 1939 to continue his law studies.

At the University of Latvia (University of Rīga) he began recruiting fellow students to an underground anti-Soviet and nationalistic opposition group, which soon attracted ex-military officers. The response accelerated hugely on the day that the Germans attacked and the *Arājs Sonderkommando* became a rallying point for patriots. Speculation surrounds the way in which Arājs came to the attention of Stahlecker who arrived in Rīga on 1 July but it was probably through an introduction made by Stahlecker's interpreter, Hans-Eugen Dressler, who had known Arājs during their time together in the Latvian army and introduced him as 'just the sort of man' Stahlecker was looking for. Most members of Arājs's group would later claim that they joined because of boredom or lack of work elsewhere but there is a body of opinion that believes many recruits were eager to show fealty to the Nazis and try to distance themselves from any risk of having been seen as too closely associated with the Soviet occupiers.

Historian Richards Plavnieks suggest that there were six principal reasons why men volunteered for the *Arājs Sonderkommando* which he lists in order of importance:

- Mis-directed anti-communist sentiment.
- Material advantage of membership.
- The aura of credibility of the occupying forces and the 'electrifying sensation' of being on the winning side.
- Pre-war authoritarian sentiments engendered by the Ulmanis regime.
- Ideological similarities between Latvian and Germans.
- Anti-Semitism.[76]

Stahlecker had a prearranged plan that was to initially incite the local population to attack Jews and 'toughen up the citizens and inure them to the wholesale massacres to follow'.[77] He summed up his approach by saying:

> In view of the future [it was necessary] to establish the unshakable and provable fact that the liberated populations themselves took the most severe measures against the Bolshevist and Jewish enemy quite on their own, so that the directions by German authorities could not be found out ... Similarly native anti-Semitic forces [in Rīga] were induced to start pogroms against Jews during the first hours after capture, though this inducement proved to be very difficult.
>
> Following out orders the Security Police were determined to solve the Jewish question with all possible means and most decisively. But it is desirable that the Security Police should not put in an immediate appearance, at least in the beginning, since the extraordinarily harsh measures were apt to stir even German circles.[78]

Arājs met Stahlecker as early as 2 July when his gang of recruits was placed under the command of the security police Chief Dr Rudolf Lange and his deputy, Rudolf Batz. It is likely that, at this stage, that Stahlecker had no particular plans for Arājs but it was soon apparent that the local population was not responding particularly well to call for 'self-cleansing' of Jews and communists in pogroms; certainly not sufficiently to make the sort of rapid progress required.

Rather than take it upon himself to rally the necessary numbers of 'volunteers' Stahlecker realised that Arājs pointed the way to a better method of implementing his agenda, but he would require very careful management. Although it had been a central ambition of Stahlecker to get locals to do his dirty work for him, when it came to the crunch, the thought of unsupervised gangs of armed Latvians rampaging through the city streets did not appeal to him.

By the next day, Arājs' men were on the street arresting Jews who had remained in Latvia and now found themselves literally surrounded by hatred. According to his trial record, one of Arājs' men, A. Proškovičs testified that it was Arājs who gave the order for the burning of the Great (Choral) Synagogue of Rīga at Gogoļa Street on 4 July by saying 'Since the people of Rīga hate Jews we must demonstrate our position by setting fire to the synagogue so that nothing of the Jewish culture remains.'[79] With several hundred people inside, the synagogue was filmed as it burned and the images shown in German propaganda newsreel. Other synagogues at Maskavas and Stabu streets suffered a similar fate. Stahlecker's interpreter, Dressler, however, would later report that it had been German troops who 'distinguished themselves by setting fire to a synagogue and committing all kinds of atrocities' but did not specify which one.[80]

Nevertheless, the newsreels clearly show that those burning the Great Synagogue were wearing German helmets while Arājs' men had been specifically instructed by Stehlecker to dress in civilian clothes to hide German involvement in their acts.[81] It should be noted however, that none of Stahlecker's written orders to Arājs survived the war. It is likely that few actually existed in the first place given that what the two men were doing was strictly outside the guidelines laid down by Heydrich, although he would certainly not have objected, and was something that neither of them would want to have documented given that it violated all the contemporary rules of warfare.

A number of books claim that one of Arājs' lieutenants, Herberts Cukurs, was present at the burning and shot victims trying to escape but Ezergailis says that Cukurs did not arrive in Rīga until 14 July.[82, 83, 84] Vilis Hāzners, who was also named by the same sources as having been present was later shown to have had no connection with the incident.

It seems as if Stahlecker had quickly decided that Arājs was going to be a useful adjunct to his *Einsatzgruppe* and proceeded to give him a measure of support by creating the *Arājs Sonderkommando* as a unit of the Latvian security police to see what developed. While the synagogue was burning the Tēvija newspaper printed an appeal calling on all 'nationally thinking Latvians, members of Pērkonkrusts, students, officers, Aizsargi, and others who wished to take part in in the cleansing of our land from harmful elements' to join the auxiliary police.

Many of his early recruits were ex-Red Army soldiers who had been soldiers of the Latvian army before that. When it was clear that recruiting numbers were low, many regular police were transferred to Arājs' auxiliary forces enticed by higher pay and the opportunity for self-enrichment through looting. The largest age group among the new auxiliary police officers was between 16 and 21. Many had no idea at first that their main occupation would be the shooting of Jews.

Arājs was allocated a walled and gated building on Valdemārs Street, with ample cellar space, in the centre of Rīga to act as its headquarters. Jewish women were held there, used for cleaning work and regularly raped, abused and murdered. Arājs' gang of violent, socially unstable young men, who came mostly from the working classes, were ready for appropriate revenge actions against the Jewish Bolsheviks. Many criminals joined up also, motivated by the prospect of quick financial benefits, and, above all criminality without legal consequences.

The German security police managed to whip into shape this 'wild and motley bunch' who had begun by 'rampaging in a manner only relatively loosely directed by [Lange]' into a functioning, disciplined and uniformed Latvian 'death squad, the actions of which were under tight German control'.[85] The structure, personnel and function of what was essentially an aggressive anti-Semitic 'mobile murder squad' was an almost unique phenomenon in the occupied eastern territories and it was this, which made the extent of the almost complete extermination of Latvian Jewry possible in the first place.

Unwilling to let the *Arājs Sonderkommando* loose without first seeing what it was made of, Stehlecker at first employed it in various guard duties and arrests of civilians in Rīga and elsewhere in Latvia. Various testimonies suggest that the commando diminished in numbers from around 300 to as little as 60 by the end of the year probably through boredom since many of the first recruits were well-educated, but after German setbacks on the Russian front at Rostov, it was considered a valuable adjunct to German forces and was greatly increased in size and its members were sent to the SD school in Fürstenberg for training.[86] The make-up of the commando at this point of enlargement meant that personnel were now drawn from the less well-educated sections of the community who had been working in jobs that required little or no qualification and involved poorly rewarded hard physical labour and who thought it a better alternative to forced mobilisation into the German army.

Upon their return to Rīga they were assigned to guard various facilities, including the Salaspils and Jumpravmuiža concentration camps as well as assisting in the execution of Jews transferred from western Europe. One unit was sent to Minsk to take part in the annihilation of Jews and combat partisans while another went to Nasva. One of their main tasks was to root out and exterminate partisans in Russia, Belorussia, the frontier regions of Poland and Latgale. When the Red Army closed on Rīga in 1944, a part of the commando was incorporated into the Latvian Legion while another unit was transferred to Germany, where they also joined the legion at a later date.

The murder of Jews in Latvia was orderly, systematic and carried out according to a fixed pattern. *Arājs Sonderkommando* units were regularly employed to escort Jewish forced labourers to camps at Salispils, Jumpravmuiža and Mežaparks, and guard them there. The Jewish victims, mostly young men, were arrested during systematic house searches or simply taken from the street by auxiliary police officers and members of the *Arājs Sonderkommando* then taken to the Rīga Central Prison where they were shot in regular nightly operations in the Bikernieki (Rumbula) forest, on the outskirts of Rīga. In his book

Bloodlands Timothy Snyder says that the Germans first carried out a demonstration shooting, and then had the *Arājs Sonderkommando* do much of the rest, but Aivars Stranga claims that it was the special closed police units (*Schutzmannschafts-Bataillione*) who played the greater part.[87, 88] Reichelt's version has it that firing squads of twenty-five men fired two shots each at their victims. Documentation is fragmented and incomplete, but it is estimated that by the end of August, some 6,000 had been killed at this site.

Moving outside the confines of the city in autumn 1941, Arājs murder squads rampaged through the countryside in their notorious 'blue buses'. First, they went to Valmiera, then to Rēzekne, Vilani and Ventspils. In each place several hundred Jews were murdered. It is estimated that in the killings of this second wave of violence against Jews, which took place until the ghettos were established, about 26,000 people died: 22,000 Jews, 2,000 communists, 2,000 Sinti, Roma and mentally ill people.

According to the German historian Dr Wolfgang Scheffler's calculation, approximately 28,000 Jews were deported from Germany, Austria and the Czechoslovakia to Rīga of which only 11,000 were taken to the Rīga ghetto. About 1,000 people died on the journey, some 2,000 perished in the Jungfernhof camp and thousands more men killed in Salaspils. The rest, numbering around 11,000 to 12,000 people, were murdered in the Bikernieki forest. According to records of the Central Prison, in 1942 1,319 people were taken from there and murdered in the forest but during 1943 it was mostly captured partisans and people who had helped them who suffered that fate. These lists suggest that overall, around 5,000 people were taken from the prison and killed in the forest during the German occupation.

In addition, Soviet prisoners of war were buried in mass graves in the Bikernieki forest during the extreme winter of 1941–42. Many of them had died of hunger, illness and the freezing cold during the deportation and had been buried in mass graves at Ziepniekkalns, Bisumuiza and in the Jewish cemetery of Smerlis. In total, over 35,000 bodies were later discovered in the mass graves at Bikernieki but many more, maybe as many as 10,000, had been dug up on Himmler's orders and burned in an attempt to hide the full scale of the crime.

This was done under the supervision of SS Standartenführer Paul Blobel, who headed the SS *Sonderkommando* 'SK-1005' all across the Eastern Front but in the Baltics, it was *Einsatzkommando 1005-B* under SS Sturmbannführer Walter Helfsgott who arrived in Rīga on 9 April 1944 to carry out the work. Lange assigned thirty Jews from the Rīga-Kaiserwald concentration camp to carry out the work. These prisoners were chained to trees during the work and had to sleep on the ground under the open sky. When they could no longer work at all they were shot, and their bodies were burned along with those they had dug up, but there were plenty more to take their place. When Soviet forces returned in 1944, they found sixty empty oil barrels that had been left behind in the Bikernieki forest.

Even in late July 1941, Himmler had realised that he needed additional defence units in the Baltics and other occupied regions and he saw that these would have to come from local populations. These emerged as *Schutzmannschafts-Bataillione* (auxiliary police battalions) distinct from the local auxiliary police. Each battalion would have no more than 500 men recruited from the local residents. Three types of public order squads were formed in the general district of Latvia and divided into battalions, companies and platoons under the supervision of German officers (*Aufsichtsoffiziere*). Five battalions, the 16th, 17th, 18th, 19th, and 20th had been formed in Rīga by January 1942, all consisted of volunteers. In February, Jeckeln launched a massive recruitment drive with newspapers advertisements and the Main Committee for the Organization of Latvian Volunteers was established, headed by Celmiņš.

At the end of September 1942, there were sixteen battalions in all comprising some 7,967 men. Altogether by 1944 there were a total of forty-eight Latvian police battalions many by now made up of men transferred from other police and military units.[89]

In his book *Himmler's Police Auxiliaries in the Occupied Soviet Territories*, US historian Richard Breitman discusses Himmler's desire to create paramilitary forces under his command from among the local Baltic populations. Successfully derailing attempts by both civilian and military institutions to take command of these forces he used them instead as mobile murder squads and hunters of partisans. Himmler also needed the police battalions to assist in the extermination of civilians, especially Jews but also Roma and other groups he considered to be of lesser worth. It was important for him, said Breitman, to maintain the level of involvement of non-Germans in the extermination of Jews but it was a problem for Himmler and a barrier to achieving his goals that, as Erich von dem Bach-Zelewski, who in 1941 had been Supreme Commander of SS and Police for Russia-Middle, put it 'Central Europeans had shown themselves unsuited to carrying out mass executions'.[90]

Again, debate rages over the level of involvement of locals and what motivations they may have had for doing so. The influential Holocaust scholar, Raul Hilberg, in his book *Perpetrators, Victims, Bystanders,* underlined the important role played by Baltic peoples in the implementation of national-socialist racist policies, but he interprets the description of voluntary to mean anyone who in some way served or worked for Germans.[91] US historian Christopher R. Browning asks, 'How could quite ordinary men turn into mass murderers?[92] Another American historian, Daniel J. Goldhagen in his book *Hitler's Willing Executioners*, argues that Ukrainians, Latvians and Lithuanians were the most important national groups who aided the Germans in slaughtering Jews and they came from cultures that had a profound hatred of Jews.[93]

German historian, Frank Golczewski, however, believes that German occupation policy in eastern Europe had no logical plan. While the Germans needed assistance from the local residents in governing the occupied regions, he says, one must not draw the far-reaching conclusion that the main responsibility lay with locals.[94]

One of the many significant things Hitler said at the Angerburg Conference on 16 July 1941 was 'It must be and remain an iron principle: It must never be tolerated that a person who is not a German carries weapons!'

It was still not clear whether these new battalions would be allowed to wear uniforms and carry arms. Both Stahlecker and Jeckeln had made strong arguments that armed alien military units should be formed but strictly within the SS framework. Supporting them was von Leeb, the Supreme Commander of German Army Group North, who had stated that the 'formation of new Lithuanian, Latvian and Estonian units would greatly relieve the [German] Army Group North'.

There was little opposition to the formation of Estonian units but Himmler told Jeckeln that 'In spite of the general shortage of weapons that would not allow us to arm adequately non-German units for battles at the front, the Führer on the whole is not in favour of the creation of such armed formations [but] the Führer has agreed to the increase in the number of *Schutzmannschafts-Bataillione* [auxiliary police battalions]'.[95] Himmler would be the only person with authority to form military units from the local populations.

While heinous crimes were being committed in their country, the bulk of the Rīga population, wherever possible, avoided going anywhere near the security services or their establishments. Overall, they tried to avoid witnessing any of the crimes and made themselves as inconspicuous as possible to the occupying forces. The daily newspapers between 1941 and 1943 made no mention of acts of terrorism or reprisals. Persecution of the Jews was seen as the unavoidable consequence of Nazi occupation. Richards Plavnieks says that there had been a 'deep societal decay' among the Latvian population due to having lived so long under a right-wing dictatorial 'political culture saturated with propaganda' leaving them afraid to show any sign of protest. The fact that Arājs had been able to gather such a sizable bunch of people willing to 'plough the furrows of hell' was, he says, ample proof that Latvian society was 'a shambles'.[96]

Of the Latvian population, it was only the Arājs squads and the Latvian auxiliary police who participated in the murder squads, but many more people took advantage of the chaos of German occupation to pillage and loot the property of those Jews who had been torn from their homes. When Jews were arrested, both the Arājs squads and the auxiliary police seized valuables and money wherever they could. The German security police and the civil administration tolerated a certain amount of robbery by Latvian accomplices and the wider population but kept the capture and seizure of the most valuable objects strictly to themselves. It was something of a bonanza that led to bitter internal battles between the German civil administration and the security police.

In the smaller villages, the less valuable possessions of the murdered Jews were auctioned off to the locals at reduced prices. Before the ghettos were established, Jews who had been turfed out of their houses and who had to look for another place to stay within a very short time, gave rise to a black market in rentals with the charging of excessively high rents. Even for urgent visits to the doctor and similar emergencies Jews would now be charged exorbitant prices. Then there was the ever-present threat of blackmail of Jews in hiding or simply afraid if being denounced to the authorities by former neighbours and acquaintances.

Greed rather than anti-Semitism per se was the main motive in most cases, which was not particularly untypical human behaviour in the extreme conditions of war and political instability. The files and the testimonies of witnesses make it clear that the reactions of many Latvians were an overall picture of an average society under the conditions of occupation, war and terror. The result of the document analysis shows that the collaborators were a relatively small proportion of active supporters, while most Latvians tended towards self-protective indifference.[97]

There were Latvians, however, who were also prepared to take the risk of helping Jews even though hiding them was punishable by death. The Jewish Documentation Centre in Latvia has a card index of over 200 cases of assistance and solidarity to persecuted Jews. In fifty-two cases the helpers were arrested and in fourteen cases they were executed. Holocaust survivor and historian Marģers Vestermanis compiled a list of the rescuers of Jews that comprises more than 400 names of rescuers, who on their turn were assisted by several hundred other persons. These altogether rescued approximately 400 Jews.

Over the course of a few years, Jānis (Žanis) Lipke saved the lives of fifty-six persecuted Jews through a highly organized network of the Rīga dock workers. Up until 1940, Lipke had worked as a dock labourer in Rīga, supplementing his meagre income with small-time smuggling. His anti-authoritarian nature was evident even then when he joined up with a left-wing organisation shielding social democrats and communists from persecution by hiding them in the holds of ships.

When the Nazis arrived, his ability to speak German and Russian as well as his native Latvian got him a position working for the Luftwaffe in warehouses near the central market and ghetto alongside Jewish inmates. Eventually he was put in charge of transporting ghetto Jews to and from their places of work and was able to arrange for some of them to slip away from time to time to be taken into hiding by a network of twenty-five family and friends such as Barnets Rozenbergs, Karl Jankovsky and Vilis Bīnenfelds. Some were hidden in a bunker under Lipke's house where they were fed and looked after by his wife, Johanna, and his older son, Alfred, who raised chickens, turkeys, geese, pigs and ducks on the land around their house. Friends had dug the hole in the ground underneath a woodshed at his house in Kipsala district in the bitter winter of 1941–42 working in shifts during the long nights.

One of the Jews they had helped, Chaim Smolyanski later described how they did it. 'The temperature was around minus 30 Celsius, we loosened the soil with blow torches, diligently tried to break it with ice picks and then carried it aside and threw snow on top, so that the neighbours wouldn't notice.' In the spring thaw the roof collapsed, and they had to rebuild it with reinforced timbers and concrete. As many as four people could hide there at any one time. One of the group, Andrejs Graubiņš, was captured and tortured by the SS but he maintained his silence and the network survived. Graubiņš died in the Dachau concentration camp.

Anna Alma Pole hid seven (some say eight) Jews in the basement of her house in Peldu iela in Rīga's old town. In summer 1943, a neighbour Isaak Vange brought to her house the Jews who had escaped from the ghetto. Pole hid them for almost a whole year. Her daughter Margarita Kestere, who had a young family would bring food to the house hidden in a pushchair. Then in August 1944, acting on a tipoff, the SS raided the house. Pole, her daughter and all the Jews were taken in to be interrogated under torture. Katrin Reichelt, however, recounts one version of the story in which the SS raided the house to be met by armed resistance during which six of the refugees were shot dead.[98] Margarita was eventually released and was able to leave Rīga but her mother and the remaining Jews were murdered.

By this time Erhard Grauel, commander of a detachment of EK2, had taken over the women's prison and used it as a detention facility for Jews and communists. Werner Hartman, a German war correspondent, reported on 6 July that this prison was so crammed full of prisoners that they were unable to lie down.[99] Grauel had seven captives executed on 7 July in retaliation for shots having been fired at German patrols in the town but his boss Stahlecker upbraided him for not executing people fast enough. Grauel immediately ordered a subordinate, Neuman, to organize the shooting of 100 Jews every day regardless of whether or not there had been any acts of sabotage. Latvian accomplices of the Germans drove the victims ten at a time into a long ditch where they were lined up in a double row and shot by either German soldiers or Latvian civilians.

On 10 July Grauel was replaced by SS Untersturmführer Wolfgang Kügler who took over the organisation of the massacres and then a few days later, Fregattenkapitän Dr Hans Kawelmacher replaced Stein as naval commander and immediately requested his superiors in Kiel to send him another 150 men to allow 'quick implementation of the Jewish problem.'[100] *Arājs Sonderkommando* units were also drafted in from Rīga.

Again, we see evidence of a policy for dealing with the Jews that is obviously understood but about which all concerned are wary of committing any specifics to paper. The implication is that Heydrich had made clear to all his commanders before the invasion that the killing of Jews would include women and children eventually but the priority during the first days would be all men suspected of having aided the Soviets with their families being dealt with later. Heydrich would have been adamant that no direct allusion to this wider policy was to be written down anywhere.

Georg Rosenstock, the commander of the 2nd Company of the 13th Police Reserve Battalion witnessed Jewish men being brought in a truck, being guarded by armed Latvians. They were then walked in groups of ten to the edge of a pit where they were shot and thrown in. These executions were witnessed by a large crowd. These killings continued all through to December albeit on a diminished scale. They took place at fortnightly intervals on the beach to the south of the lighthouse. Initially the execution squads were Germans, but were later replaced by Arājs Sonderkommandos. Estimates of those murdered during this time are about 600 Jews, 100 communists and 100 Roma.

A study of the Liepāja executions concluded that these were public executions and 'in many ways a festival' and a form of grotesque 'execution tourism', to which German soldiers travelled long distances to get the best places to witness the mass shootings.[101] Richard Wiener photographed the *Einsatzgruppen* killings in July and August and found German soldiers standing around the execution site, not as participants, but as spectators. The December shootings at Šķēde were photographed by SS Scharführer Strott.

These pictures were discovered by David Zwirzon, who worked as an electrician at the SD office in Liepāja. He stole the film, had prints made, and returned the originals before they were missed. The prints were put in a metal box and buried behind the stables of the police building. They were later retrieved, handed over to the Soviets and later used in war crimes trials and displayed in museums around the world. Philippe Labrune saw one of photograph in the Jewish Museum in Rīga and began an investigation to find out who the people in the photograph were (see plate section). The best evidence suggests that the 10-year-old girl was Sorella Epstein and the woman who she was hiding behind was her mother Roza. The two other women were probably Sorella's cousin Mia Malka Epstein and her mother Emma Rathaus.

The first reported killing of Roma in Latvia was in August 1941 at Baltinava, which was followed by other murders in Liepāja in November when 173 Roma victims were recorded amongst the many thousands of Jews. Documentation is scarce but German records that survived the war have details of all the victims which is a clear indication that these murders were carried out by *Einsatzgruppe* personnel. Eyewitness accounts tell of Roma killings in many places including Kalvene county, Aizpute county and Zolmežs.[102]

Documents in the Latvian State Archives show that 311 Roma of Rēzekne district were killed and on 6 January 1942 Roma from Ludza were taken to Gabari forest in Zvirgzdene county and killed. Most of the murders were committed against small numbers of Roma but incidents were widespread across the country and continued for many months. Mention must be made of those who risked their lives to protect Roma. Talsi district commissioner, Kārlis Krūmiņš, made urgent representation to the German authorities to put Roma to work rather than kill them. He was successful but was later punished by the Soviets as a Nazi collaborator. The mayor of Sabile, Mārtiņš Bērziņš, was later honoured by the state for preventing the massacre of around 200 Roma on 13 September 1941 in the Svente forest. The fact that he was able to stand down the execution squad suggests that they were native Latvians rather than *Einsatzgruppe* soldiers.

As the war turned against the German armies in the east, former Latvian Ambassador Voldemārs Salnais began trying to bring all the disparate resistance movements together. In Rīga, Leonīds Siliņš established the Central Council of Latvia (CCL) on 13 August 1943, with representation from the Latvian Social Democratic Workers' Party, the Latvian Farmers' Union, the Democratic Centre and the Latgalian Christian Farmers' Party. The aim of the CCL was to re-establish independence based on the 1922 constitution. Contacts were now established between the CCL and the Western powers. In December 1943, they sent a memorandum to the US State Department entitled 'Declaration in the Name of the People of Lithuania, Latvia and Estonia' in which it is assumed that Germany will lose the war but that 'the only country which at present constitutes a danger to independence is the Soviet Union'.[103]

During 1944, the CCL convened on three occasions, the first of which was on 8 January when CCL chair Konstantin Čakste with other Latvian delegates Bruno Kalniņš and Ludwigs Sēja met Lithuanian Stepanos Kairys. The Estonian representative failed to arrive in time, but their man Ernst Kull was able to hold a conference with Čakste in his private apartment in Rīga on 15 March. When the CCL next met on 15 April, they discussed the prospect of the Soviets returning and planned to resist them with 'weapons in hand, with all [our] strength under all circumstances to protect [our] country and to fight for restoration of [our] sovereign against a united enemy, taking advantage of any outside help'.[104]

This proved to be something of a distant hope when several resistance activists were arrested. The Lithuanian Kazys Ambraziejus was taken in Tallinn on 21 April and there followed arrests of more than 100 Estonian and 6 Latvian activists. German security had also intercepted CCL documents being taken out of the country that contained names. One version has it that a Lithuanian courier got drunk and was picked up by the authorities and another suggests that the wife of one of the resistance members had an affair with a German officer and betrayed the movement.

Throughout its existence under German occupation the CCL's most important contribution was the way it shared information about the situation in the Baltics with western intelligence agencies. One of the main conduits for this transmission of information was Antanas Valiukėnas one of the founders of the LAF who had fled Lithuania during the Soviet occupation and was living in Germany. Otherwise, it was across the Baltics to Finland that couriers took their valuable intelligence to be forwarded to the Secret Intelligence Service (SIS) in London and the Office of Strategic Services (OSS) in Washington.

Evidence shows that three long reports on conditions in Latvia were sent to Sweden in 1942, even before the establishment of the CCL, on Swedish merchant ships with the cooperation of Rīga Port Police Lieutenant Indriķis Ruckulis. Latvian activists Valdis Puriņš, Alberts Dullis and Alīda Niklase were three of the many resistance workers imprisoned by the Germans for passing information to British Intelligence.

A Latvian military organisation was established by General Jānis Kurelis in July 1944 from the Aizsargi of Rīga district as the Military Commission of the CCL. This group led by Captain Kristaps Krišs Upelnieks had the official goal of defending the Dvina river between Pļaviņas and Ķegums in case of German retreat and forming partisan groups in the rear of the Soviet Forces. The SIS maintained contact with this group through Salnais in Stockholm. Its main sources of intelligence on the ground were Pēteris Klibiķis and German Abwehr Lieutenant Ervin Haselmann.[105] The US War Department noted that 'among the best intelligence materials found during the war there were those obtained in Stockholm from our contacts with representatives of the Baltic states'.[106]

If the CCL thought this would get them western support against the Soviet Union they were soon to be disabused of that notion. Čakste and his colleagues fervently hoped that their cooperation would encourage the Western powers to think positively about sovereignty of the Baltic states but there is little evidence to suggest that they ever had any interest in that. It was a foregone conclusion in Western intelligence circles that the Baltics would remain as part of the Soviet Union after the war.

On 29 April 1944, the Gestapo had Čaksti, Kalniņš and Sēja transferred to Salaspils concentration camp from where they were taken to Danzig on 10 September before being thrown into Stutthof concentration camp. Chakste died on 22 February 1945 whilst being transferred to Lauenburg concentration camp. Eight leading Kurelian officers were sentenced to death by an SS and police court in Liepāja on 18 November 1944 and shot in the naval prison there, after which 1,300 men were arrested and sent to concentration camps in Germany.

Nazi action against Jews in occupied territories proceeded according to a carefully orchestrated sliding scale of destructive measures. Initially, laws were introduced defining and identifying who was and who was not a Jew. Then Jewish property was confiscated, and the Jews denied gainful employment. This was followed by the removal of Jews from their homes to specially designated areas, usually sealed-off ghettos, out of sight of the general populations. They were herded in like animals to await the judgement of the German authorities who would know where to find them all when they had decided what to do with them.

Up until these ghettos were established, however, those Jews who had avoided arrest were required to wear yellow stars on their clothing and were forbidden to leave their premises without an official permit. In Jelgava, they were dismissed from their employment, banned from places of public entertainment and many public areas. Association with non-Jews was strictly forbidden, Jewish businesses and houses were looted and synagogues were burned down. Only one remained standing, thanks to its proximity to Latvian homes.

When the ghettos were set up in autumn 1941 they were always in the poorest parts of towns. In Jelgava, one such was in a building recently used for stabling horses. In Ludza and Varakpjini ghettos were unfenced, but inmates were not allowed to leave except for specific purposes such as forced labour. Many ghettos were surrounded by barbed wire, though, and the perimeter was patrolled by members of the Latvian self-defence force.

Each ghetto was meant to be only a temporary measure in a process leading to the final murder of the Jews, either through mass killings or transfer into labour and concentration camps. All ghettos were in the most dilapidated parts of urban centres, where overcrowding, epidemics, starvation and death were a normal progression. Many laws and directives were aimed at the ghetto inhabitants and the severest punishment, usually death, followed transgression of any of them. Violations might also result in the murder of an unspecified numbers of other ghetto inhabitants who had no connection to the deed. A secondary objective of ghettos was to humiliate and degrade the Jews to reinforce the message of the Jews' 'inferiority' and make it somewhat easier for less motivated members of the German forces to carry out their gruesome duties. Higher-status Jewish men were especially singled out for particularly debasing treatment.

The three main ghettos were established in Rīga, Daugavpils and Liepaja. The Rīga Jews, who had survived the rampages of terror were ordered to relocate to a ghetto and create a Jewish council *(Judenrat)* in accordance with the directives of 18 August 1941. The ghetto was bounded by a 2-meter-high barbed wire fence along Lāčplēša, Maskavas, Jersikas, Ebreju, Lauvas, Lielā Kalna, Krāslavas and Jēkabpils streets. It was sealed on 25 October 1941 when a total of 29,602 Jews were registered as ghetto residents and confined to an area that had previously been occupied by a third of that number. The approximately 21,000 women and children among them were the families of men who had already been killed. Conditions in the ghettos were appalling with up to twenty people squashed into a single room. Things got even worse when Jews were brought in from surrounding villages such as Kjrsava. In Ludza the ration was 300 grams of bread per person per day, but food distribution was haphazard, and many went without food altogether and starved to death. Sexual assault by ghetto guards was an everyday occurrence.

Against all odds, the Council of Elders (*Ältestenrat*) headed by Mihails Eļjaševs, the Jewish police headed by Michael Rosenthal and council departments attempted to alleviate the worst of the depravations by operating a hospital, clinic, pharmacy, old-age home and other services. One of the prime functions of the ghetto was to provide slave labour and so thousands of men, and about 1,000 women had jobs, some of them outside the ghetto. Any institution or company in the city could apply for Jewish labour.

Working conditions in the firms and offices varied from almost concentration camp-like conditions to so-called good firms. Jewish work columns became a common sight on the streets of Rīga in the early morning and evening. To avoid the daily march to the firms furthest away from the ghetto, so-called 'barracks' of varying quality were erected in some factories and offices. When they left the ghetto and when they returned, they were searched so that nothing prohibited, including food, would be taken out or brought into the ghetto. Attempts to bring food to the ghetto were punished by hanging in a square near Sarkanā Street.

Then, in November 1941, Jeckeln, who had been so effective as the 'outstanding entrepreneur of violence' and mass murderer of Jews in Ukraine, emptied the Rīga ghetto of Jews.[107] This had been precipitated by Hitler's authorisation to Heydrich and Himmler in September to deport German Jews from the Reich. It had been assumed prior to this that deportations would not take place until after the war, so no actual preparations had been made for carrying out the directive. The only large ghetto in existence at that time was in Łódź in occupied Poland but the authorities there pleaded that an estimated 60,000 deportees could not possibly be crammed in, so an alternative was urgently sought.

After Łódź was eventually forced to take 20,000 Jews, Roma and Sinti, Himmler looked further east and saw that Minsk and Rīga, which were already under German control offered a solution. Minsk, however, was vetoed by the Wehrmacht who were starting to become stalled on their drive on Moscow due to the bitterly cold weather and thought it too close to the front. Stahlecker also objected to the Rīga plan claiming that camps were already full there but Jeckeln, eager to please Himmler and prove his worth came up with a plan to clear the Rīga ghetto by killing all 25,000 inmates thus making space to bring in the deportees.

Jeckeln, a native of Rīga, had been involved with the mass shooting of Jews previously at Kamianets-Podilskyi in August while he had been Higher SS and Police Leader for Reichskommissariat Ukraine and now he brought his industrial shooting methods to Latvia. His approach had bcn to involve all German units, be they SS, police or army, in mass coordinated shootings of Jews. Jeckeln had developed his technique of killing by introducing what he called the 'sardine method,' where victims were made to lie down in rows in a pit before they were shot. The next group would lie directly upon that layer of corpses, and so on until the pit was full. This form of industrial murder allowed more than 10,000 individuals to be shot on a single day and was Jeckeln's personal innovation.[108] The weapon of choice for this action was the captured Soviet PPD-40 machine gun set to fire a single shot.

Deportations started before Jeckeln had been able to get things ready, however, and the first five transports went instead to Kaunas even though there were no facilities there to accommodate them. The 2,934 people (1,159 men, 1,600 women and 175 children) from Berlin, Munich and Frankfurt am Main, who arrived there on 25 November were taken to Fort IX death camp and murdered by Jäger's EK3, the German order police and Lithuanian volunteers.

Four days later, another transport brought more Jews (893 men, 1,155 women and 152 children) from Vienna and Wroclaw all of whom met a similar fate. Jäger's officers included SS Obersturmführer Peter Eisenbarth (Gestapo), SS Obersturmführer Paul Müller (SD), SS Obersturmführer Johannes (Hans) Schäfer (Kripo), SS Obersturmführer Heinrich Schmitz (Gestapo), SS Obersturmführer Erich Wolff (SD) and SS Hauptsturmführer Gerhard Kortkampf (SD). After the war, Jäger avoided detection by working as a farm hand near Heidelberg under an assumed name until March 1959 when he was arrested and charged with his crimes. He committed suicide by hanging himself while awaiting trial in Karlsruhe on 22 May 1959.

On 1 December, Jäger submitted one of the most chillingly detailed reports to survive the war in which he wrote:

> In Lithuania there are no more Jews, apart from Jewish workers and their families … I consider the Jewish action more or less terminated as far as EK3 is concerned. Those working Jews and Jewesses still available are needed urgently and I can envisage that after the winter this workforce will be required even more urgently. I am of the view that the sterilization program of the male worker Jews should be started

> immediately so that reproduction is prevented. If despite sterilization a Jewess becomes pregnant, she will be liquidated.

It is significant that up until 19 August the number of Jewish men killed on any one day exceed the number of women and children but on 23 August that changed dramatically when 4,602 women and 1,609 children were murdered against 1,312 men. 'I wanted to eliminate the working Jews and their families as well,' he wrote, 'but the Civil Administration (*Reichskommissar*) and the Wehrmacht attacked me most sharply and issued a prohibition against having these Jews and their families shot'. He therefore set up a specially selected mobile commando under the command of SS Untersturmführer Joachim Hamann, who 'adopted [his] aims fully and who was able to ensure the co-operation of the Lithuanian Partisans and the Civil Authorities concerned'. Hamann, the son of a Baltic German and a 'fanatical hater of Jews'[109] had been a paratrooper in Poland and France before being assigned to the security police in Berlin during summer 1940. This move, in effect, halted an investigation into his conduct for mistreating men under his command, which says much about his appointment as training officer of EK3.

Historian Michael Mills claims that the massive death toll claimed by Jäger could not have been reached without the assistance of Lithuanian auxiliaries working under his guidance.[110] Jäger's report of 1 December lists the killing of Jews (46,403 men 55,556 women, 34,464 children), 1,064 communists, 653 persons with mental disabilities, and 134 others, from 2 July to 1 December 1941. This raises the question of whether Stahlecker had planned to use local volunteers in such numbers or whether he was taken by surprise. Despite his contact with the Pērkonkrusts before the attack, it seems unlikely that he could have anticipate such enthusiastic support and when he saw the strength of local feeling, he moved quickly to supress it and disarm the killers.

On 27 November a fence was built along Daugavpils and Ludzas streets in the Rīga ghetto. This sealed off the so-called 'small ghetto' where about 4,500 able-bodied men were imprisoned. Elsewhere about 300 women seamstresses were imprisoned in the Term Prison, and later moved to a building complex at No. 66 Ludzas Street. The other prisoners were told to be ready to move to another place of detention, so they had to pack up their belongings and wait in the streets of the ghetto. About 800 people who could not or did not want to leave their apartments were shot in the streets and homes of the ghetto. Later, their bodies were collected by a special Jewish team, which buried them in the Old Jewish Cemetery.

In two large-scale operations on 29–30 November and 8–9 December 1941, prisoners were assembled in columns of around 1,000 at a time and taken from the ghetto to the forest guarded during their 10-kilometre march by Latvian guards who had been given full deadly authority to deal with attempted escapees. The 'particularly vicious'[111] Dr (of law) SS Lieutenant Colonel Edward Strauch believed that the Latvians would not have the stomach for mass executions, however, and used his own men of *Einsatzkommando 2* to carry out the actual killing. When the prisoners arrived at the previously dug 'cavernous' pits with 'ramps carved into the sides' they were stripped of clothing and valuables before descending into the pits where they were shot according to Jeckeln's 'sardine method'.[112] The first transportation of approximately 730 Berlin Jews to arrive in Rīga was also caught up in the clearance of the Rīga ghetto on 30 November.

The Rīga ghetto had not been completely cleared when another four transportations of 3,984 people arrived in Rīga during the first few days of December from Nuremberg, Stuttgart, Vienna and Hamburg so the deportees were taken to the Jungfernhof camp run by Rudolf Seck. There they were forced to live in desolate barns and cowsheds. An estimated 800 inmates died of frostbite, malnutrition or rapidly spreading diseases during the winter months. Immediately afterwards a transportation arrived from Cologne. This time the Jews were taken directly to the ghetto. On an icy-cold, humid Sunday, they had to walk from the station to the ghetto but children, the elderly and the weak, who could not cope with this long walk on icy roads, were put onto buses, which took them directly to the Bikernieki forest where they were murdered.

Steven Springfield had been a very fit young man, capable of work and he was able to survive incarceration and deportation to Germany at the end of the war before being liberated by the Soviets. He describes the murders, 'when the people got there they were told to undress, put the shoes in one pile, clothing in another pile, driven to the edges of these mass graves, and machine-gunned. It was going on all night and the next day. Fifteen thousand of our people were massacred on that particular day.'[113] Another eye-witness account says that the victims had to descend to a pit on a special slope, lie face down on the ground, and were shot in the back of the head. Each group that was shot was thrown onto the bodies of the previous group.

Murder squads worked in shifts and the killings went on all day until dark. At Nuremberg, Blobel dispassionately described executions he had overseen,

> Since [the victims] were kneeling on the brink of the mass grave [they] fell as a rule at once in the mass grave. I have always used rather large execution squads, since I declined to use the men who were specialists in shots in the neck (*Genickschuss*). Each squad shot for about an hour and was then replaced. The persons who still had to be shot were assembled near the place of execution and were guarded by members of those squads which at the moment did not take part in the execution.[114]

Jews selected for deportation from the Reich were told by the Department for Jewish Affairs at the Head Office for Reich Security that they were going to the newly occupied eastern territories to find accommodation and work to help reconstruct these areas. The local headquarters of the state police then organised all deportations within their jurisdiction and readied them for transportation in cooperation with the German National Railway. The local German police force even accompanied the transportations as far as Rīga so it was clear to them what was actually happening. A great many people in the authorities were aware of the deportation of the German Jews, and the councils were heavily involved. The National Socialist Public Welfare Organisation auctioned and distributed the possessions of the deported as soon as the tax offices and other authorities had helped themselves to personal effects for their own purposes.

Any concern over the legality of stealing private property was cleared up by the issuing of Regulation 11 of the Reich Citizenship Law, which stipulated that a Jew 'leaving the Reich' would lose not only his nationality but also his property. The Reich Association of Jews in Germany were made to compile the deportation lists in accordance with Gestapo guidelines. Finally, the Jewish people themselves had to suffer the ultimate ignominy of having to pay for their deportation by means of special contributions to the 'Special Account W' of the Reich Association. To amplify the fiction that they were travelling to work, each person was allowed to take a packed suitcase. The guidelines stipulated that the people chosen for deportation had to pack only their absolute necessities, but everything was searched intensively by the Gestapo at the assembly points when any valuables were impounded. In the severe winter of 1941–42 only unheated goods trains were provided, and this inevitably and predictably led to numerous transportation passengers freezing to death during the journey.

In December further transportations followed from Kassel, Düsseldorf, Münster-Bielefeld and Hanover. Those who died during transport, numbering around 1,000 were buried where the trains stopped at Skirotava railway station. In Rīga, the deportees were accommodated in the homes previously occupied by the murdered Latvian Jews in what became known as the 'German ghetto'. These homes were painfully cramped, especially as two further transportations arrived from Theresienstadt ghetto, three from Berlin, two from Vienna, one from Leipzig and one from Dortmund. Many men from the ghetto and Jungfernhof concentration camp who were fit for work were taken to the site of the future detention camp in Salaspils where they found a half-finished barrack with a leaky roof and missing windows on a snow-covered meadow. They had to build their own accommodation in the ice-cold conditions and then build the entire camp. It is estimated that around 1,000 people died during the construction of the camp in icy conditions with inadequate food and complete lack of hygiene. Salaspils was later used as a detention camp for Russian prisoners.

The commandant of the Rīga ghetto, Kurt Krause, had already set up a ghetto council before the massacres of Rīga Jews and this was revived to ensure that the German intake was capable of self-administration. As each transport arrived, they select an elder to represent them and this person became part of the council run by Max Leiser. There was also a uniformed Jewish ghetto police force to maintain order. The old and weak from the ghetto and Jungfernhof concentration camp were recorded and separated out, ostensibly to be assigned to less strenuous work at a canning factory in Dünamünde but the transport only took them as far as the Bikernieki forest where they were shot by Latvian auxiliaries under the direction of the German security police and buried in mass graves. An estimated 5,000 people died in this way. Those who remained were given varying types of work to do such as cleaning apartments, or craft-based jobs for those with skills. They received no money. For ghetto residents, possession of money was punishable by death. Any wages paid by firms using ghetto residents was paid to the district commissioner.

The Jews suffered immense shock and distress at the conditions they had endured during transport and situation they found at Rīga. On arrival, they were herded like cattle in the bitterly cold weather with much shouting and sometimes violence to Jungfernhof concentration camp or the ghetto. The appalling conditions saw some 800 die in the winter months in Jungfernhof alone. In Salaspils the death rate was particularly high because of the barbaric living and working conditions. Only a fraction of the men taken there returned to the Rīga ghetto in summer 1942, on completion of the building of the camp, in a state of total exhaustion. Several hundred Jews in the Rīga ghetto organized a resistance group who tried to escape from the ghetto and join partisans. In October 1942, German police discovered one escape party and, as reprisal, more than 100 Jewish ghetto police were executed. The Germans destroyed the ghetto in December 1943, and deported the last Jews to Kaiserwald.

Himmler decided on 15 March 1943, that a better way of accommodating the Jews being transported east from German was to construct a concentration camp in Rīga and this led to the phased dissolution of the ghetto. In June of the same year, he ordered all Jews in Latvia to be shipped out to Auschwitz, Kaiserwald and its subcamps to make space for Jews who were now brought in from Germany, Austria and Czechoslovakia. The ghetto inmates discovered that their misery could be even greater when they were transferred to the new Kaiserwald concentration camp in a suburb of Rīga where conditions were significantly worse than those experienced in the ghetto. The clearance of the ghetto, which began in summer 1943, dragged on until late autumn.

All those who were considered to be unfit for work were gathered together in the ghetto, and more than 2,000 of them were deported to Auschwitz at the beginning of November. Only a small team of cleaners remained in the empty ghetto until 1944. Even when the great majority of the workers continued to live in the firms' barracks, Kaiserwald concentration camp remained the coordinating point for all prisoners. All the atrocities associated with this institution happened here too. Medical experiments, torture, arbitrary executions, selections etc. The concentration camp doctor, Dr Eduard Krebsbach, also managed the 'Children's Action', in which all remaining children were dragged off to be murdered. The Jews of Dobele were all murdered by 13 July and those in Silene by 22 July.

In Latvia, as in Lithuania, a Sonderaktion 1005 unit was set up to eradicate all evidence of mass murders.

The SS has been using Jews as 'corpse units' (*Leichenkommandos*) since 1942 to excavate mass burial sites and burn the corpses. They were often chained to prevent escape while they carried out their grotesque, macabre work. These units acquired the colloquial title of 'suicide squads' (*Himmelfahrtskommandos*) because after completion of their work were also shot and their bodies added to the pyres. It was considered vital that the remaining Jewish prisoners in the Baltic region should under no circumstances be left to be found by the approaching Soviet army, so the 14,350 Jews who had survived thus far were deported on 'death marches' to the nearest concentration camp, Stutthof near Danzig. Since this camp was already overcrowded, many prisoners were sent on to other concentration camps in the territory of the Reich such as Dachau or Neuengamme. The mortality rate during these death marches was very high. Of the approximately 25,000 Jews who were deported from the Greater German Reich to Rīga, only 1,000 survived the war.

On 16 March 1998, some 500 uniformed veterans of the Latvian SS Volunteer Legion went on their annual march through Rīga to remember comrades who fell in battle on the bank of the River Velikaya, south-east from Ostrov. Their demonstration met with virulent attacks from the Russian press. Since the end of the war, debate had raged over whether the legion had been essentially a force of coerced soldiers fighting for freedom against the Soviet occupiers or whether they had been volunteers operating as an integral part of the Nazi SS establishment involved in the mass killings of Jews and other civilians. The legion had been formed on 10 February 1943 on Hitler's orders and by August it had 17,971 members with another 12,000 joining by January 1944. The 15th Division went into battle against the Soviets in December 1943 followed by the 19th Division a few months later.

Even though formally the Latvian Legion was subordinate to the SS organisation, it was a regular component of the German military forces that fought against the Red Army. The setbacks suffered by the German armies in the Soviet Union had meant compulsory conscription in either labour or military battalions of young men throughout the Baltics and elsewhere. Latvian military leaders General Rudolf Bangerskis and Colonel Arturs Silgailis realised that allowing them to be conscripted into labour units would have them dispersed all across the continent and chose instead to champion the creation of a Latvian military unit under Latvian command that would at least have the merit of keeping them on home soil and might even be able to elicit guarantees of broader national self-determination from the Western powers eager to contain the Bolsheviks after the war. To this end they called up former commissioned and non-commissioned officers of the Latvian army around which to create the force.

The Russian Ministry of Foreign Affairs claimed that the 1998 march had provoked indignation in Moscow by commemorating 'the blood and suffering of thousands of people' when the Legion had 'murdered tens of thousands of Jews, Russians and Belarusians in 1944'. Criticising the Latvian authorities for allowing the march and with a blind eye to the history of the Soviet Union, the mayor of Moscow, Yuriy Luzhkov, said 'I do not know of any other countries where human rights are breached so openly.'

It had clearly been Soviet post-war policy to exaggerate the extent to which the people of Latvia, and other eastern European countries, had been complicit in genocidal war crimes and, after the collapse of the Soviet Union, to create the impression that the Baltics were still controlled by fascist elites. Even the Danish press were taken up with the event and wrote that although members of the legion were mostly conscripts rather than volunteers 'Latvian members of the [legion had] actively and enthusiastically taken part in the extermination of Jews' but that was qualified by the Simon Wiesenthal Centre in Jerusalem who said that the Legionaries were not involved in crimes against humanity but many of their number had 'previously served in the security police and had actively participated in the mass murder of civilians.' On 27 May, a majority of the Latvian parliament, which had not sanctioned the march, voted to dismiss the Latvian armed forces commander, Juris Dalbins, for participating in it in full uniform.[115]

Since the 1960s, the Soviet Union had targeted the Baltic nations and Ukraine through KGB Moscow show trials and executions of individuals accused of genocide whose presence at the scene of the alleged crimes was shown by contrary evidence to have been improbable if not impossible. When the Soviet called for the deportation of Vilis Hāzners, a former Latvian legionnaire and leader of the 'Latvian Hawks of the Daugava River' they presented their evidence in the form of a document entitled *Daugavas Vanagi: Who are they?*, which few consider to be little more than pernicious propaganda. The US Office of Special Investigations was not convinced of the authenticity of the evidence against him and refused to comply.

In a rebuttal of charges laid against the legion, the following points may be made:

- The legion was constituted after the bulk of Jewish murders were committed.
- The legionnaires 'oath of allegiance to Hitler' was compulsory for all personnel in the German armed forces and probably meant little to the majority of them.
- The majority were fighting *against* the Soviets rather than *for* the Nazis.

Although Lange had reported on the growth of anti-German sentiment in Latvia, the fear of a second Soviet occupation had motivated many to join the legion. One German general, Adolf Ax, wrote: 'They wish to achieve a sovereign Latvian nation state. Forced to choose between Germany and Russia they have chosen Germany, because they strive at co-operation with Western civilization. They regard German overlordship as the least evil. Their hatred for Russia was deepened by the occupation of Latvia.' There is no reason at all to associate the Latvian Legion, whose formation began in early 1943, with war crimes committed by some earlier military or paramilitary units. Latvian legionnaires did not take part in repressive activities but fought exclusively at the front against the Red Army.[116]

In an effort to gain political advantage through the legion, Latvian leaders had submitted a formal request to Otto-Heinrich Drechsler, General Commissioner of Latvia, for the restoration of Latvian independence. Drechsler was in favour of it and Himmler saw the sense in offering Latvia and Estonia national independence even to the extent that a decree was drafted for Hitler's signature. Rosenberg, however, tried to scupper the idea it when it was discovered that in the Moscow Conference of Ministers of Foreign Affairs of October 1943 it became known that British Foreign Minister Anthony Eden and US Secretary of State Cordell Hull had agreed to the post-war incorporation of the Baltic states into the Soviet Union. It was finally laid to rest when von Ribbentrop prevailed upon Hitler to reject it.

As early as 1942, the Soviet Union had established an Extraordinary State Commission to investigate war crimes of the Nazis and their collaborators in the Baltics during the Second World War. The findings of this commission, however, should not be taken at face value since the person charged with editing its reports was Andrei Vyshinsky, who had been Moscow's Plenipotentiary in Latvia during the 1940–41 occupation and who had been notorious for organising Stalin's show trials during the 1930s. In 1943, the Presidium of the Supreme Soviet of the Soviet Union passed a law 'on the penalties for German-fascist evildoers, guilty of murdering and torturing the Soviet civilian population and Red Army prisoners-of-war, and for Soviet citizens [guilty of] spying and treason of the Motherland, and for their accomplices'.

Consequently, military tribunals across the Soviet Union convicted roughly around 2.5 million people of offences relating to the German occupation. One trial took place in Rīga on 3 February 1946 and resulted in the conviction and execution of seven German ex-officials of the Rīga military district. Friedrich Jeckeln, Generalmajor Hans Paul Kupper, Generalleutnant Siegfried Ruff, SA Standartenführer Alexander Bocking, Generalleutnant Wolfgang von Ditfurth, Generalleutnant Albrecht Baron Digeon von Monteton and Generalmajor Bronislav Pavel.

All were found guilty and publicly hanged immediately after the trial.

Estonia

Germany and Estonia had been close economic trading partners for most of the 1930s and Estonia's economy was very dependent on that relationship. Throughout the first Soviet occupation, Estonia had looked to Germany for salvation and when it came they were keen to prove their worth with an eye to becoming a solid partner in the future national socialist order. Germany offered security against the reimposition of Bolshevism, while many racial theorists in Berlin viewed the Estonians as the most racially developed group in eastern Europe. Estonia was to become 'probably the only country in occupied Eastern Europe without armed anti-German resistance.'[117]

Eradication of European Jewry was one of the Reich's overriding war aims and many in Estonia were ready to cooperate with that ambition in order to ingratiate themselves to their new German masters. Identifying with the Nazis in their anti-Bolshevist campaign would also help to wipe away the shame of Soviet occupation. Snyder claims that the most enthusiastic were those who had actually worked hand in hand with the Soviets and were anxious to obfuscate and divert attention from their past actions. It should be noted also that the type of person who collaborated with the Soviets in the persecution of civilians were in possession of just those qualities that the Germans would also find useful. They were all set to became 'eager collaborators' in the Holocaust. One such was Ain-Ervin Mere who had been a Soviet agent and who now became commander of Estonian security police who would play a major role in the murder of Jews.[118] According to Anton Weiss-Wendt, 8,614 Jews died in Estonian territory during the war.

In 1961, a prosecution was mounted against Mere, commander of the Estonian security police, Ralf Gerrets, deputy commandant of the concentration camp at Jägala, and Jaan Viik, a guard at the same camp. The charge was mass murder of Jews. Gerrets and Viik were found guilty and duly executed but Mere had moved to Britain and the British government declined to extradite him, citing a lack of evidence. He died in 1969 in Leicester, England. A year later, Juhan Jüriste, Karl Linnas and Ervin Viks were charged with murdering 12,000 civilians at a concentration camp in Tartu. All three defendants were convicted and sentenced to death, but only Jüriste was executed. Australia would not extradite Viks but the US agreed to deport Linnas who died in a Soviet prison hospital.

The State Archive of the Russian Federation and the Central Archive of the FSB of Russia made available documents relating to the interrogation of members of the Estonian 36th Police Battalion.

Excerpts from the transcripts are included here and it is up to the reader to decide what credence to give them.

27 July 1948: Interrogation of Juhanes-Oswald Rahumeel
RAHUMEEL Juhanes-Oswald Juhanovich, B 1916, in the Kärla volost, of the Saaremaa uyezd ESSR, Estonian, citizen of the USSR, non-party member, education of 6 classes, engaged in agriculture.
Lives in the farm Ratra in the Iempa village, volost Kärla, uyezd Saaremaa

Question: Were you conscripted into the Soviet Army in 1941?
Answer: Yes, I was mobilized to the Soviet Army in 1941 and was appointed to one of the coastguard units in Saaremaa where I served up to October 5, 1941.

Question: Were you a member of an organization named Omakaitse (Estonian auxiliary police self-defence force)?
Answer: I had entered the organization Omakaitse at my own free will in the middle of October 1941 and had been a member up to February 1942, i.e., before my entry into the 36th police battalion. When I was a member of the Omakaitse, I was given a Russian rifle and 30 live cartridges. Moreover, I received a salary of 60–70 DM.

Question: When did you join the 36th police battalion?
Answer: I joined the 36th police battalion voluntarily at the beginning of February 1942.

Question: What was the 36th police battalion busy with, while situated in Novogrudok?
Answer: The main object of our 36th battalion was arresting Soviet citizens, mostly Jews, and afterwards convoying them to execution. Our soldiers and officers also took part in executions of Soviet citizens which took place at the Novogrudok region.

Question: What was your own role in the extermination of Soviet citizens?
Answer: Our 36th police battalion carried out exterminations mostly in 3 places, namely the Novogrudok region, the Novoelnya station, and near the Dyatlovo Village, which is about 20–30 kilometres away from Novogrudok. My personal role was that I once convoyed Soviet citizens – Jews to execution.

Question: Tell me in detail, how was the execution carried out in the Dyatlovo village?
Answer: Approximately on the 10th of August 1942, our company (the 2nd company) including me, except the 3rd platoon, was loaded onto trucks and we were taken to the Dyatlovo Village, which is 20–30

> kilometres away from Novogrudok where a Jewish camp was situated. When we arrived at this camp, we encircled it. Afterwards, we drew the Jews out their houses. All in all, about 1,000–1,500 Jews were gathered there. Later on, after we had drawn the Jews out their homes on one square, we ordered them to lie down on their stomachs, not letting them to get up. Around them were guards from our company, including myself. In the morning trucks and a mobile gas chamber pulled up to the Jewish camp. When the vehicles arrived, all of us soldiers started driving these Jews together, I personally put Jews into the mobile gas chamber, and also into a vehicle. Then we took them to the place of execution. This place was located a few hundred meters away form the Dyatlovo Village. All in all, about 1,000 Jews were executed.

Another man, Rudolf Mjaeorga, testified as follows:

> **Question:** Tell me in detail, how the executions of Jews took place.
> **Answer:** Before the execution, soldiers of the 36th Police Battalion, including myself, had arrested a group of Jews. Some of them had been put into vehicles, others had been sent afoot out of town, where the arrested dug out large pits – ditches that were about 30–60 metres lengthwise, 1.5 meters in depth and about 2.5 metres wide. After the ditches were ready, we shot the Jews that were digging them. I personally shot 10 Jews. Afterwards, other Jews, in groups of 20–30 people, were brought to these ditches; among them were women and children.

After the start of the war, a forced migration policy for the Jews had become much more difficult to implement and mandatory resettlement became the default option. Short-term measures and interim plans were drawn up for concentrating more and more Jews in occupied Poland, but this turned out to be impracticable due to the huge numbers involved.

When it was clear that ghettoization was a temporary phase, the intolerable conditions in the Jewish settlements and ghettos ceased to be an issue and became a guarantee that they would soon be cleared out. The main objective was to draw a distinction between Jews who were capable of work and those who were not. The Jewish question soon found new 'solutions' when the Nazis invaded the Soviet Union. Now the way was open for resettlement much further east, especially given plans to resettle millions of Russians in Siberia.

In 1939, there were approximately 4,400 Jews living in Estonia about 2,200–2,300 of them in Tallinn, 1,000 in Tartu and the rest spread out in the countryside which made them, as a percentage of the population, a tenth of that in Latvia. At this time, Jews in Estonia enjoyed cultural autonomy and received support directly from the state for cultural activities such as language and sporting activities, but the Estonian public generally regarded the Jews, who were in many ways isolated from mainstream culture and society, with indifference. There was little evidence of anti-Semitism even among the radical Right who were more focused on the Baltic Germans as the main stumbling block on the road to a resurgence of Estonian nationalism.

The turning point for Estonian Jews came with the Soviet occupation that had demoralised and humiliated the Estonian people who found the Jews to be a convenient scapegoat for their traumas. Many were influenced by Nazi propaganda and came to believe that the special Soviet terror battalions had contained a significant number of Jews which fuelled a growing conviction that Jews and communists had been and still were colluding against them. Most of the Jews managed to evacuate to the Soviet Union in summer 1941 when the war between Germany and USSR had broken out. However, by the time of the German forces' arrival, there were approximately 500 Jews still left in Tallinn and the Holocaust in Estonia would play out rather differently than in the other two Baltic states.

On 12 July, Kurg, who had been officially appointed by the Germans as commander of Tartu after his leadership in its capture from the Soviets, ordered the incarceration of all Jews in the city in the Turu Street synagogue before relocating them to the Tartu concentration camp in the Kuperjanov Barracks on Vystavochnaia Ploshchad. They would later be taken out and shot. Forty-two Jewish men were arrested in the first three days. Widespread anti-Jewish repressions began in September when the German security police and the head of SD gave an order to arrest all Jewish men over the age of 16. Over 200 Jewish men arrested in Tallinn were sent to Tallinn Central Prison (so-called Patarei Labour and Correctional Camp) and executed by early October. Jewish women and children were sent to the Harku prison camp near Tallinn; by mid-October 1941, there were 400 of them there. By summer 1942, approximately 640 Jews had been executed in Tallinn, 518 of whom were originally from Tallinn and the rest from other Estonian towns.

There were relatively few Jews in the country which persuaded the German authorities, under Oberst Hans Gosebruch, that ghettoization was not a practical solution. Where confinement was decreed, often single houses would be designated as places of incarceration before transfer to a concentration camp. Tallinn Central Prison became the most important detention centre of the Estonian Roma. There were over 240 Roma in the Tallinn Central Prison in spring 1942. They were soon sent to the Harku camp near Tallinn, where they were executed within a few months. In winter 1943, another 500 Roma were brought to Tallinn Central Prison. It is unknown how many of them were executed or died.

All the Jews who had been arrested in 1941 in Tallinn had been executed by 1942. However, several hundred Jews that had been brought to Estonia from late 1942 to September 1944 passed through Tallinn as they were kept for some time in Tallinn Central Prison. Then with the closure of the Jägala camp in autumn 1943, all surviving Czech and German Jews that had been brought to Estonia in 1942 were sent to Tallinn. Many female prisoners were soon taken to the Vaivara concentration camp but the fate of men is not recorded. Deportations from the west continued with approximately 300 Jews brought to Tallinn Central Prison from France in summer 1944. By the end of August, forty had survived, thirty-four of whom made it to the Stutthof concentration camp in occupied Poland during the evacuation.

Following the German invasion, many Estonian Jews were evacuated, fled in time, or were recruited into the Red Army. Some 400 of the 10,000 Baltic Jews deported to Siberia by the Soviets in June 1941 were from Estonia. When the Germans drove the Soviets out in 1941, police investigations had been carried out against the Jews still remaining in the country. Evidence from police files shows that prosecutions against these Jews proceeded on the basis of their disputed allegiance to the Estonian state.[119] Files were stamped either 'communist suspect' or 'accused of subversive activities' with little reference to the Jewishness. By the beginning of 1942, all arrested Jews had been secretly executed. Only a few individuals managed to hide until the end of the war.

In the months after September 1942 some 12,500 Jews were brought to Estonia from Germany and occupied countries. The first to arrive were about 1,000 Jews from the Terezín (Theresienstadt) ghetto in Bohemia who arrived by train at Raasiku station. Shortly afterwards another 1,000 arrived from Frankfurt am Main and Berlin. Between 400–500 of the younger ones were placed in Jägala camp near Tallinn. The remainder were murdered by Estonian camp guards and police at Kalevi-Liiva. In June 1944, approximately 300 men from the Drancy transit camp in France (Convoy 73) were sent to a camp in Tallinn.

After 1933, the Third Reich had maintained a 'Gypsy' policy that alternated between expulsion and *Seßhaftmachung* (resettlement). Existing measures to harass the Roma population such as charging them high rents for substandard living conditions, sudden closing or destruction of camping areas were compounded by the setting up of fenced and guarded camps. The fate of Roma communities was of little concern to local administrations. 'Anti-Gypsy' sentiments became common in the press and in professional journals, as some 500 Roma were sterilised under the Law to Prevent Genetically Deficient Offspring in 1934. The Law for the Protection of German Blood and German Honour and the 1935 Marital Health Law were also applied to ban on marriage between 'Aryans' and 'members of alien [*artfremden*] races.'

In 1940, 2,800 Roma had been resettled in the Lodz Ghetto in Poland and soon another 5,000 followed from the Austrian Burgenland. When the *Einsatzgruppen* began operating in the occupied territories after the Nazi invasion of the Soviet Union, traveling Roma were murdered when they were encountered but were not the subject of specific searches. As non-Christian, non-white, Asian people possessing no territory in Europe, Roma were outsiders in everybody's country.

The unambiguously racist attitude to Roma was linked to the notion of crime prevention that saw antisocial behaviour in some sectors of the population as being explained by hereditary factors. In this way, over 2,000 Roma, branded as 'asocial,' were sent to concentration camps in 1938.[120]

Himmler signed a decree at the end of 1938 calling for a 'resolution of the Gypsy question appropriate to the character of this race,' which marked the transition from a 'Gypsy' policy conceived as part of a program to remove 'aliens' from the community to one of persecution in its own right. Thousands of 'antisocial' Sinti and Roma were taken into 'preventive police custody' or sent to various concentration camps in April and June 1938. Hardly any of them survived internment in a camp. Others were subjected to forced sterilization on the grounds of their allegedly inherent antisocial behaviour.[121]

Records of the Tallinn Council show that Roma had been in Estonia since 1533 probably having arrived from Rothenberg in Germany. By the end of the nineteenth century there were some 150 living in Estonia but they were in three distinct linguistic groups. The oldest of these groups, the *Lajenge Roma* lived just north of Tartu and had been fairly well assimilated into the local population. During the inter-war years there was an influx of Roma from Latvia and other Russian speakers moved in from the east and settled around Narva. Generally, these Roma communities retained their own traditions but there were high levels of illiteracy. By 1939, it is estimated that there were around 1,000 all told.

Despite partial assimilation of the Roma communities into the Estonian majority there remained social and racial prejudices against what the Estonians called *mustlased,* which means dirty or black. Prejudice against the Roma was similar to anti-Semitism in that it was encouraged by the Church from where most of the derogatory popular images and clichés came but there was minimal interaction between the Roma and Jewish communities. While Roma dress and habits were engaging, they also served to differentiate them from Estonian society. Negative representation of Roma was widespread. For instance, thefts onmarket days were often ascribed to Roma, especially if they involved horses. It was commonly accepted that Roma were dishonest and such attitudes were handed down through the generations. Children were warned to keep away from the 'tribe of beggars and thieves.' Only a small minority of Estonians were neutral toward the Roma but even here their 'otherness' was recognised.[122]

When the Soviets took control in Estonia in 1940 and 1941 the Roma communities, being somewhat separated from the rest of the population and essentially apolitical, were largely unaffected. The Soviets did, however, with little success try to Encourage Roma into employment and their children into education. Whether or not this mildly positive attitude by the Soviets towards the Roma was responsible, there grew during the Soviet occupation an unwarranted assumption that somehow the Roma and communists were in collusion.

In the Soviet Union, the idea of Roma as social outcasts was endemic, and the words 'Gypsy' and criminal became virtually synonymous while it was common for people to think of them as pests or parasites. As early as 1933, 5,000 itinerant Roma had been deported from Moscow to internal exile for putting kinship loyalty above loyalty to the state. There was no sense that this was an ethnic cleansing, however, but more of a purge of what were seen as criminal or socially harmful elements. In Germany, at this time, the Nazis also appeared to look on the Sinti and Roma as merely asocial but on 8 December 1938, Himmler issued a decree for 'Combating the Gypsy Plague', which put a whole different complexion on the issue by giving it a racial aspect.

Ideas put forward by the distinguished historian Ruth Bettina Birn, about attitudes to Roma in Estonia in the 1930s are uncorroborated but are worth stating. The 'respectable' Estonian elite, Birn maintains, saw themselves as threatened by the 'lawless underclass' of lazy, promiscuous non-Estonian ethnicities.[123] The Jews, however, experienced none of the outbursts of violent antisemitism seen in other eastern European countries nor did the Jewish minority suffer any restrictions of its cultural autonomy during the period of independence.

Debate continues over whether Roma were explicitly included in Nazi extermination plans or whether they were just caught up in the category of 'racially undesirable elements'. Whatever the case, they fell to the mobile killing units of *Einsatzgruppe A* that had moved into the

Baltics hot on the heels of the Panzers in June 1941 with instructions from SS Brigadeführer Bruno Streckenbach, Director of AMT1, the staff department of the Reich Main Security Office (RSHA). Streckenbach had gone to Pretzsch, near Leipzig, in May 1941 to conduct a three-week course for handpicked members of the SD, Gestapo and the police, who were training for service in the *Einsatzgruppen*. He detailed their mission, which was to seize and destroy all political and radical enemy groups such as political commissars, Bolsheviks, Roma, partisans and Jews. He further ordered that all enemies of the Third Reich were to be deported to concentration camps and the Jews were to be singled out for 'special treatment'.[124] Heydrich's order to Higher SS and police leaders on 2 July 1941, however, does not mention 'Gypsies'.

An operational plan, *Generalplan Ost* was drawn up by Standartenführer Hans Ehlich and Oberführer Konrad Meyer, which anticipated that 'As many as ten million people in this region will be surplus and will either need to die or be driven into Siberia.' At a conference at Wewelsburg in June, Himmler warned that it was his intention to change the ethnic makeup of eastern Europe by 'eliminating' Jews, Roma, Slavs and other 'inferior' people to make way for future German settlers.[125]

In all, the *Einsatzgruppen* comprising some 3,000 men, would go on to kill over 1 million people. Their instructions allowed for broad selection of targets and left them considerable leeway to interpret their instructions as they saw fit. *Einsatzgruppe A* in the Baltics calculated the number of its victims up to 1 February 1942, to be 240,410 of which 218,000 were Jews. That did not count the approximately 5,500 killed in pogroms. They listed their victims as 'Lithuanians crossing the border, communists, partisans, mentally ill' and 311 others. Listing the numbers of dead brings with its own tragedy given that each victim was an individual in their own right whose personal catastrophe is swamped by the magnitude of the crimes.

In his book *Centuries Will not Suffice*, Prit Buttel says: 'We can condemn the mass murder of six million Jews during the Second World War, but do we really think of these deaths as individual people, each of whom had a past full of triumphs and failures, a future full of hopes and fears, a life that was suddenly cut short? Six million futures destroyed.'[126]

Rounding off the number of those murdered to the nearest thousand or the nearest fifty seems grossly disrespectful to each one of them but the fact is that the numbers cannot be verified accurately because of the circumstances in which they were killed. 'Each one of them died a different death, since each one of them had lived a different life' wrote

Timothy Snyder and the Russian poet Anna Akhmatova wrote in her requiem, 'I'd like to call you all by name.'[127]

When the *Einsatzgruppe* had begun exterminating the Jews it was not difficult to extend their remit to take in Roma who were handed over by Wehrmacht troops left behind the advance on Leningrad to 'mop up'. These Wehrmacht administrators provided the organisational and technical assistance required to carry out such a massive campaign of murder then when the mobile killing units were transformed into stationary units of the security police, they also received support from civil occupation authorities in their systematic killing of the Roma.

Unlike the situation in the Ukraine, where many Roma were branded as partisans or spies, Roma rounded up in the Baltics were automatically listed as mere subversive elements. In no case were Roma officially targeted as a blanket category and neither did the killings start immediately. In Estonia it was not *Einsatzkommando 1a* but indigenous collaborators who murdered Roma during the first months of the German occupation in the Tartu concentration camp, which was set up as the result of a local initiative and only approved by the Germans ex post facto. The camp initially operated under the auspices of the Omakaitse. The first 100 prisoners, Jews and Roma, taken into the camp by the Omakaitse were quickly executed while itinerant Roma families were ordered into a separate building across the Emajõgi River from where, in October, they were accused of rioting, sent to a concentration camp and murdered.

Such judicial procedures as existed were carried out in the concentration camp and it was the guards themselves who volunteered to carry out the executions. Other Roma were subjected to compulsory labour. All this time the Roma were persecuted as 'criminals' rather than for their ethnicity so exact figures of Roma murdered is impossible to ascertain. On 10 September, the head of *Einsatzkommando 1a*, Dr (of Law) Martin Sandberger, issued an order authorizing the arrest of all Jews in Estonia but Roma were swept up in the purge also.

According to Bentamin Ferencz, a prosecutor at the Nuremberg *Einsatzgruppen* trial, Sandberger was 'an active and probably even an industrious member of the gang of murderers that killed hundreds of thousands of innocent people.' He had been a fanatical Nazi and member of the SD ever since his time at Tübingen University. Reichsstudentenführer Gustav Scheel called him 'one of the most capable and best men of the SD-OA Südwest. He is determined, bright, quick and with a sound judgment. Highly gifted, industrious and not shy. He possesses a sharp logic and is available for anything.'[128]

In October 1939, Heydrich personally appointed him as chief of the recently established *Einwanderzentrale Nord-Ost* (Immigration office north-east) in Gotenhafen to take charge of deportations to create room for ethnic German emigrants, so called Volksdeutsche, from were expected to return from the Baltic states and the Soviet Union. It was in summer 1941 that Sandberger would be made head of *Einsatzkommando 1a* that was first active in Latvia and Lithuania before arriving in Tallinn on 28 August.

In his report of September 1941, Sandberger said:

> Generally speaking, the population is used to the fact that the Germans now call the shots in Estonia. All measures taken are being carried through obediently. The Estonians make any effort you can think of to support the Wehrmacht and to show their good will. In tracking down Estonian Bolshevists and taking them to court, the Omakaitse in particular, have frequently shown the desired co-operation.[129]

While Estonian Jews were targeted by Sandberger's *Sonderkommando 1a*, it had been initially hoped that the local population could be incited to carry out pogroms but anti-Semitism among the Estonian population as a whole never rose to the level where this was possible.

Within five days there were eighty-seven Jews and thirty Romani 'political prisoners' in the Pärnu concentration camp. A decree issued by Heinrich Lohse, Reich Commissioner of the Reichskommissariat Ostland, in December 1941 was aimed at itinerant 'Gypsies who wander about in the countryside ... spreading disease' are unfit for work and constitute a threat as potential spies. These were to be treated in the same way as the Jews. While executions of almost 2,000 Roma were carried out unimpeded in Latvia between April 1942 to March 1943, the police did not start screening the Roma population in Tallinn, Haapsalu, Paide and Saaremaa until 23 January 1942.

The Estonian police apparatus had been created as soon as the Germans took control of the country in June and retained much of the pre-war character but in May 1942 it was divided into a German (Group A) and an Estonian (Group B) with the Punishment Planning Commissions (*Strafprojektierungskommissionen*) operating between the two sections. Both Sandberger, commander of the Security Police and Security Service in Estonia, and Obersturmführer Heinrich Bergmann, head of the Criminal Division of the German Kripo in Estonia, had always stressed the important role the Estonians were to play in the fight against 'asocial elements and incorrigible offenders' such as

Gypsies, prostitutes, habitual criminals, and the work-shy. Again, it was emphasised that Roma were to be treated in the same way as the Jews. Sedentary Roma engaged in regular work, however, should be tolerated, but remain under police supervision.

In the case of habitual criminals, preventive police custody was the order of the day but for anti-social elements with a significant history of previous convictions execution was considered appropriate. Those taken into custody might find themselves incarcerated in a concentration camp euphemistically called 'work and education' camps (*Arbeitserziehungslager, or AEL*). By June 1942, itinerant Roma had all but disappeared in Estonia and, according to a report by Bergmann, the 'Gypsy Problem' in Estonia had been completely resolved but this proved to be more wishful thinking than fact.

On 11 June, Dr Otto Bräutigam, head of the General Politics Department of the Ministry of the Occupied Eastern Territories (RMO), expressed his opinion that sedentary Roma should be shot along with their itinerant brethren and Jews. Even though a decree to this effect 'The Treatment of Gypsies in the Occupied Eastern Territories,' was not effective until mid-1943, it provides the context in which the mass murder of a significant proportion of the Estonian Roma population took place. Without conclusive evidence, it is suspected that it was Bergmann who was behind the local initiative to murder 91 men and 152 women at Harku camp at the end of October. If this is the case, he was probably acting on reports indicating that Goebbels and Dr Otto Thierack of the Justice Ministry had agreed, on 14 September, that 'Gypsies should be exterminated unconditionally as 'necessary security measures'.[130]

During the last week of January and the first week of February 1943, on the orders of Sandberger, all remaining Roma were herded into Tallinn and its vicinity. On 31 January 1943, there were altogether eighty-seven Roma – thirty-three men and fifty-four women – living in the province area. Name, birthdate, place of residence, and occupation were recorded and all those fit for work were employed in agriculture. All Roma property, mostly equipment associated with horses, was impounded. On 9 February 1943, forty-seven were taken to Tallinn for deportation alongside sixty-nine from Haapsalu and seventy-three from Petseri. The deportation order included all working Roma.

Those Roma unfit for work were sent to Jagala 'work and education camp', which already held Jews who had been brought in on *Judentransporte* (transport of Jews) from the Theresienstadt ghetto and who were murdered on arrival. It was still cold in early March 1943 and the freshly dug pit in Kalevi-Liiva, the usual place for executions at the Jagala camp, was full of snow. After having received instructions from the Estonian Sipo in Tallinn, Alexander Laak, the commandant, notified his subordinates about the forthcoming execution of Roma. A group of Roma under escort of Sipo officials arrived earlier than scheduled: a small bus with some twenty-five Romani women and the elderly from Tallinn Central Prison, and on a truck about the same number of 5- and 6-year-olds from Vasalemma. The bus stopped in front of a pit already surrounded by guards from the Jagala camp.

All of the personnel of the camp, including Commandant Laak, were Estonians. Deputy Commandant Ralf Gerrets directed the arrivals toward the pit. After realising what was going on, the women started crying hysterically. Insensitive to their cries, the guards drove them, one by one, to the pit, where Laak dispatched them with a single shot to the back of the head. The last one was an old woman without legs. Only after she had handed over to the guards, by then well drunk, her last money and a gold ring, was she carried, instead of being dragged, toward the mass grave. After the bus drove away, the truck pulled up. Gerrets threw the children, shivering in the cold and screaming in terror, onto the ground. Guards took two children each to the pit. This time, a departure from the usual practice, the children were not even ordered to remove their clothes, dirty and full of holes as they were. And another departure, Laak, whose seemingly limitless ability to kill was restrained only by the size of the pit he had to fill, could not bring himself to start shooting. The guard Ian Viik saved everyone's face by opening fire first.[131]

Evidence suggests that the Final Solution of the 'Gypsy' question had not been completed in Estonia before early October 1943. It is known that Otto Koslovsky, a 19-year-old Romani was arrested on 24 September so at least some Estonian Roma were still alive at the time. It was in October that the remaining Estonian Gypsies, included the Mitrowski, Kozlowski and Burkewiecz families, were shot in the town of Hargla, near Tallinn. Elsewhere, teenagers from the Laitse were told that they were going to meet their parents, and they were issued holiday clothing. They were shot in Kalevi-Liiva.

Actual total figures of Roma murdered in wartime Estonia are unknown but two reputable independent studies put the estimates at between 800 and 850.[132] In 1943, it was decided to transfer all 2,000–3,000 itinerant Roma of eastern Europe to Auschwitz-Birkenau where the SS had set up the special 'Gypsy' section.

Under German occupation, Estonians attitude toward Roma hardened. Estonian and Russian communities, for the most part, were indifferent to their fate. The rural population would have been keenly aware that both Jews and, especially Roma, were disappearing from their communities and made no protest and expressed no negative comments. The Estonians generally saw the Roma as a nuisance while the Russians hoped that persecution of Roma would divert public animosity away from them. There is no evidence, however, that either of these two groups supported a programme of extermination, merely a removal. It was the officials of the Estonian secret police who exhibited the most vitriolic racist attitudes and made no effort to disguise their anti-Semitism.

The massacre of the Roma was public knowledge but hardly anyone criticized it and very few helped them. Not one of the European resistance movements took a stand for the Roma. All the European and non-European states refused to grant Roma refugees asylum.[133] After the war, the victors made no effort to punish the Germans for their crimes against the Roma and the issue was not addressed at the trials of the major German war criminals in Nuremberg. Alex J. Kay believes that the Allies failed to address the genocide of the Roma because it would have meant them having to safeguard the rights of the surviving Roma in obtaining some kind of restitution for their suffering. Furthermore, in 1956 the Federal Court of Justice in Karlsruhe refused to accept that the killing of Roma had been racially motivated but carried out as part of the purge of 'anti-social' elements as so the surviving Roma were not granted restitution payments for their traumas. Kay asks why the pan-European genocide of the European Roma plays such an insignificant role in European memory.[134]

According to Sandberger's records, during the first year of occupation, 5,634 people were executed, 5,623 placed in concentration camps and 18,893 imprisoned. These figures do not include victims of the Estonian militia. Sandberger also saw to the deportation of the 'racially inferior' population of the Estonian part of the region of Ingermanland, also known as Ingria. These people were earmarked for forced labour in Germany and their former home region was designated for settlement of Volksdeutsche (people of Germany origin but not German citizens) immigrants.

An Estonian International Commission for the Investigation of Crimes against Humanity was set up in 1998 by Estonian President Lennart Meri to investigate the historical record of the massive violation of human rights in Estonia during and after the Second World War. They estimated that the total number of Roma murdered in Estonia at somewhere between 400 and 1,000, men, women and children. Some 6,000 ethnic Estonians, apart from Jews and Roma, were also killed during this period as well as around 1,000 people of uncertain citizenship, mostly ethnic Russians. Most of these killings took place before to the spring of 1942. Later around half of the 30,000 Soviet prisoners of war held in Estonia died during captivity either as the result of neglect or deliberate killings.

The commission apportioned responsibility for these crimes in two ways. Firstly, there were those who were held responsible because of the positions they had held at the time. These were primarily the most senior members of the Estonian Self-Administration (the directorate) reporting directly to Hjalmar Mäe. Then there were those whose individual actions rendered them culpable regardless of whether they were volunteers in the service of the occupying power or had been conscripted. The directorate, a voluntary organisation, was seen to have been a convenient structure for the administration of the territory of Estonia limiting the need for the Germans to use their own resources for this purpose. In particular, they cooperated with the Germans in rounding up and killing Estonian Jews and Roma, and in seeking out and killing Estonians deemed to be opponents of the occupiers.

The following were named as persons with responsibility for all criminal actions carried out in Estonia, and beyond its borders by military units or police battalions raised with their consent, during the period of the German occupation; Hjalmar Mäe, Oskar Angelus, Alfred Wendt (or Vendt), Otto Leesment, Hans Saar, Oskar Öpik, Arnold Raadik, Johannes Soodla. The police Group B and the Estonian security police, headed by Ain-Ervin Mere and later by Julius Ennok were also complicit in actions against Estonians. The commission particularly singled out the roles of Ain-Ervin Mere; Julius Ennok; Ervin Viks and Evald Mikson, who signed numerous death warrants; Karl Linnas and Aleksander Koolmeister, commandant and senior officer respectively at camps in Tartu and Tallinn; and Aleksander Laak, commandant at Jägala and later in Tallinn.

The commission also reviewed the role of the *Miško Broliai*, a small number of whom were responsible for a number of killings of alleged communist sympathisers and the round-up of Jews during the first two months following the German invasion. The role of Estonian military units and police battalions in was also investigated to identify units, which took part in deportations of Jews, guard duties at concentration camps and a number of mass shootings, and which took place in Poland and Belarus. In one well-documented instance, the 36th Police Battalion participated in the gathering together and shooting of almost all the Jews still surviving in the town of Nowogródek on 7 August 1942. The 286th, 287th and 288th police battalions participated at various times in the killing of prisoners at camps in Estonia.

Efforts to discover documents in Estonian archives pertaining to the murder of Roma proved largely fruitless. It is known that according to the regulations of German occupying powers in Estonia only the roaming Roma belonged to the category of persons who were rounded up and later executed. It is known, however, that a number of adolescent Roma boys were kept in a special facility for young 'criminals' in Laitse, and a few, together with the young people of other nationalities survived the war.

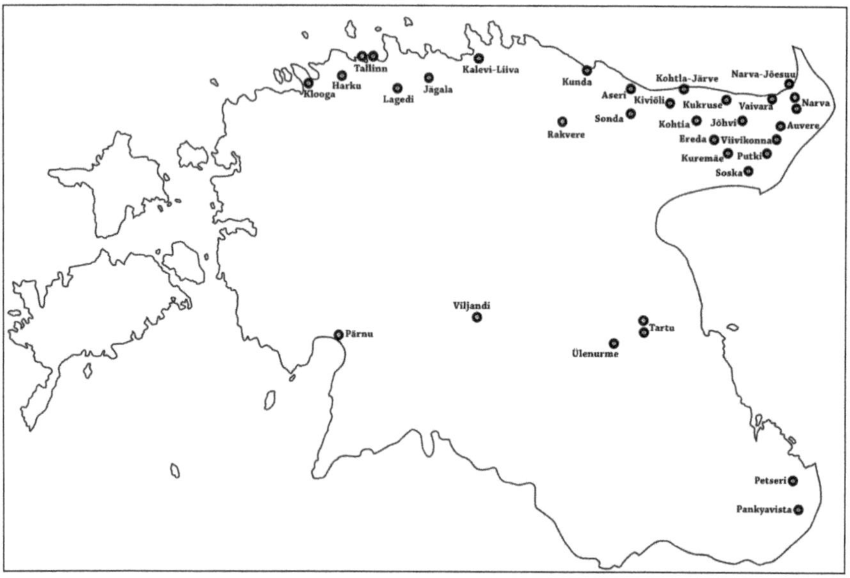

Estonian Concentration Camps

Vaivara concentration camp was the main camp (Stammlager) of a network of more than twenty labour camps located in the region of the Estonian shale oil industry operating under the authority of the *SS Wirtschafts-Verwaltungshauptamt* (SS Main Economic and Administrative Office). Camp commanders were Hans Aumeier, Otto Brennais and Franz von Bodman. The camp had approximately 10,000 Jewish inmates and a large part of them performed slave labour in the shale oil industry in eastern Estonia. Most of them were deported in 1943 from ghettos in Lithuania, others came from Latvia and, in 1944, some from territories controlled by Hungary.

Nearly one third of the inmates died in Estonia as a result of the severe conditions, or of being deemed unfit for work and then being sent to other camps where they were executed. Another third was evacuated by sea in August of 1944 to Stutthof concentration camp, and the remaining third were murdered when the camp was disbanded. The last couple of thousand inmates of the Vaivara camp system were sent to Klooga; only 100 or so managed to escape the final mass murder on 19 September 1944.

Other camps in the Vaivara complex were as follows:

Klooga: September 1943 to September 1944

It was one of the largest of the Vaivara camps and saw a mass murder of Jews that could not be evacuated when it was closed. According to a post-war Soviet investigative committee, 108 Jews survived the mass murder. Klooga's prisoners were mostly used in the timber and concrete industry. The number of prisoners in Klooga was usually between 1,800 and 2,100. It is estimated that about 3,000 Jews passed through the camp. Prisoners here lived in stone buildings that had functioning plumbing and running water. Inmates that had medical training worked in the prison hospital located in the camp territory. When the camp was overrun by Soviet forces they reported:

> Corpses of men and women randomly lay in front of the door in the premises of the ground floor of the building, and also in the first and second aisles between plank beds. The bodies in the aisles lay with their faces down in two-three rows lengthwise the aisle, one on another, like a tile roof; heads of the top corpses lay on the middle of the body that is bellow, with their legs towards the doors. There are 79 corpses in total, with their outer clothing on. The corpses have bullet wounds in the nape; all bodies are in the stage of decomposition. 200 meters away from the camp, to the north from the railway, near a ditch, there is a burned down building with a stone base and two pipes remaining. At a corner of the base on a stone the date of 7/21/1944 is engraved. The base is 45 centimetres high. On the site of fire, in ashes, there are plenty of burnt skulls, vertebras, and other bones and remains of corpses.[135]

Kiviõli: September 1943 to August 1944

This labour camp was divided into two sections: Kiviõli I and Kiviõli II. The first Jewish forced labourers to arrive in Kiviõli were 358 men and 89 women but by November there were around 600 in total. Despite a typhus epidemic breaking out in December, this figure had more than doubled to 1,300 by February 1944. In August 1944, the 2,000 prisoners in the camp were evacuated to the Lagedi camp near Tallinn and from there to the Stutthof concentration camp in occupied Poland.

Ereda: July 1943 to July 1944
The camp was divided into two parts: Upper-Ereda and Lower-Ereda (the camp of the sick). Prisoners and children incapable of work were transferred there from other Vaivara network camps. By the end of 1943 there were about 1,000 prisoners working in road and railway construction and agriculture. In late July 1944, most of the prisoners were evacuated to the Lagedi camp near Tallinn and from there to the Stutthof concentration camp in occupied Poland. It is known that a Jewish mass murder was organised in Ereda when the camp closed. There is no reliable data concerning the number of its victims.

Kukruse
There is no exact data concerning the establishment and liquidation of the Kukruse labour camp.

Viivikonna: September 1943 to February 1944
There were two labour camps in Viivikonna where prisoners worked for the oil shale industry. The exact number of Jews in Viivikonna is unknown but estimates put it at 1,500–2,000. The camps were closed as Soviet forces approached in early 1944 and 872 Jews in Viivikonna I were transferred to Vaivara camp and another 700 Jews from Viivikonna II were sent to the Ereda camp.

Auvere: September 1943 to January 1944
Auvere labour camp held approximately 500–700 prisoners who mainly worked on the railways. More than eighty are known to have died during a typhus epidemic in November. One of the first camps to close as the Soviets moved west prisoners were taken to Vaivara and Kiviõli labour camps.

Narva-Jõesuu: October 1943 to January 1944
Of the 261 Jews in the camp in December 1943, 33 of died of abdominal typhus and the camp was shut down in January 1944 when all the prisoners were taken to Vaivara.

Narva: October 1943 to January 1944
Narva was one of the largest of all the camps in Vaivara network. Its inhabitants were mainly Jews from Vilnius. It is known that seventeen Roma were executed in Narva in 1941. The last surviving Czech Jewish

men from Jägala were put in Narva were among the eighty prisoners that were sent to the Jalaka anti-tank trench already in November to dig up and burn the bodies of the Tartu concentration camp victims. Over 100 prisoners died in the December typhus epidemic. When the Soviet forces reached Narva in January 1944, the prisoners were evacuated to Vaivara. According to testimonies, executions of Jews took place during the liquidation of the camp.

Kuremäe: October 1943 to March 1944
The first 150 Jewish prisoners arrived at the camp in late October 1943, but numbers rapidly increased to around 850 when the nearby Soska camp was closed down. It is known that around eighty prisoners who were unfit for work were murdered when the camp was abandoned ahead of approaching Soviet forces and prisoners were transferred to the nearby Kohtla labour camp.

Soska: October 1943 to February 1944
This labour camp on the left shore of Narva river belonged to the Vaivara concentration camp network. The camp was established in autumn 1943. In November, 495 Jewish forced labourers lived there, including many that were sick and elderly. Thirty-one prisoners died due to diseases and overwork. The Red Army crossed Narva river in early February 1944 and therefore posed a threat to Soska. Consequently, the camp was hastily evacuated. Most of the camp's 437 Jews were sent to the nearby Kuremäe camp.

Jõhvi: October 1943 to January 1944
There is no data concerning the number of Jews in the camp. Based on testimonies, some executions were carried out by Germans working in the camp. Some of the prisoners were transferred to Vaivara camp following a typhus outbreak in December. The rest were taken to Vaivara after the closure of Jõhvi camp in January 1944.

Kohtla-Järve: October 1943 to July 1944
In Kohtla-Järve Jewish forced labourers worked for the shale oil industry.

Kunda: October 1943 to August 1944
Kunda was a small camp with around 200 prisoners. After the camp was liquidated, the Jews from there were evacuated to the Stutthof concentration camp in occupied Poland via the Lagedi camp near Tallinn.

Pankjavitsa: November 1943 to February 1944
In November, 250 Jews arrived at Pankjavitsa from Vaivara concentration camp most of whom were later transferred to Petseri and Ülenurme camps in early 1944.

Ülenurme: January to March 1944
About 100 Jewish prisoners were brought to Ülenurme from Pankjavitsa camp in Petseri county and taken to Rīga in March 1944.

Petseri: January to March 1944
Approximately 100 Jewish prisoners were brought to Pesteri from Pankjavitsa and taken to Rīga in March 1944.

Kohtla: January to July 1944
The first prisoners were some fifty women that had survived the Jägala camp and Tallinn Central Prison, and who had arrived in Estonia in 1942 from Germany and Czechoslovakia. Numbers here swelled considerably in early March by transfers from Kuremäe camp, which had been closed. In late July all the prisoners were evacuated to Lagedi camp near Tallinn and from there to the Stutthof concentration camp in occupied Poland.

Sonda: February to August 1944
Sonda was a little bigger than Kunda with some 300 prisoners. Survivors of Sonda considered living conditions there to be the best of all the camps where Jews were treated humanely. However, during the evacuation of prisoners in summer 1944, some Jews were allegedly shot in the camp. The survivors were evacuated to the Stutthof concentration camp in occupied Poland.

Aseri: May to August 1944
Aseri had space for about 200 prisoners. According to witnesses, forty to fifty people (mostly children, women and the elderly) were taken away from the camp and executed in July 1944, when the evacuation of the camps began. The rest were relocated to Kohtla labour camp in late July.

Other camps were:

Harku: September 1941 to October 1942
Jewish women and children were among 400 prisoners taken to Harku from Tallinn in October 1941. Many of those detained were executed in

late 1941 or early 1942. One report gives a figure of 1,133 prisoners in July 1942 with Roma listed separately, as interned persons. Numbers were 328 Roma of which 170 were men and 158 women and 189 of whom were under the age of 18. On 27 October 1942, 243 of these, 91 men and 152 women, were murdered there. Children under the age of 11 who had been separated from their families at Harku were taken to 'education colonies' in Laitse, also Harju Province.

Lagedi

Lagedi camp was established in August 1944 as a transit camp to evacuate the Jews from Vaivara concentration camp to the Stutthof concentration camp in occupied Poland. Most of the Jews in Lagedi were evacuated on 19 August, but a few days later, another 500 Jews were brought in from the Klooga camp. With the German evacuation from Tallinn on 18 September 1944, a mass murder of the remaining Jews in Lagedi took place. There are no solid data concerning the number of people that were executed.

Tartu: July 1941 to Spring 1944

Most of the 1,000 Jews living in Tartu before the war evacuated to Russia when the Germans invaded in June 1941. About 160 remained and were rounded up by the Germans. Detained Jewish men were murdered in July and August, women and children in August and September. They were executed at the Jalaka anti-tank trench near Tartu that had been established in summer 1941. It was later decided that the bodies must be burned. This task was given to eighty Jews that had been brought from Narva labour camp in November 1943. Digging up and burning of the bodies lasted until April 1944. Most of the Jewish prisoners had been executed by then. The last twenty-two were murdered right after the works had ended.

Jägala: September 1942 to September 1943

Jägala was run by an Estonian Aleksander Laak. It was termed a labour and re-education camp housing about 2,000 Czech and German Jews who worked both locally and elsewhere. During the first month of its existence, the camp saw the arrival of some 3,000 Jews from Terezin. All those considered infit to work were taken to Kalevi-Liiva and shot. Others were transferred to Tallinn and Tartu.

Kalevi-Liiva: September 1942 to September 1943

Some 1,002 mainly Czech Jews from the Terezin ghetto and another 1,049 Jews followed from Frankfurt am Main and Berlin.

Approximately 1,600 Jews were executed on the day of their arrival. Another 400 prisoners from Jägala camp, Jews and Roma, were also brought to Kalevi-Liiva and murdered there. On 5 September 1942, Estonian police officers murdered over 1,000 Jewish children, women and men from the Theresienstadt ghetto in the Kalevi-Liiva dunes on the Baltic coast. Further transports followed, carrying Jews from cities like Frankfurt and Berlin.

In total, up to 6,000 Jews from the German Reich and Poland as well as 110 Estonian Roma perished on the site in 1942–43. There have been seven known ethnic Estonians (Ralf Gerrets, Ain-Ervin Mere, Jaan Viik, Juhan Jüriste, Karl Linnas, Aleksander Laak and Ervin Viks) who have faced trials for crimes against humanity committed during the Nazi occupation in Estonia. The accused were charged with murdering up to 5,000 German and Czech Jews and Roma people near the Kalevi-Liiva concentration camp in 1942–43.

Rakvere

In Rakvere, the executions of Jews took place in August and December 1941. Altogether, twenty-two local Jews were killed.

Narva

According to the Estonian security police's data from 1942, thirty-one Jews were executed in Narva.

Pärnu

There were approximately 250 Jews living in Pärnu before the war. More than 100 of them evacuated to Russia in June 1941 and by mid-September, most Jewish men who remained had been murdered. On 2 November, thirty-three women were executed in a forest near Pärnu and twenty-eight children in a synagogue. Altogether, 137 Estonian Jews were murdered in Pärnu in 1941.

Viljandi

Some eighteen Jews from Viljandi were executed during the German occupation. Roma incarcerated in Viljandi prison including women, children and the elderly were murdered there by the Estonian Omakaitse militia.

Chapter 7

ON THE BATTLEFRONT

The first six months of Operation *Barbarossa* had seen the Red Army's defences shattered all along the front as the Germans encircled the bulk of the Soviet 3rd, 4th and 10th armies west of Minsk. Once across the two main defensive lines of the Dvina and the Dnepr rivers, they forged ahead towards Leningrad and Smolensk. From the very first day of the German attack, Stalin and the Stavka (Soviet Military High Command) consistently and repeatedly made every effort to halt and drive back the Germans. All through June to September they ordered a series of counterattacks and, in on one occasion, a full-fledged counteroffensive, but all proved to be clumsy poorly coordinated attempts. These actions included virtually suicidal counterattacks by the 3rd and 12th mechanized corps at Raseinai.

Von Leeb's German Army Group North captured Rīga and Pskov achieving a partial encirclement of the Soviet 16th, 19th and 20th armies in the process. When von Leeb's forces had broken through to the south of Pskov and headed toward Luga they looked as if they might reach the outskirts of Leningrad within a couple of weeks but the Panzers, as usual, had raced far ahead of their logistical support and their supply lines were overextended.

Then in late August Hitler's plans were thwarted by the ferocious Soviet defence of Smolensk led by Field Marshal Semyon Timoshenko, which caused the Germans to temporarily halt the drive on Leningrad and Moscow to concentrate on Kyiv and central Ukraine. The Soviets had thrown 80,000 men of the Baltic fleet into their path and although they slowed the Germans, it was only a temporary hold-up that was overcome once the panzers were re-supplied with fuel and ammunition. The Soviet Smolensk counteroffensive suddenly collapsed and weakened the whole defensive front when the Soviet 5th, 21st, 26th and 37th armies were eventually scattered.

Meanwhile, the German Army Group South had made good progress towards Kyiv destroying the Soviet 6th and 12th armies on the way and threatened the Black Sea port of Odesa. On 17 September 1941, Hitler finally decided that the main prize was Moscow and transferred Reinhardt's XXXXI Panzer Corps from the Leningrad Front leaving von Leeb stalled without his mobile armour, unable to mount an offensive and forced to adjust his strategy to one of encirclement of the city with a view to starving its defenders out. Leningrad was within touching distance by the end of August 1941 but the Soviet troops inside the city were told bluntly to 'defend their city to the death.'[1] German Army Group Centre had been given three of the Wehrmacht's four Panzer groups to launch a concerted offensive to capture Moscow.

Even though the advancing German forces seized huge tracts of open countryside across the entire front, they made little impact on the cities, towns, and major roads so that by late February of 1942 the front was a patchwork quilt of overlapping Soviet and German forces, and neither side was able to overcome the other. Stalin ordered the Leningrad and Volkhov fronts to raise the siege of Leningrad by attacking across the Neva and Volkhov rivers against German Army Group North but although Lieutenant General Andrei Andreyevich Vlasov's 2nd Shock Army broke through the German lines, they became isolated and destroyed by German counterstrokes between May and July. Attempts to relieve Vlasov by Korovnikov's 59th Army and Yakovlev's 52nd Army was undermined by defections of Vlasov's force to the Germans talking with them details of Soviet plans. On 11 July Vlasov, himself, defected to the Wehrmacht. At the end of the war, he was captured by Soviet forces and hanged as a traitor on 1 August 1946.

After the Red Army's winter offensive collapsed in late April 1942 both sides took the opportunity to reorganized and refitted their forces and look for ways to regain the strategic initiative. Confident that his forces could still achieve many of Operation *Barbarossa*'s original aims, Hitler and his High Command planned a new campaign to realise their most ambitious strategic objectives. For his part, Stalin completely accepted that the Red Army would emerge victorious only after it could organise a massive strategic counteroffensive along the entire front and all Soviet hopes were pinned on that.

The soviets tried and failed over many months to break the siege of Leningrad which eventually wore down German Army Group North in a series of bloody battles, but they held the city as both sides became wasted by attrition. The Germans were forced onto the defensive, however, as the Soviets steadily built up their reserves and readied for their planned counterattack. The balance of power was tipping inexorably in favour of the Soviet forces. The Luftwaffe was losing control of the skies above the battlefields and Soviet armament production was, with help from Britain and the US beginning to outstrip that of the Germans.

By early December, having just failed to take Moscow the combination of harsh weather, alien terrain and a fiercely determined enemy, ground the German offensive to a halt. Soviet reserves had piled in and unleashed a devastating counteroffensive at Tikhvin, east of Leningrad, and at Rostov in the south, driving German forces back along all three principal strategic axes and away from Moscow. The stunning effectiveness of the Soviet response threatened to sorely test the Wehrmacht's resilience.

Hitler feared a collapse of his front and issued his famous 'Halt Order' on 18 December. Commanders were ordered to stubbornly defending every inch of ground even in 'impossible circumstances' and all requests to withdraw were denied. Colonel Günther Blumentritt, Chief of Staff of the German 4th Army claimed that this 'fanatical order that the troops must hold fast regardless in every position, and in the most impossible circumstances, was undoubtedly correct.'[2]

General Georg von Küchler had replaced von Leeb but his two infantry armies lacked mobile units and had to dig in to hold its position as the Soviets built up its Leningrad and Volkhov fronts. The Soviet 8th, 54th and 59th armies massed for a drive to break through the German front at Siniavino and lift the siege of Leningrad. With his southern flank under threat, von Küchler appealed to Hitler for permission to withdraw but Hitler denied him.

It was the fact, however, that senior, and even comparatively junior, army officers interpreted the order in their own way to avoid suicidal and ineffective actions. They had been trained to adopt *Auftragstaktik* (actions taken without orders, but which support the intentions of ones commander), which encouraged decentralized initiative within an overall strategic framework, and they were not going to abandon their doctrine even if it meant ignoring the halt order. Even von Bock realised that 'units will probably pull back without orders' and Heinz Guderian, commander of the 2nd Panzer Army admitted that such 'impossible orders' were 'simply nerve-wracking'. Field Marshal Günther von Kluge who took over from von Bock said 'No area is to be given up unnecessarily but neither is it to be held if troops are to be wiped out as a result'.[3] Early in 1942, Stalin ordered a general offensive all along the front from Leningrad to the Black Sea.

Hitler deployed Manstein's 11th Army to the Leningrad sector to reignite the assault on the city having assumed that Stalingrad would be taken before the winter set in. This did not happen because, as before, German intelligence significantly underestimated the strength of Soviet reserves and came under a concerted pre-emptive attack. On the Leningrad and Volkhov fronts the Soviets launched a massive offensive, Operation *Polar Star*, against German Army Group North at Siniavino. It ultimately failed and resulted in the destruction of the 2nd Shock Army for the second time in a single year, but it also ripped the guts out of Manstein's 11th Army that was now incapable of mounting any further assault to take Leningrad. Despite the failure of the Soviet Operation *Polar Star*, it was a dress rehearsal for the January 1944 offensive that ultimately liberated Leningrad.

The Stavka had consistently expanded its strategic horizons to take advantage of any local collapse that might occur in the German front while the Red Army was conducting major offensive operations. One such subsidiary operations took place at the very end of the Leningrad-Novgorod offensive when the Govorov and Popov's Leningrad and 2nd Baltic Fronts pounded the Wehrmacht's Panther Line defences in the Narva, Pskov, Ostrov and Pustoshka sectors along the Estonian border for a period of almost six weeks.

The Leningrad Front's 2nd Shock, 59th and 8th armies repeatedly attempted to encircle and destroy German Army Group North's forces at Narva and thrust deep into Estonia but failed. To the south, the Soviet 42nd, 67th and 54th armies attacked at Pskov and Ostrov but could not break into either city. Meanwhile, to the south, on the Leningrad Front's left flank, the 2nd Baltic Front's 1st and 3rd Shock, 10th Guards, and 22nd armies achieved only limited success in heavy fighting against German Army Group North's 16th Army at Pustoshka.

Throughout the entire winter of 1943, the Red Army's 1st Baltic, Western and Belorussian fronts continued their assaults across the entire front. Bagramian's 1st Baltic Front struck north and north-east of Vitebsk in near constant offensive operation from late December 1943 and severed communications between German forces in Vitebsk and Polotsk. The winter and early spring now became an unremitting struggle for survival. It is worth noting the special attention that Stalin had paid to the Baltic front when the Belorussia offensive stalled. While Hitler's 'Halt Order' failed to stop the Red Army's Leningrad-Novgorod offensive it was markedly more successful in holding the Panther-Wotan Line (Ostwall), which stretched from Narva on the Baltics along the line of the Dnieper.

After a 515-day siege, the Soviets broke through to Leningrad on 18 January 1944 and threatened to push the Germans all the way back to the coast of the Baltic Sea and weaken the left flank of the German central forces. Küchler was replaced by Generalfeldmarschall Walter Model who was more to Hitler's liking. Model sent out an order to all commanders in the field that they were to build defence lines where they stood, not take a single step backwards and fight to the bitter end. It was impossible, of course and Hitler now agreed to a tactical retreat of the 18th Army to the west bank of the Narva River, which narrowed the defensive line considerably and where a crucial battle would be fought.[4]

A stalemate of sorts developed until March when the Soviets launched an air and artillery bombardment of the city of Narva. Infantry attacks were driven back in bitter hand to hand fighting and amid the quagmire of an early spring thaw, German lines held. To the south, however, the Soviets had decimated seventeen German divisions in Operation *Bagration* and pushed on towards Vilnius threatening to split the German Army North Group and German Army Centre Group. Despite Hitler demanding that the city be held at all costs, it fell to the Soviets in mid-July at a cost of 13,000 German dead after which Hitler ordered his forces to consolidate along the Tannenberg Line west of the Narva. Two Soviet rifle divisions with air cover launched an attack before the Germans could dig in, however, threatening an early breakthrough but the German lines held. Stalin issued the order to break through to Tallinn 'at all costs'.

The 2nd Shock Army attacked across the Narva river on 25 July. Defenders ran out of ammunition and were cut down by Soviet fire. Suicidal defensive actions were unable to prevent further Soviet advances along the road to Tallinn. With the loss of Narva on 10 August, the German position was now hopeless. Guderian wanted to relocate thirty divisions to Germany for a brief rest and resupply before reinforcing the line in Poland but Hitler would not hear of it. In mid-September, General Ferdinand Schorner decided to evacuate all German troops from Estonia south to Pärnu in Latvia.

The Soviets continued their inexorable advance towards Tallinn and took it on 22 September. Rīga fell on 13 October but there was fierce resistance in Courland by German and Latvian troops by now well versed in defensive tactics. The battles here were prolonged, intense and costly for both sides. Hitler designated the area Fortress Courland and decreed that it was not to be evacuated under any circumstances. They were still holding out in May days after Hitler had shot himself.

Chapter 8

SECOND SOVIET OCCUPATION

The Sovietisation of the Baltics after 1944 was little more than a continuation of the policy that had been adopted as early as the reign of Tsar Peter I (1682–1725), continued by Tsar Nicholas I (1825–1855) and implemented by the Bolsheviks after the Russian Revolution in 1917. This essentially meant the subjugation of all territories in the Imperial Russian Empire (and later the Soviet Union) to the interests of Russian power invested in a supreme leader and enforced through terror. After 1944 this involved occupation, annexation, integration and colonisation.

The post-war fate of the Baltic states had been determined as early as 1942 when Anthony Eden had visited Moscow to prepare the ground for Western-Soviet cooperation against the Nazis. He had been left in no doubt that any would be subject to several conditions one of which was that the western governments would not interfere with Soviet claims to the Baltics. Lord Halifax, who was the British ambassador to the United States, gave voice to what had been agreed at that meeting when he told the US that 'Mr. Eden cannot incur the danger of antagonizing Stalin, and the British War Cabinet have … agree[d] to negotiate a treaty with Stalin, which will recognize the 1940 frontiers of the Soviet Union.'[1]

Churchill followed that up a few weeks later in a letter to US President Franklin D. Roosevelt saying, 'I hope therefore that you will be able to give us a free hand to sign the treaty which Stalin desires as soon as possible'.[2] Roosevelt saw no possibility of arguing the case and concurred by saying 'The European people will simply have to endure Russian domination, in the hope that in ten or twenty years they will be able to live well with the Russians'.[3] The Yalta Conference of February 1945 rubber stamped these Soviet demands and consigned the Baltics to Soviet domination for more than forty years.

When they returned to power in the Baltics, the Soviets adopted a twofold policy. The Baltic states were a vital part of their political and military strategy. As well as extending Soviet power westwards to the Baltic Sea coast the three states acted as a barrier to Western incursion. Together with the fact that they had been part of the Imperial Russian Empire and the Soviets still claimed historical rights to dominion, Estonia, Latvia and Lithuania did not become satellite states after 1945 but were fully and forcefully incorporated into the Soviet Union.

This required a repudiation of Lenin's concept of a socialist world in which aggressive nationalism was abjured and subjugation of other states rejected but Lenin was long dead, and Stalin had other ideas which, in many ways, harked back to an imperial mentality. Russian culture and influence was promoted over other subordinate cultures with a belief that 'Eurasian peoples could be fused ... into a single, essentially Russian-oriented people.'[4] The two most effective methods of achieving this in the Baltics were the suppression of local cultures and manipulation of the ethnic composition. Russian was declared to be the official language and all dealings with authority of any description had to be carried out in Russian. The main underground opposition, the *Miško Broliai, were* hunted down with brutal intensity.

Lithuania was unprepared for the second Soviet occupation. There was certainly a feeling among the people that there must be resistance but there was no sign of effective political or military leadership. Almost all the high-ranking military leaders had fled or been deported. Some 30,000 Lithuanians joined resistance movements that sprang up, but they had little understanding of partisan warfare. Small partisan groups amalgamated into larger units, and subsequently into districts. A district would typically have between two and five brigades. Some sort of military order and discipline was brought in under the leadership of Jonas Žemaitis-Vytautas with the wearing of military uniforms the imposition of statutes, rules and regulations.

The first encounter with Soviet troops was on 3 August 1944 when there were clashes in the Kaunas district and again on 16 December resulting in the deaths of three Soviet soldiers for which fifty-six Lithuanian civilians were executed in reprisals. In December also, in a much bigger confrontation, Soviet troops and Lithuanian partisans fought in Kedainys district when some ninety Soviet soldiers were killed. The insurgency spread with twenty-four partisans and eighty Soviet soldiers dying in battles in the Ukmerge district on 12 January 1945. An enraged Soviet administration brought in 2 NKVD divisions

(2nd and 4th) and employed up to 7,000 local destruction battalions (*stribai*) hurling 10,000 troops against the rebels during the summer months but still the death toll was heavily biased against them.

The Soviet forces were encouraged to enact brutal rape, theft and murders of non-combatant Lithuanians to force the partisans to stand down. General Vetrov of the 4th NKVD division, was particularly murderous when it completely eradicated a number of villages and their inhabitants in the Dzukija region towards the end of December 1944. When partisans were captured, they were tortured before being shot as a means of intimidating and discouraging their compatriots. The Soviet Poliburo member M.A. Suslov came to see for himself and vowed that 'There will be a Lithuania but without Lithuanians.'[5] To make the point, 200,000 Lithuanian Poles were transported to Poland in trains carrying the sign 'Going Home' despite their families having lived in Lithuania for many generations. Lithuanians in the Klaipėda region were sent to Germany along with a total of 170,000 other Baltic Germans at the same time as cities like Vilnius were heavily settled by Soviet immigrants.

The following year saw a number of major encounters between partisans and Soviet forces. In March 1945, in the forest of Labanoras, partisans of the Tigras unit found themselves surrounded and out of ammunition. They armed all their remaining hand grenades, stood in a group and exploded them preferring death to the inevitable gruesome experience of capture. No number of such encounters was ever going to influence Soviet policy in Lithuania except to double down on terror and suppression but attacks such as the one led by Adolfas Ramanauskas-Vanagas carried out at the end of 1945 when NKVD headquarters in Merkinė were temporarily occupied by rebels undoubtedly nourished the national spirit of resistance to Soviet occupation. The Lithuanian Constitutional Court in 2014 suggested the Soviet repressions that attempted to 'exterminate the basis of the political nation of Lithuania' directed at the 'most active political and social groups' had been tantamount to genocide.[6]

When the Red Army returned to Latvia it did so in massive numbers intent on turning the country into a vital military outpost against the West. Along with the military came political controls. The Soviets had been preparing for this by training former residents of Latvia who had been evacuated to the Soviet Union and who could speak the local language and were familiar with the local situation. The first wave, some of whom had held these posts previously, included the of heads of all central institutions of the Communist Party and the municipal and district divisions of the NKVD. The Bolsheviks held absolute power to the eliminate all remaining political, economic and spiritual leaders and the destruction of the European-style socio-political structure.

Most Latvians did not regard the Red Army as a liberator, merely another occupation power that had replaced the Germans. For this reason, it was important for the authorities to create, within the population, a loyal support group made up mostly of demobilised soldiers and officers of the Red Army. It was not difficult to persuade many ex-servicemen to stay in the country given that it had suffered less ravages than the western Soviet Union and had a significantly higher standard of living. The massive deportations had left many dwellings unoccupied, and the authorities decreed that 10 per cent of all new buildings were allocated to Soviet ex-servicemen and their families.

Latvian resistance to Soviet occupation was merely a continuation of a movement that had begun in 1940 when all the Baltic states had become embroiled in a war completely against their will. Partisans had been active all through the German occupation and had little trouble changing the focus of their attention to the Soviets once more. By this time the resistance groups were made up mostly of draft dodgers and deserters from the Red Army rather than the 'criminal elements and bandits' depicted by Soviet propaganda, although there were a few of those also.[7]

The Soviets took the threat of armed resistance seriously and deployed a large number of troops to combat their activities, but it must be said that they did so with little success. The partisans had, by now, become well versed in the methods of subversive warfare. It was only when the Soviets were able to engage up to 3,500 secret informers and agents into the population that they eventually began to have any success.

More than one in ten of the population of Estonia had served in German volunteer legions, police battalions or Waffen-SS but many who did so had been pressed into service. Up to 95 per cent of security police employees in Estonia were ethnic Estonians and served at the centre of the German repressive apparatus. Estonian cooperation and collaboration with the Germans had reached a higher level than in many other occupied territories with the result that Moscow considered almost all adult males compromised and meant to purge the state of these 'criminals' when they regained control. When this became a near certainty towards the end of September 1944, the population of Estonia had declined by one quarter relative to 1939. About 20,000 Baltic Germans left in 1940, and another 100,000 had gone because of Soviet evacuation, mass deportation, mobilisation and arrests. The Germans killed approximately 8,000 people, 30,000 died in the war, 7,000 ethnic

Swedes resettled to Sweden and more than 70,000 Estonians fled abroad.[8]

As German troops left Estonia, they helped to set up a number of anti-Soviet partisan groups while others who had been hiding from the Germans in the forests, fearing arrest or mobilisation by the Soviets, created their own units. When the Germans left Tallinn, an interim administration was established under Otto Tief on 18 September and the city saw the Estonian flag flying from public buildings. It was ripped down by Soviet forces four days later.

The Soviet Union had been preparing for its return to Estonia almost as soon as their forces had left in 1941. The Bureau of the Central Committee of the Estonian Communist Party, which had been set up in Moscow and then moved to Leningrad after the siege was lifted, did what it could to support partisans. Courses were arranged to train evacuees and Estonians in the Red Army to full administration posts with special attention given to preparations for purges making full use of Estonian archives that had been grabbed by the NKVD in 1940.

In all three Baltic states, they created lists of 'politically coloured persons'. In Estonia alone they recorded 37,794 names. Historian Gottlieb Ney wrote that in 'the [Soviet Union] the main task of archives is to expose class enemies in order that they be destroyed.'[9]

Throughout 1944, the head of the Department of the Estonian Archives, Bernhard Veimer, had his staff trawl through newspapers that had been published in Estonia during German occupation to search for references to 'anti-Soviet elements' in all areas of Estonian life from farmers to priests to soldiers. Three operational groups were set up and trained ready to return to Estonia after liberation. Their task was to find individuals who had cooperated with the Germans, liquidate Nazi and espionage cells, destroy anti-Soviet partisan units, and organise counterintelligence services.

In the late summer and autumn 1944, Stalin had taken a personal interest and met the first party secretaries of the Baltic republics in August 1944. It was agreed that destroyed infrastructure was the first economic priority with rebuilding of electric power stations and bridges. Next would be the expansion of heavy industry and energy supply with housing provision, food and consumer goods production coming last.

The class war with 'enemies' in the villages was ramped up as plenipotentiaries went from villages to village searching with local activists for 'active collaborators. More land was confiscated from farmers and in September 1945 houses, farm equipment, animals and personal belongings of some 9,000 households was confiscated.

As part of the 'cleansing of 'Estonian military-fascist and bourgeois-nationalist organisations', Tief and his associates were arrested almost immediately, and all passports had to be renewed, which was an efficient way of screening the population. [10] Within weeks there were some 4,200 people in Estonian prisons as a result and this increased to 8,900 by April 1945. A total of 381 death penalties were documented. Tief was given a ten-year prison sentence in Siberia. Destruction battalions were re-established with a view to using them as sort of auxiliary state security with special responsibility to root out partisans, but their military value was limited due to poor discipline and their propensity for criminal activity.

The armed, anti-Soviet resistance in Estonia was decentralised and lacking in leadership because potential leaders had been arrested. Consequently, it was far weaker than in Lithuania or western Ukraine. There was a peak in armed resistance activity in 1945, which saw 565 partisans killed and 3,894 arrested. Amnesties were adopted as a tactic of control and the first one was declared in Estonia in October 1944, and a second, larger one in May 1945. By the end of 1945, some 3,000, mostly draft dodgers, had been legalised but were required to pass on information about others as part of their 'cleansing'.

APPENDICES

Appendix I

COMPOSITION OF EINSATZGRUPPE A

Formed in Gumbrinnen on 23 June 1941
Headquarters: Danzig
Commander

SS Brigadeführer unde Generalmajor der Polizei Dr Franz Walter Stahlecker (killed on 23 March, 1942 in a battle with Soviet Partisans)
SS Brigadeführer und Generalmajor der Polizei Heinz Jost (March 1942 – 10 September 1942)
SS Oberführer und Oberst der Polizei Dr Humbert Achamer-Pifrader (10 September 1942 – 4 September 1943)
SS Oberführer Friedrich Panzinger (5 September 1943 – 6 May 1944)
SS Oberführer und Oberst der Polizei Dr Wilhelm Fuchs (6 May – 10 October 1944)

Sonderkommando 1a

SS Obersturmbannführer Dr Martin Sandberger (June 1941 – 1943)
SS Obersturmbannführer Bernhard Baatz (1 August 1943 – 15 October 1944)

Sonderkommando 1b

SS Oberführer und Oberst der Polizei Erich Ehrlinger (June – November 1941).
SS Sturmbannführer Walter Hoffmann (Deputy) (January – March 1942)
SS Obersturmbannführer Dr Eduard Strauch (March – August 1942)
SS Sturmbannführer Dr Erich Isselhorst (30 June – 1 October 1943)

Einsatzkommando 1a
SS Obersturmbannführer Dr Martin Sandberger (June 1942 – 1942)
SS Obersturmbannführer Karl Tschierschky (1942)
SS Sturmbannführer Dr Erich Isselhorst (November 1942 – June 1943)
SS Obersturmbannführer Bernhard Baatz (June – August 1943)

Einsatzkommando 1b
SS Sturmbannführer Dr Hermann Hubig (June – October 1942)
SS Sturmbannführer Dr Manfred Pechau (October – November 1942)

Einsatzkommando 1c
SS Sturmbannführer Kurt Graaf (1 August – 28 November 1942)

Einsatzkommando 2
SS Obersturmbannführer Rudolf Batz (June – 4 November 1941)
SS Obersturmbannführer Dr Eduard Strauch (4 November – 2 December 1941)
SS Obersturmbannführer Dr Rudilf Lange (3 December 1941 – 1944)
SS Obersturmbannführer Dr Manfred Pechau (October 1942)
SS Obersturmbannführer Reinhard Breder (26 March 1943 – July 1943)
SS Obersturmbannführer Oswald Poche (30 July 1943 – 2 March 1944)

Einsatzkommando 3
SS Standartenführer Karl Jäger (June 1941 – 1 August 1943)
SS Oberführer und Oberst der Polizei Dr Wilhelm Fuchs (15 September 1943 – 27 May 1944)
SS Sturmbannführer Hans-Joachim Böhme (11 May – July 1944)

Appendix II

VICTIMS OF THE TELŠIAI MASSACRE OF 25 JUNE 1941

Juozas Antanavičius, Antanas Antanavičius, Jonas Antanavičius, Liudvikas Bachmanas, Kazys Baltrimaitis, Povilas Balsevičius, Stasys Balsevičius, Albinas Baltramiejūnas, Juozas Beimavičius, Kostas Bučys, Juozas Bumblys, Steponas Bubelė, Adolfas Butkus, Antanas Čiužas, Andrius Čiurinskas, Pranas Daukša, Stasys Daknevičius, Antanas Dibisteris, Henrikas Glazauskas, Pranas Gužauskas, Augustinas Gaudutis, Vaclovas Gailius, Ignas Geležinis, Kazimieras Galdikas, Juozas Jablonskis, Aleksas Jankauskas, Jonas Jakštas, Stasys Jocys, Adolfas Jogminas, Kazys Katkus, Kazimieras Kaulius, Juozas Kvedaras, Petras Kavolis, Boleslovas Kavolis, Povilas Kardelis, Povilas Kazlauskas, Karolis Kiševičius, Vladas Kaveckas, Boleslovas Korza, Leonas Kusa, Bronius Križinauskas, Vitoldas Lileikis, Mikas Lengvenis, Mikas Lionginas, Pranas Lukauskas, Liudas Malakauskas, Petras Maskolenka, Jonas Milius, Antanas Montvydas, Vladas Motuza, Motiejus Norvaiša, Liudas Pakalniškis, Zigmas Parafionovičius, Vaclovas Pabarščius, Kazys Puškorius, Vladas Petronaitis, Kazys Paulauskas, Andrius Rudokas, Jonas Rudokas, Adomas Rakas, Zigmas Sakelis, Adomas Simutis, Julius Simutis, Feliksas Stuka, Vladas Songaila, Česlovas Šalkauskas, Zenonas Šakenis, Edmundas Šalčius, Jonas Šleinius, Jonas Telšinskis, Juozas Truška, Zenonas Tarvainis, Jurgis Vičius, Povilas Vilčinskis, Herminegildas Žvirzdinas and Georgijus Michejevas.

Appendix III

STATISTICS OF THE TRANSPORTS

The following data stems from Wolfgang Scheffler und Diana Schulle, *Book of Remembrance: The German, Austrian and Czechoslovakian Jews deported to the Baltic States,* Munich: De Gruyter, 2003:

Date of Departure	Place of Departure	Passengers	Date of Arrival	Survivors	Note
27.11.1941	Berlin	1,053	30.11.1941	0	All were killed in forest of Rumbula after arrival
29.11.1941	Nürnberg	1,008	02.12.1941	52	Detained in camp Jungfernhof
01.12.1941	Stuttgart	1,013	04.12.1941	43	Detained in camp Jungfernhof
03.12.1941	Wien	1,001	06.12.1941	18	Detained in camp Jungfernhof
06.12.1941	Hamburg	964	09.12.1941	35	Detained in camp Jungfernhof
07.12.1941	Köln	1,011	10.12.1941	87	
09.12.1941	Kassel	1,034	12.12.1941	100	
11.12.1941	Düsseldorf	1,007	13.12.1941	98	
13.12.1941	Münster Osnabrück Bielefeld	1,031	16.12.1941	102	

Date of Departure	Place of Departure	Passengers	Date of Arrival	Survivors	Note
15.12.1941	Hannover	1,001	18.12.1941	68	
09.01.1942	Theresienstadt	1,005	12.01.1942	110	
11.01.1942	Wien	1,000	15.01.1942	31	
13.01.1942	Berlin	1,034	16.01.1942	15	
15.01.1942	Theresienstadt	997	19.01.1942	18	
19.01.1942	Berlin	1,002	23.01.1942	19	
21.01.1942	Leipzig Dresden	773	24.01.1942	47	
25.01.1942	Berlin	1,044	30.01.1942	13	
26.01.1942	Wien	1,201	31.01.1942	36	
27.01.1942	Gelsenkirchen Dortmund	938	01.02.1942	121	
06.02.1942	Wien	1,003	10.02.1942	36	
15.08.1942	Berlin	938	18.08.1942	1	
20.08.1942	Theresienstadt	1,000	Unknown	0	
31.08.1942	Berlin Insterburg	797	03.09.1942	6	All were killed after arrival except 80 men
19.10.1942	Berlin	959	22.10.1942	17	All were killed after arrival except 81 men
26.10.1942	Berlin	798	29.10.1942	0	All were killed after arrival
	In total	24,612		1,073	Less than 4 per cent survived

Appendix IV

THE JÄGER REPORT, 1 DECEMBER 1941

The Jäger Report is a complete tabulation of executions carried out in the Einsatzkommando 3 zone up to 1 December 1941 written by its commander Standartenführer Karl Jäger. This document was retrieved from the archives of Shamash: The Jewish Internet Consortium:

On my instructions and orders the following executions were conducted by Lithuanian partisans:

4.7.41	Kauen-Fort VII	416 Jews, 47 Female Jews	463
6.7.41	Kauen-Fort VII	Jews	2,514

Following the formation of a raiding squad under the command of SS Obersturmführer Hamman and eight to ten reliable men from the Einsatzkommando, the following actions were conducted in cooperation with Lithuanian partisans:

7.7.41	Mariampole	Jews	32
8.7.41	Mariampole	14 Jews, 5 Comm. officials	19
8.7.41	Girkalinei	Comm. officials	6
9.7.41	Wendziogala	32 Jews, 2 Female Jews, 1 Lithuanian (f.), 2 Lithuanian Comm., 1 Russian Comm.	38
9.7.41	Kauen-Fort VII	21 Jews, 3 Female Jews	24
14.7.41	Mariampole	21 Jews, 1 Russ., 9 Lith. Comm.	31

17.7.41	Babtei	8 Comm. officials (incl. 6 Jews)	8
18.7.41	Mariampole	39 Jews, 14 Female Jews	53
19.7.41	Kauen-Fort VII	17 Jews, 2 Female Jews, 4 Lith. Comm., 2 Comm. Lithuanians (f.), 1 German Comm.	26
21.7.41	Panevezys	59 Jews, 11 Female Jews, 1 Lithuanian (f.), 1 Pole, 22 Lith. Comm., 9 Russ. Comm.	103
22.7.41	Panevezys	1 Jew	1
23.7.41	Kedainiai	83 Jews, 12 Female Jews, 14 Russ. Comm., 15 Lith. Comm., 1 Russ. O-Politruk	125
25.7.41	Mariampole	90 Jews, 13 Female Jews	103
28.7.41	Panevezys	234 Jews, 15 Female Jews, 19 Russ. Comm., 20 Lith. Comm.	288

Total carried forward	3,384

sheet 2			
Total carried forward			3,384
29.7.41	Rasainiai	254 Jews, 3 Lith. Comm.	257
30.7.41	Agriogala	27 Jews, 11 Lith. Comm.	38
31.7.41	Utena	235 Jews, 16 Female Jews, 4 Lith. Comm., 1 robber/murderer	256
31.7.41	Wendziogala	13 Jews, 2 murderers	15
1.8.41	Ukmerge	254 Jews, 42 Female Jews, 1 Pol. Comm., 2 Lith. NKVD agents, 1 mayor of Jonava who gave order to set fire to Jonava	300
2.8.41	Kauen-Fort IV	170 Jews, 1 US Jewess, 33 Female Jews, 4 Lith. Comm.	209
4.8.41	Panevezys	362 Jews, 41 Female Jews, 5 Russ. Comm., 14 Lith. Comm.	422
5.8.41	Rasainiai	213 Jews, 66 Female Jews	279
7.8.41	Utena	483 Jews, 87 Female Jews, 1 Lithuanian (robber of corpses of German soldiers)	571
8.8.41	Ukmerge	620 Jews, 82 Female Jews	702
9.8.41	Kauen-Fort IV	484 Jews, 50 Female Jews	534
11.8.41	Panevezys	450 Jews, 48 Female Jews, 1 Lith. 1 Russ.	500
13.8.41	Alytus	617 Jews, 100 Female Jews, 1 criminal	719
14.8.41	Jonava	497 Jews, 55 Female Jews	552
15–16.8.41	Rokiskis	3,200 Jews, Female Jews, and J. Children, 5 Lith. Comm., 1 Pole, 1 partisan	3,207
9–16.8.41	Rasainiai	294 Female Jews, 4 Jewish children	298
6–14.8.41	Rokiskis	493 Jews, 432 Russians, 56 Lithuanians (all active communists)	981
18.8.41	Kauen-Fort IV	689 Jews, 402 Female Jews, 1 Pole (f.), 711 Jewish intellectuals from Ghetto in reprisal for sabotage action	1,812
19.8.41	Ukmerge	298 Jews, 255 Female Jews, 1 Politruk, 88 Jewish children, 1 Russ. Comm.	645

22.8.41	Dunanburg	3 Russ. Comm., 5 Latvian, incl. 1 murderer, 1 Russ. Guardsman, 3 Poles, 3 Roma (m.), 1 Roma (f.), 1 Romani child, 1 Jew, 1 Jewess, 1 Armenian (m.), 2 Politruks (prison inspection in Dunanburg	21

Total carried forward	16,152

sheet 3			
Total carried forward			16,152
22.8.41	Aglona	Mentally sick: 269 men, 227 women, 48 children	544
23.8.41	Panevezys	1,312 Jews, 4,602 Female Jews, 1,609 Jewish children	7,523
18–22.8.41	Kreis Rasainiai	466 Jews, 440 Female Jews, 1,020 Jewish children	1,926
25.8.41	Obeliai	112 Jews, 627 Female Jews, 421 Jewish children	1,160
25–26.8.41	Seduva	230 Jews, 275 Female Jews, 159 Jewish children	664
26.8.41	Zarasai	767 Jews, 1,113 Female Jews, 1 Lith. Comm., 687 Jewish children, 1 Russ. Comm. (f.)	2,569
28.8.41	Pasvalys	402 Jews, 738 Female Jews, 209 Jewish children	1,349
26.8.41	Kaisiadorys	All Jews, Female Jews, and Jewish children	1,911
27.8.41	Prienai	All Jews, Female Jews, and Jewish Children	1,078
27.8.41	Dagda and Kraslawa	212 Jews, 4 Russ. PoWs	216
27.8.41	Joniskia	47 Jews, 165 Female Jews, 143 Jewish children	355
28.8.41	Wilkia	76 Jews, 192 Female Jews, 134 Jewish children	402
28.8.41	Kedainiai	710 Jews, 767 Female Jews, 599 Jewish children	2,076
29.8.41	Rumsiskis and Ziezmariai	20 Jews, 567 Female Jews, 197 Jewish children	784
29.8.41	Utena and Moletai	582 Jews, 1,731 Female Jews, 1,469 Jewish children	3,782
13–31.8.41	Alytus and environs	233 Jews	233
1.9.41	Mariampole	1,763 Jews, 1,812 Female Jews, 1,404 Jewish children, 109 mentally sick,1 German subject (f.), married to a Jew, 1 Russian (f.)	5,090
Total carried over			47,814

sheet 4			
Total carried over			47,814
28.8–2.9.41	Darsuniskis	10 Jews, 69 Female Jews, 20 Jewish children	99
	Carliava	73 Jews, 113 Female Jews, 61 Jewish children	247
	Jonava	112 Jews, 1,200 Female Jews, 244 Jewish children	1,556
	Petrasiunai	30 Jews, 72 Female Jews, 23 Jewish children	125
	Jesuas	26 Jews, 72 Female Jews, 46 Jewish children	144
	Agriogala	207 Jews, 260 Female Jews, 195 Jewish children	662
	Jasvainai	86 Jews, 110 Female Jews, 86 Jewish children	282
	Babtei	20 Jews, 41 Female Jews, 22 Jewish children	83
	Wendziogala	42 Jews, 113 Female Jews, 97 Jewish children	252
	Krakes	448 Jews, 476 Female Jews, 97 Jewish children	1,125
4.9.41	Pravenischkis	247 Jews, 6 Female Jews	253
	Cekiske	22 Jews, 64 Female Jews, 60 Jewish children	146
	Seredsius	6 Jews, 61 Female Jews, 126 Jewish children	193
	Velinona	2 Jews, 71 Female Jews, 86 Jewish children	159
	Zapiskis	47 Jews, 118 Female Jews, 13 Jewish children	178
5.9.41	Ukmerge	1,123 Jews, 1,849 Female Jews, 1,737 Jewish children	4,709
25.8–6.9.41	Mopping up in: Rasainiai Georgenburg	16 Jews, 412 Female Jews, 415 Jewish children all Jews, all Female Jews, all Jewish children	843 412
9.9.41	Alytus	287 Jews, 640 Female Jews, 352 Jewish children	1,279
9.9.41	Butrimonys	67 Jews, 370 Female Jews, 303 Jewish children	740
10.9.41	Merkine	223 Jews, 640 Female Jews, 276 Jewish children	854
10.9.41	Varena	541 Jews, 141 Female Jews, 149 Jewish children	831

11.9.41	Leipalingis	60 Jews, 70 Female Jews, 25 Jewish children	155
11.9.41	Seirijai	229 Jews, 384 Female Jews, 340 Jewish children	953
12.9.41	Simnas	68 Jews, 197 Female Jews, 149 Jewish children	414
11–12.9.41	Uzusalis	Reprisal against inhabitants who fed Russ. partisans; some in possession of weapons	43
26.9.41	Kauen-F.IV	412 Jews, 615 Female Jews, 581 Jewish children (sick and suspected epidemic cases)	1,608

Total carried over	66,159

sheet 5			
Total carried over			66,159
2.10.41	Zagare	633 Jews, 1,107 Female Jews, 496 Jewish children (as these Jews werebeing led away a mutiny rose, which was however immediately put down; 150 Jews were shot immediately; 7 partisans wounded)	2,236
4.10.41	Kauen-F.IX	315 Jews, 712 Female Jews, 818 Jewish children (reprisal after German police officer shot in ghetto)	1,845
29.10.41	Kauen-F.IX	2,007 Jews, 2,920 Female Jews, 4,273 Jewish children (mopping up ghetto of superfluous Jews)	9,200
3.11.41	Lazdijai	485 Jews, 511 Female Jews, 539 Jewish children	1,535
15.11.41	Wilkowiski	36 Jews, 48 Female Jews, 31 Jewish children	115
25.11.41	Kauen-F.IX	1,159 Jews, 1,600 Female Jews, 175 Jewish children (resettlers from Berlin, Munich and Frankfurt am main)	2,934
29.11.41	Kauen-F.IX	693 Jews, 1,155 Female Jews, 152 Jewish children (resettlers from Vienna and Breslau)	2,000
29.11.41	Kauen-F.IX	17 Jews, 1 Jewess, for contravention of ghetto law, 1 Reichs German who converted to the Jewish faith and attended rabbinical school, then 15 terrorists from the Kalinin group	34
EK 3 detachment in Dunanburg in the period 13.7–21.8.41:		9,012 Jews, Female Jews and Jewish children, 573 active Comm.	9,585
EK 3 detachment in Wilna:			
12.8–1.9.41	City of Wilna	425 Jews, 19 Female Jews, 8 Comm. (m.), 9 Comm. (f.)	461
2.9.41	City of Wilna	864 Jews, 2,019 Female Jews, 817 Jewish children (*Sonderaktion* because German soldiers shot at by Jews)	3,700
Total carried forward			99,084

sheet 6			
Total carried forward			99,804
12.9.41	City of Wilna	993 Jews, 1,670 Female Jews, 771 Jewish children	3,334
17.9.41	City of Wilna	337 Jews, 687 Female Jews, 247 Jewish children and 4 Lith. Comm.	1,271
20.9.41	Nemencing	128 Jews, 176 Female Jews, 99 Jewish children	403
22.9.41	Novo-Wilejka	468 Jews, 495 Female Jews, 196 Jewish children	1,159
24.9.41	Riess	512 Jews, 744 Female Jews, 511 Jewish children	1,767
25.9.41	Jahiunai	215 Jews, 229 Female Jews, 131 Jewish children	575
27.9.41	Eysisky	989 Jews, 1,636 Female Jews, 821 Jewish children	3,446
30.9.41	Trakai	366 Jews, 483 Female Jews, 597 Jewish children	1,446
4.10.41	City of Wilna	432 Jews, 1,115 Female Jews, 436 Jewish children	1,983
6.10.41	Semiliski	213 Jews, 359 Female Jews, 390 Jewish children	962
9.10.41	Svenciany	1,169 Jews, 1,840 Female Jews, 717 Jewish children	3,726
16.10.41	City of Wilna	382 Jews, 507 Female Jews, 257 Jewish children	1,146
21.10.41	City of Wilna	718 Jews, 1,063 Female Jews, 586 Jewish children	2,367
25.10.41	City of Wilna	1,776 Female Jews, 812 Jewish children	2,578
27.10.41	City of Wilna	946 Jews, 184 Female Jews, 73 Jewish children	1,203
30.10.41	City of Wilna	382 Jews, 789 Female Jews, 362 Jewish children	1,553
6.11.41	City of Wilna	340 Jews, 749 Female Jews, 252 Jewish children	1,341
19.11.41	City of Wilna	76 Jews, 77 Female Jews, 18 Jewish children	171

19.11.41	City of Wilna	6 PoWs, 8 Poles	14
20.11.41	City of Wilna	3 PoWs	3
25.11.41	City of Wilna	9 Jews, 46 Female Jews, 8 Jewish children, 1 Pole for possession of arms and other military equipment	64
		Total	133,346

		Prior to EK3 taking over security police duties, Jews liquidated by pogroms and executions (including partisans)	4,000
		Total	137,346

Appendix V

NUREMBERG MILITARY TRIBUNAL II-A

On 10 September 1947, the US Military Government for Germany created Military Tribunal II-A to try Case No. *United States v. Otto Ohlendorf, et al.*, usually referred to as the Einsatzgruppen Case. The twenty-four defendants were all leading members of Einsatzgruppen that operated on the Eastern Front during the Second World War.

The men had been indicted on 29 July 1947 for their role in murdering between 723,661 and 1 million people 'as part of a systematic program of genocide' between June 1941 and July 1943. The indictment listed three charges:

- Crimes against humanity.
- War crimes.
- Membership in organizations declared criminal by the International Military Tribunal.

Amongst those charged were Otto Ohlendord, Heinz Jost, Paul Blobel, Gustav Noske and Martin Sandberger.

Chief prosecutor Ben Ferencz based his case solely on wartime SS reports and in his opening statement said,

> It is with sorrow and with hope that we here disclose the deliberate slaughter of more than a million innocent and defenceless men, women, and children. This was the tragic fulfilment of a program of intolerance and arrogance ... Each of the defendants in the dock held a position of responsibility or command in an extermination unit. Each assumed the right to decide the fate of men, and death was the intended result of his power and contempt. Their own reports will show that the slaughter

> committed by these defendants was dictated, not by military necessity, but by that supreme perversion of thought, the Nazi theory of the master race.

Each defendant pleaded 'not guilty'. Even those who admitted playing a role in the mass killings denied their culpability. They argued that they had acted legally and in obedience to superior orders.

The tribunal rendered its judgment on 8–9 April 1948. It found twenty defendants guilty on all three counts. Two of the defendants were found guilty on only count three. The tribunal noted in its judgment that 'the charge of purposeful homicide in this case reaches such fantastic proportions and surpasses such credible limits that believability must be bolstered with assurance a hundred times repeated.'

The sentences were announced on 10 April 1948, fourteen defendants were sentenced to death, two were sentenced to life terms, and five received sentences that ranged from ten to twenty years. Matthias Graf was released with time served. Ultimately, only four of the fourteen death sentences were carried out. Ohlendorf, Naumann, Blobel and Braune were hanged on 7 June 1951.

REFERENCES AND NOTES

Chapter 1

1. Tulun, Mehmet Oğuzhan, *Russification policies imposed on the Baltic People by the Russian Empire and the Soviet Union*, Başkent University, 2012, p. 23
2. Parrot, Andrew, *The Baltic States from 1914 to 1923: The First World War and the Wars of Independence*, Baltic Defence Review No 8 Vol. 2, 2002, p. 140
3. Mačiulis, Dangiras and Staliūnas, Darius, *Lithuanian Nationalism and the Vilnius Question, 1883–1940*, Verlag Herder-Institut, Marburg, 2015, p. 51
4. ibid, p. 56
5. Lumans, Valdis O., *Latvia in World War II*, Fordham University Press, 2006, p. 19
6. Ruutsoo, Rein, *The Estonians: Identity of Small Nation in Past and Present*, Anthropological Journal on European Cultures, Vol. 6, No. 1, 1997, p. 75

Chapter 2

1. Stresemann, Memorandum from 13 January 1925, cited in Schot, Stresemann, Der Deutsche Osten, p. 6
2. Gerwarth, Robert and Horne, John, *Vectors of Violence: Paramilitarism in Europe after the Great War, 1917–1923*, The Journal of Modern History, Vol. 83, No. 3, 2011, p. 510
3. Balkelis, Tomas, *Demobilization and Remobilization of German and Lithuanian Paramilitaries after the First World War*, Journal of Contemporary History, Vol. 50, No. 1, 2015, p. 42
4. ibid, p. 43
5. ibid, p. 51
6. ibid, p. 53
7. https://straysatellite.com/Rīga
8. ibid
9. ibid
10. ibid

Chapter 3

1. Valge, Jaak, *Foreign Involvement and Loss of Democracy, Estonia 1934*, Journal of Contemporary History, Vol. 46, No. 4, 2011, p. 791
2. ibid, p. 794
3. ibid, p. 797
4. Haynes, Rebecca, *Reviewed Work(s): The Radical Right in Interwar Estonia by Andres Kasekamp*, The Slavonic and East European Review, 2003, p. 580

5. The Baltic Germans and German Policy towards Latvia after 1918, The Historical Journal, Vol. 13, No. 2, 1970, p. 298
6. ibid, p. 316
7. Lūmans, p. 27
8. Housden, M. and Smith, D.J., *Forgotten Pages in Baltic History: Diversity and Inclusion*, Brill Academic, 2011, p. 203
9. Lūmans, p. 42
10. Kalijarvi, Thorsten, *The Problem of Memel*, The American Journal of International Law, Vol. 30, No. 2, 1936
11. Nikžentaitis, Alvydas, *Germany and the Memel Germans in the 1930s (On the Basis of Trials of Lithuanian Agents before the Volksgerichtshof, 1934–45*, The Historical Journal, Vol. 39, No. 3, 1996, p. 778
12. Nikžentaitis, Alvydas, *The Elections in Meme*, Bulletin of International News, Vol. 15, No. 25. p. 193
13. Mačiulis,and Staliūnas, p. 73
14. Ken, Oleg and Rupasov, Alexander, *Moscow and the Baltic States: Experience of Relationships, 1917–1939*, E-International Relations, 2018, p. 56
15. Piirimai, Kaarel, *Review: 'Masters of the Baltic': Soviet Objectives Towards the Baltic on the Eve of the Second World War*, Journal of Contemporary History, Vol. 47, No. 4, 2012, p. 878
16. ibid, p. 880

Chapter 4

1. Sagatienė, Dovilė, *The Debate about Soviet Genocide in Lithuania in the Case Law of The European Court of Human Rights*, European Humanities University, Vilnius, 2021, p. 780
2. Snyder, Timothy, *Black Earth*, Random House, Kindle edition, p. 120
3. Chodakiewicz, Marek Jan, *The Debate about Soviet Genocide in Lithuania in the Case Law of The European Court of Human Rights*, Routledge, 2017, p. 117
4. Senn, Alfred Erich, *Baltic Battleground*, p. 21
5. Chodakiewicz, p. 112
6. Lenin, Vladimir, *Neizvestnye dokumenty. 1891–1922*, Moskva: Rosspen, 1999, p. 358
7. Rei, August, *Nazi-Soviet Conspiracy and the Baltic States*, University of Michigan, 2006, p. 41
8. Anušauskas, Arvydas, *Lessons of History: The Silent Occupation of 1940*, Lietuvos Respublikos Seimo kanceliarija, Vilnius, 2014, p. 6
9. Kersten Report, Wahington DC 1954, Wm. S. Hein and Co., p. 288
10. Mačiulis, and Staliūnas, p. 181
11. Mälksoo, Lauri, *The Baltic States Between 1940 and 1991: Illegality and/or Prescription*, downloaded from https://brill.com 07/01/2023, p. 73
12. League of Nations Treaty series LNTS, Vol. 2, p. 29
13. League of Nations Treaty series LNTS, Vol. 131, p. 309
14. Mälksoo, p. 83
15. ibid, p. 85
16. ibid, p. 91
17. Lithuanian Central State Archives, f. 648, ap. 2, b. 582, l., p. 186
18. Truska, Liudas, *The Upsurge of Anti-Semitism in Lithuania in the Years of the Soviet Occupation*, downloaded from https://komisija.com, p. 1
19. Truska, Liudas and Variekis, Vygantas, *The Preconditions for the Holocaust: Anti-Semitism in Lithuania*, Vilus: Margi raštai, 2004, p. 131
20. Smetona, Antanas, *Antanas Smetona's correspondence 1940–1944*, Vytautas the Great University Publishing House, 1999, p. 373

21. Sužiedėlis, Saulius, *Lithuanian Collaboration during the Second World War: Past Realities, Present Perceptions, in Kollaboration in Nordosteuropa: Erscheinungsformen Und Deutungen Im 20. Jahrhundert, ed. Joachim Tauber*, Harrassowitz, 2006, p. 149
22. Senn, Alfred Erich, *Lithuania in March 1941, An American Diplomat's Report*, Journal of Baltic Sudies, Vol. 26, 1995, p. 154
23. Matthäus, Jürgen, *Key Aspects of German Anti-Jewish Policy, Lithuania and the Jews: The Holocaust Chapter, Symposium Presentations*, United States Holocaust Memorial Museum Center for Advanced Studies, 2004, p. 18
24. eng.lsm.lv, 2019
25. Helmreich, E.C., *The Return of the Baltic Germans*, The American Political Science Review, Vol. 36, No. 4, 1942, p. 715
26. Saburova, Irina, *The Soviet Occupation of the Baltic States Author*, The Russian Review, Vol. 14, No. 1, 1955, p. 39
27. Vilums, Jānis, *Non-Violent Resistance to the Soviet Occupation Regime in Latvia in 1940–1941*, Symposium of the Commission of the Historians of Latvia Vol. 29, 2021, p. 54
28. Šneidere, Irēne, *The First Soviet Occupation Period in Latvia 1940–1941; The Hidden and Forbidden History of Latvia under Soviet and Nazi Occupation 1941–1991*, Institute of the History of Latvia, University of Latvia, 2005, p. 36
29. ibid, p. 33
30. Plavnieks, Richards, *Nazi Collaborators on Trial during the Cold War: The Cases against Viktors Arājs and the Latvian Auxiliary Security Police*, University of North Carolina, 2013, p. 29
31. Vilums, p. 59
32. Saburova, p. 43
33. Riekstiņš, Jānis, *The 14 June 1941 Deportation in Latvia; The Hidden and Forbidden History of Latvia under Soviet and Nazi Occupation 1941–1991*, Institute of the History of Latvia, University of Latvia, 2005, p. 65
34. Šneidere, p. 41
35. Juris Pavlovičs, *Change of Occupation Powers in Latvia in Summer 1941*, p. 95
36. ibid, p. 100
37. Rahi-Tamm, Aigi, *Human Losses, in: Salo, ed., The White Book, O˜ ispuu, ed., Crimes of Soviet Occupation* p. 38
38. ibid, p. 12
39. ibid, p. 14
40. Goldberg, Rubin B., *Russian and Soviet Nationalities Policy in the Baltic States, 1855–1991*, University of Vermont, 2015, p. 35
41. Senn, Alfred Erich, *Baltic Battleground*, p. 17
42. Gitelman, Zvi, *Soviet Reactions to the Holocaust, 1945–1991*, Armonk, NY, p. 4
43. Levin, Dov, *The Lesser of Two Evils: Eastern European Jewry under Soviet Rule, 1939–1941*, Philadelphia, 1995, p. 44
44. Levin, Dov, *Baltic Jews under the Soviets 1940–1946*, Jerusalem, 1994, p. 92
45. Senn, Alfred Erich, *Baltic Battleground; The Hidden and Forbidden History of Latvia under Soviet and Nazi Occupation 1941–1991*, Institute of the History of Latvia, University of Latvia, 2005, p. 45
46. Rahi-Tamm, p. 38

Chapter 5

1. Haslam, Jonathan, *Stalin and the German Invasion of Russia 1941: A Failure of Reasons of State?*, International Affairs, Vol. 76, No. 1, 2000, p. 137
2. ibid, p. 136

3. Erickson, John, *The Soviet High Command*, Macmillan & Co., 1962, p. 585
4. Rotundo, Louis, *Stalin and the Outbreak of War in 1941*, Journal of Contemporary History, Vol. 24, No. 2, Studies on War, 1989, p. 291
5. Kokoshin, Andrei, *The German Blitzkreig Against the USSR, 1941*, Belfer Center for Science and International Affairs, 2016, p. 43
6. Rotundo, p. 285
7. ibid, p. 379
8. Kokoshin, p. 46
9. Rotundo, p. 288
10. Stolfi, Russel H.S., *Barbarossa Revisited: A Critical Reappraisal of the Opening Stages of the Russo-German Campaign (June–December 1941)*, The Journal of Modern History, Vol. 54, No. 1, p. 31
11. ibid, p. 35
12. Erickson, p. 587
13. Werth, Alexander, *Russia At War, 1941–1945*, Pan, 1965, p. 154
14. Erickson, p. 598
15. Kokoshin, p. 50
16. Goldberg, Rubin B., p. 35
17. Šiušaitė, A. and Landsbergis, V., *Forgotten Soviet War Crime Rainiai in Lithuania 24–25th June, 1941*, AB Baltijos kopija, 2007, p. 10
18. ibid, p. 89

Chapter 6

1. https://ibiblio.org/pha/policy/1941/410824a.html
2. Snyder, Timothy, *Black Earth*, p. 83
3. Tenenbaum, Joseph, *The Einsatzgruppen*, Jewish Social Studies Vol. 17, No. 1, 1955, p. 45
4. ibid, p. 43
5. ibid, p. 46
6. Streim, Alfred, *The Tasks of the SS Einsatzgruppen*, https://museumoftolerance.com/education/archives-and-reference-library
7. Snyder, Timothy, *Black Earth*, p. 147
8. Tenenbaum, p. 47
9. Buttar, Prit, *Centuries Will Not Suffice: A History of the Lithuanian Holocaust*, Amberley Publishing, Kindle edition, 2023, p. 40
10. Zentrale Stelle der Landesjustizverwaltungen zur Aufklarung von NS-Verbrechen, Ludwigsburg, 201 AR-Z 76/59, Vol. 9, p. 100
11. Breitman, Richard, *Plans for the Final Solution in 1941*, German Sudies Review, Vol. 17, No. 3, 1994, p. 490
12. US Military Tribunal II, Case 9, *United States v. Otto Ohlendorf and others*, Official Transcripts, p. 316
13. Browning, Christopher R., *The Nazi Decision to Commit Mass Murder*, German Studies Review, Vol. 17, No. 3, 1994, p. 475
14. ibid, p. 479
15. Truska, Liudas and Variekis, Vygantas, p. 40
16. Snyder, Timothy, *Black Earth*, p. 147
17. Buttar, p. 89
18. Truska, Liudas and Variekis, Vygantas, p. 191
19. Lithuanian Special Archives, f. K-1, ap. 58, b. 12949/3, l. 25–26
20. Rudashevski, Yitskhok, *Diary of the Vilna Ghetto*, Israel: Ghetto Fighters' House, 1973, p. 27

21. Schalkovsky, Samuel, *The Clandestine History of the Kovno Jewish Ghetto Police*, Bloomington: Indiana University Press, 2014, p. 69
22. Buttar, p. 101
23. Arad, Yitzhak, Gutman, Yisrael and Margaliot, Abraham, *Documents on the Holocaust, Selected Sources on the Destruction of the Jews of Germany and Austria, Poland and the Soviet Union*, Yad Vashem, Jerusalem Document No. 177, 1981, p. 389
24. Vanagaitė, Rūta and Zuroff, Efraim, *Our People*, Rowman & Littlefield Publishers, Kindle edition, 2020, p. 4
25. Szarota, Tomasz, *On the Threshold of the Holocaust. Anti-Jewish Riots and Pogroms in Occupied Europe: Warsaw–Paris–The Hague–Amsterdam–Antwerp–Kaunas*, Frankfurt am Main: Peter Lang, 2015, p. 180
26. Arad, Yitzhak, *The Final Solution in Lithuania in the Light of German Documentation*, www.yadvashem.org, p. 240
27. Vanagaitė and Zuroff, p. 63
28. Arad, Yitzhak *The Final Solution*, p. 243
29. Vanagaitė and Zuroff, p. 74
30. ibid, p. 99
31. ibid, p. 112
32. Buttar, p. 131
33. Dieckmann, Christoph and Sužiedėlis, Saulius, *The Persecution and Mass Murder of Lithuanian Jews during Summer and Fall of 1941*, Vilnius: Margi raštai, 2006, p. 147
34. Arad, Yitzhak *The Final Solution*, p. 246
35. Nuremberg War Trials, Document L-180, Vol. IV, p. 161
36. Tenenbaum, p. 58
37. Nuremberg War Trials, Vol. iv, p. 35. Cf. Bach-Zelewski's testimony in IMT, p. 475
38. Tenenbaum, p. 59
39. ibid, p. 60
40. Arad, Yitzhak *The Final Solution*, p. 248
41. ibid, p. 252
42. Chodakiewicz, p. 144
43. Kay, Alex J., *Transition to Genocide, July 1941: Einsatzkommando 9 and the Annihilation of Soviet Jewry*, Holocaust and Genocide Studies, Vol. 27, No. 3, 2013, p. 413
44. Tenenbaum, p. 47
45. ibid, p. 53
46. Kay, Alex J., *Transition to Genocide*, p. 415
47. ibid, p. 417
48. ibid, p. 419
49. ibid, p. 420
50. ibid, p. 421
51. ibid, p. 426
52. Judgement of the Assize Court attached to the Regional Court in Berlin, 3 P (K) Ks 1/62, from 22 June 1962, in: UniA GI, Promotionen und Dissertationen an der Universität Gießen von 1894 bis 1945, Jur. Prom. Nr. 775, fols. 36–159, here fols. 38–39, 106, 120 and 146
53. Arad, Yitzhak, *The Toll of the Extermination Operations (July–December 1941) Ghetto in Flame*, KTAV Publishing House, 1980, p. 209
54. Arad, Yitzhak *The Final Solution*, p. 259
55. *Time* magazine website time.com
56. Janavičienė, Audronė, *Soviet Saboteurs in Lithuania (1941–1944)*, Genocide and Resistance Research Center of Lithuanian Population, 2004

57. Feldmanis, Inesis, *Latvia under the Occupation of National Socialist Germany 1941–1945; The Hidden and Forbidden History of Latvia under Soviet and Nazi Occupation 1941–1991*, Institute of the History of Latvia, University of Latvia, 2005, p. 85
58. ibid, p. 86
59. Bassler, Gerhard P., *Alfred Valdmanis and the Politics of Survival*, University of Toronto Press, 2000, p. 114
60. Ezergailis, Edward, *The German Times 1941–1945, Liberation, Volunteering, Self-Defense, Revenge*, Yearbook of the Museum of the Occupation of Latvia, 2002, p. 164
61. Lūmans, p. 161
62. Zellis, Kaspars, *The Holocaust in Rezekne: Research Problems, Questions, Perspective*, University of Latvia, 2017, p. 96
63. Anders, Edward and Dubrovskis, Juris, *Who Died in the Holocaust? Recovering Names from Official Records*, Holocaust and Genocide Studies, Oxford University Press, 2003, p. 217
64. Zellis, p. 99
65. Reichelt, Katrin, Lecture at the book presentation *'Latvia under German occupation 1941–1944. The Latvian Part in the Holocaust'*, https://riga-komitee.eu/en/history/latvia-under-german-occupation-1941–1944
66. ibid
67. Gilbert, Martin, *The Holocaust: The Human Tragedy*, Rosetta Books, 2015, p. 154
68. Reichelt, Katrin, Lecture at the book presentation
69. https://holocaustinlatvia.org/index.php?en/German/review-1100-ElephantsReichelt
70. Vercrumba, p. 3
71. Rislakki, Jukka, *The Case for Latvia: Disinformation Campaigns against a Small Nation*, Rodopi, 2008, p. 135
72. Arad, Gutman, and Margaliot, p. 389
73. Plavnieks, p. 4
74. Latvia under German Occupation: 1941–1943, Washington, DC: The Press Bureau of the Latvian Legation, 1943. p. 111–112.
75. Neiburgs, Uldis, *Resistance Movement in Latvia during Nazi German Occupation (1941–1945)*, Museum of the Occupation of Latvia, 2011, p. 6
76. Plavnieks, p. 49
77. Tenenbaum, p. 55
78. Document L-180, in Trials of War Criminals Before the Nuernberg Military Tribunals (Washington 1949–51), Vol. IV, p. 155
79. Testified by A. Proškovičs, E. Jurģītis and others, LVA, fonds 1968, file 45285, Vol. 2, p. 4; Vol. 8, p. 190
80. Vercumba, p. 6
81. ibid, p. 7
82. Press, B., *The Murder of the Jews in Latvia*, Museum of the Occupation of Latvia, 2011, p. 46
83. Schneider, Gertrude, *Journey into Terror, Story of the Riga Ghetto*, Westport Praeger, Kindle edition, 2001
84. Vercumba, p. 5
85. Plavnieks, p. 39
86. Vīksne, Rudīte, *Members of the Arājs Commando in Soviet Court Files; The Hidden and Forbidden History of Latvia under Soviet and Nazi Occupation 1941–1991*, Institute of the History of Latvia, University of Latvia, 2005, p. 194
87. Snyder, Timothy, *Bloodland*, Random House Kindle edition, p. 193
88. Stranga, Aivars, *The Holocaust in Occupied Latvia: 1941–1945; The Hidden and Forbidden History of Latvia under Soviet and Nazi Occupation 1941–1991*, Institute of the History of Latvia, University of Latvia, 2005, p. 163

89. Kangeris, Kārlis, *'Closed' Units of Latvian Police – Lettische Schutzmannschafts-Bataillone; The Hidden and Forbidden History of Latvia under Soviet and Nazi Occupation 1941–1991*, Institute of the History of Latvia, University of Latvia, 2005, p. 113
90. ibid, p. 106
91. Hilberg, Raul, *Perpetrators, Victims, Bystanders: The Jewish Catastrophe 1933–1945*, Harper Collins, 1992, p. 96
92. Browning, Christopher R., *Ordinary Men: Reserve Police Battalion 101 and the Final Solution in Poland*, Harper Collins, 1992, p. 107
93. Goldhagen, Daniel J., *Hitler's Willing Executioners: Ordinary Germans and the Holocaust*, Harper Collins, 1996, p. 409
94. Golczewski, Frank, *Organe der deutschen Besatzungsmacht: Die ukrainischen Schutzmannschaften*, Wolfgang Benz, 1998, p. 173
95. Himmler's telegram to Jeckeln, 27 January 1942, BA–B, NS 19/1462
96. Plavnieks, p. 74
97. Reichelt, Katrin, *Latvia under German Occupation 1941–1944: The Latvian Part in the Holocaust*, Metropol-Verlag, 2021
98. Reichelt, Katrin, *Rescue Knows no Conventions: Help for Persecuted Jews in German-Occupied Latvia 1941–1945*, Lukas Verlag, 2016
99. Ezergailis, Edward, *The Holocaust in Latvia 1941–1944: The Missing Center*, Historical Institute of Latvia in association with USHMM, 1996, p. 290
100. Anders and Dubrovskis, p. 126
101. Klee, Ernst, Dressen, Willi and Riess, Volker, *The Good Old Days - The Holocaust as Seen by its Perpetrators and Bystanders*, Macmillan, 1991
102. Kretalovs, Deniss, *The Roma Genocide in Latvia*, Roma Culture Centre Berlin, 2017, p. 7
103. National Archives II, College Park, MD (NA), Record Group 226, Entry 16, Box. 817, 67897C
104. Siliņš, Anderson E., *Latviešu nacionālā pretestības kustība. 1943–1945*, Latvijas Centrālā padome, 1994, p. 76
105. Bower, T., *The Red Web: MI6 and the KGB Master Coup*, Aurum Press, 1989, p. 43
106. US War Department, SSU Unit, War Report of the OSS / Vol. 2, New York: Walker & Co, 1976, p. 261
107. Snyder, Timothy, *Black Earth*, p. 173
108. ibid, p. 176
109. Buttar, p. 53
110. https://forum.axishistory.com/viewtopic.php?t=76709
111. Tenenbaum, p. 51
112. Plavnieks, p. 44
113. Holocaust encyclopedia encyclopedia.ushmm.org/content/en/article/Rīga
114. Nuremberg War Trials, Document No. 3824, Vol. IV, p. 443
115. Botcher, Bjarke W., *The Debate on the Latvian SS Volunteer Legion*, Baltic Defence Review No. 3, 2000
116. Feldmanis, Inesis, *Waffen-SS Units of Latvians and Other Non-Germanic Peoples in World War II; The Hidden and Forbidden History of Latvia under Soviet and Nazi Occupation 1941–1991*, Institute of the History of Latvia, University of Latvia, 2005, p. 131
117. Weiss-Wendt, Anton, *Murder Without Hatred: Estonians and the Holocaust*, Syracuse University Press, 2009, p. 74
118. Snyder, Timothy, *Black Earth*, p. 214
119. Weiss-Wendt, Anton, *Murder Without Hatred: Estonians and the Holocaust*, Syracuse University Press, 2009, p. 158
120. Zimmermann, Michael, *Jews, Gypsies and Soviet Prisoners of War: Comparing Nazi Persecutions In: The Roma: A Minority in Europe: Historical, Political and Social Perspectives [online]*, Central European University Press, 2007

121. Kay and Stahel, p. 82
122. Weiss-Wendt, Anton, *Murder without hatred* p. 34
123. Birn, Ruth Bettina, *Collaboration with Nazi Germany in Eastern Europe: The Case of the Estonian Security Police*, Contemporary European History, 2001, p. 197
124. Maclean, French L., *The Field Men*, Schiffer Military History, 1999
125. Buttar, p. 46
126. ibid, p. 20
127. Snyder, Timothy, *Bloodlands*, p. xv
128. https://tracesofwar.com/articles/4748/Sandberger-Martin.htm
129. ibid
130. Reich Ministry for the Occupied Eastern Territories RMO, Dept. III to Dept. I (Politics), October 23, 1943, BA (Dahlwitz-Hoppegarten), R-90/147, p. 754
131. Weiss-Wendt, Anton, *Extermination of the Gypsies in Estonia during World War II: Popular Images and Official Policies*, Holocaust and Genocide Studies, Vol. 17, No. 1, 2003, p. 47
132. Weiss-Wendt, Anton, *Extermination of the Gypsies* p. 49
133. Kay, Alex, J. and Stahel, David, *Mass Violence in Nazi-Occupied Europe*, Indiana University Press, Kindle edition, p. 87
134. Kay, Alex, J. and Stahel, David, *Mass Violence*, p. 89
135. State Archives of the Russian Federation, Fund 7021, List 97, File 17a, p. 12

Chapter 7

1. Baxter, Ian, *The Crushing of Army Group North 1944–1945 on the Eastern Fron*, Pen & Sword, Kindle edition, p. 23
2. Blumentritt, Günther, *Moscow: The Fatal Decisions Six Decisive Battles of The Second World War From The Viewpoint Of The Vanquishe*, Michael Joseph, 1956, p. 66
3. Briefe von Heinz Guderian an seine Frau Margarete' BA-MA N 802/46 (16 December 1941)
4. Baxter, p. 23

Chapter 8

1. Harrimann, Averell & Abel, Elie, *Special Envoy to Churchill and Stalin 1941–1946*, Random House, 1974, p. 1135
2. Potts, Joanna and Berthon,Simon, *Warlords: An Extraordinary Re-Creation of World War II Through the Eyes and Minds of Hitler, Roosevelt, Churchill, and Stalin*, Da Capo Press and Methuen, 2006, p. 138
3. Gannon, Robert, *The Cardinal Spellman Story*, Doubleday, 1962, p. 222
4. Huttenbach, Henry R., *Introduction: Towards a Unitary Soviet State: Managing a Multinational Society, 1917–1985*, Mansell Publishing, 1990, p. 3
5. Staöaitis, Arûnas, *Lithuania's Struggle against Soviet Occupation 1944–1953*, Baltic Defence Review, No. 3, 2000, p. 117
6. Sagatienė, p. 780
7. Strods, Heinrihs, *Resistance in Latvia 1944–1991; The Hidden and Forbidden History of Latvia under Soviet and Nazi Occupation 1941–1991*, Institute of the History of Latvia, University of Latvia, 2005, p. 288
8. Mertelsmann, Olaf and Rahi-Tamm, Aigi, *Cleansing and Compromise: The Estonian SSR in 1944–45*, Cahiers du Monde russe Vol. 49, No. 2/3, 2009, p. 330
9. Ney, Gottlieb, *From Scientist to Chekist in The Estonian State and Nation in the Second World War: The Red Year*, Stockholm, 1956, p. 154
10. Mertelsmann and Rahi-Tamm, p. 332

SOURCES

Anders, Edward and Dubrovskis, Juris, *Who Died in the Holocaust? Recovering Names from Official Records*, Holocaust and Genocide Studies. Oxford University Press, 2003

Anušauskas, Arvydas, *Lessons of History: The Silent Occupation of 1940*, Lietuvos Respublikos Seimo kanceliarija, Vilnius, 2014

Arad, Yitzhak, *The Final Solution in Lithuania in the Light of German Documentation*, https://yadvashem.org

Arad, Yitzhak, *The Toll of the Extermination Operations (July–December 1941) Ghetto in Flames*, KTAV Publishing House, 1980

Arad, Yitzhak, Gutman, Yisrael and Margaliot, Abraham, *Documents on the Holocaust, Selected Sources on the Destruction of the Jews of Germany and Austria, Poland and the Soviet Union*, Yad Vashem, Jerusalem Document No. 177, 1981

Balkelis, Tomas, *Demobilization and Remobilization of German and Lithuanian Paramilitaries after the First World War*, Journal of Contemporary History Vol. 50, No. 1, 2015

Bassler, Gerhard P., *Alfred Valdmanis and the Politics of Survival*, University of Toronto Press, 2000

Baxter, Ian, *The Crushing of Army Group North 1944–1945 on the Eastern Front*, Pen & Sword, Kindle edition,

Birn, Ruth Bettina, *Collaboration with Nazi Germany in Eastern Europe: The Case of the Estonian Security Police*, Contemporary European History, 2001

Blumentritt, Günther, *Moscow: The Fatal Decisions Six Decisive Battles of The Second World War From The Viewpoint of The Vanquished*, Michael Joseph, 1956

Botcher, Bjarke W., *The Debate on the Latvian SS Volunteer Legion*, Baltic Defence Review No. 3, 2000

Bower, T., *The Red Web: MI6 and the KGB Master Coup*, Aurum Press, 1989

Breitman, Richard, *Plans for the Final Solution in 1941*, German Sudies Review, Vol. 17, No. 3, 1994

Browning, Christopher R., *Ordinary Men: Reserve Police Battalion 101 and the Final Solution in Poland*, Harper Collins, 1992

Browning, Christopher R., *The Nazi Decision to Commit Mass Murder*, German Studies Review, Vol. 17, No. 3, 1994

Buttar, Prit, *Centuries Will Not Suffice: A History of the Lithuanian Holocaust*, Amberley Publishing, Kindle edition, 2023

Cepinskyte, Agne, *The Weimar Republic's Policies Towards the Baltic Germans*, King's College London, 2019

Chodakiewicz, Marek Jan, *Intermarium: The Land between the Black and Baltic Seas*, Routledge, 2017

Chodakiewicz, Marek Jan, *The Debate about Soviet Genocide in Lithuania in the Case Law of The European Court of Human Rights*, Routledge, 2017

Dieckmann, Christoph and Sužiedėlis, Saulius, *The Persecution and Mass Murder of Lithuanian Jews during Summer and Fall of 1941*, Vilnius: Margi raštai, 2006

Erickson, John, *The Soviet High Command*, Macmillan & Co., 1962

Ezergailis, Edward, *The Holocaust in Latvia 1941–1944: The Missing Center*, Historical Institute of Latvia in association with USHMM, 1996

Ezergailis, Edward, *The German Times 1941–1945: Liberation, Volunteering, Self-Defense, Revenge*, Yearbook of the Museum of the Occupation of Latvia, 2002

Feldmanis, Inesis, *Latvia under the Occupation of National Socialist Germany 1941–1945; The Hidden and Forbidden History of Latvia under Soviet and Nazi Occupation 1941–1991*, Institute of the History of Latvia, University of Latvia, 2005

Feldmanis, Inesis, *Waffen-SS Units of Latvians and Other Non-Germanic Peoples in World War II; The Hidden and Forbidden History of Latvia under Soviet and Nazi Occupation 1941–1991*, Institute of the History of Latvia, University of Latvia, 2005

Gannon, Robert, *The Cardinal Spellman Story*, Doubleday, 1962

Gerwarth, Robert and Horne, John, *Vectors of Violence: Paramilitarism in Europe After the Great War, 1917–1923*, The Journal of Modern History, Vol. 83, No. 3, 2011

Gilbert, Martin, *The Holocaust: The Human Tragedy*, Rosetta Books, 2015

Gitelman, Zvi, *Soviet Reactions to the Holocaust, 1945–1991: The Holocaust in the Soviet Union*, Armonk, NY, 1993

Golczewski, Frank, *Organe der deutschen Besatzungsmacht: Die ukrainischen Schutzmannschaften*, Wolfgang Benz, 1998

Goldberg, Rubin B., *Russian and Soviet Nationalities Policy in the Baltic States, 1855–1991*, University of Vermont, 2015

Goldhagen, Daniel J., *Hitler's Willing Executioners: Ordinary Germans and the Holocaust*, Harper Collins, 1996

Harrimann, Averell & Abel, Elie, *Special Envoy to Churchill and Stalin 1941–1946*, Random House, 1974

Haslam, Jonathan, Stalin and the German Invasion of Russia 1941: A Failure of Reasons of State?, International Affairs, Vol. 76, No. 1, 2000

Haynes, Rebecca, *Reviewed Work(s): The Radical Right in Interwar Estonia by Andres Kasekamp*, The Slavonic and East European Review, 2003

Helmreich, E.C., *The Return of the Baltic Germans*, The American Political Science Review, Vol. 36, No. 4, 1942

Hiden, J.W., *The Baltic Germans and German Policy Towards Latvia After 1918*, The Historical Journal, 1970

Hilberg, Raul, *Perpetrators, Victims, Bystanders: The Jewish Catastrophe 1933–1945*, Harper Collins, 1992

Housden, M. and Smith D.J., *Forgotten Pages in Baltic History: Diversity and Inclusion*, Brill Academic, 2011

Huttenbach, Henry R., *Introduction: Towards a Unitary Soviet State: Managing a Multinational Society, 1917–1985*, Mansell Publishing, 1990

Janavičienė, Audronė, *Soviet Saboteurs in Lithuania (1941–1944)*, Genocide and Resistance Research Center of Lithuanian Population, 2004

Kalijarvi, Thorsten, *The Problem of Memel*, The American Journal of International Law, Vol. 30, No. 2, 1936

Kangeris, Kārlis, *'Closed' Units of Latvian Police – Lettische Schutzmannschafts-Bataillone; The Hidden and Forbidden History of Latvia under Soviet and Nazi Occupation 1941–1991*, Institute of the History of Latvia, University of Latvia, 2005

Kasekamp Andres, *Fascism by Popular Initiative: The Rise and Fall of the Vaps Movement in Estonia*, Brill Academic, 2015

Kay, Alex J., *Transition to Genocide, July 1941: Einsatzkommando 9 and the Annihilation of Soviet Jewry*, Holocaust and Genocide Studies, Vol. 27, No. 3, 2013

Kay, Alex J. and Stahel, David, *Mass Violence in Nazi-Occupied Europe*, Indiana University Press, Kindle edition, 2021

Ken, Oleg and Rupasov, Alexander, *Moscow and the Baltic States: Experience of Relationships, 1917–1939*, E-International Relations, 2018

Klee, Ernst, Dressen, Willi and Riess, Volker, *The Good Old Days: The Holocaust as Seen by its Perpetrators and Bystanders*, Macmillan, 1991

Kokoshin, Andrei, *The German Blitzkreig against the USSR, 1941*, Belfer Center for Science and International Affairs, 2016

Kretalovs, Deniss, *The Roma Genocide in Latvia*, Roma Culture Centre Berlin, 2017

Lenin, Vladimir, *Neizvestnye dokumenty, 1891–1922*, Moskva: Rosspen, 1999

Levin, Dov, *Baltic Jews under the Soviets 1940–1946*, Jerusalem, 1994

Levin, Dov, *The Lesser of Two Evils: Eastern European Jewry under Soviet Rule*, 1939–1941, Philadelphia, 1995

Lūmans, Valdis O., *Latvia in World War II*, Fordham University Press, 2006

Mačiulis, Dangiras and Staliūnas, Darius, *Lithuanian Nationalism and the Vilnius Question, 1883–1940*, Verlag Herder-Institut, Marburg, 2015

Maclean, French L., *The Field Men*, Schiffer Military History, 1999

Mälksoo, Lauri, *The Baltic States Between 1940 and 1991: Illegality and/or Prescription*, downloaded from https://brill.com 07/01/2023

Matthäus, Jürgen, 'Key Aspects of German Anti-Jewish Policy,' *Lithuania and the Jews: The Holocaust Chapter, Symposium Presentations*, United States Holocaust Memorial Museum Center for Advanced Studies, 2004

Mertelsmann, Olaf and Rahi-Tamm, Aigi, *Cleansing and Compromise, The Estonian SSR in 1944–45*, Cahiers du Monde russe Vol. 49, No. 2/3, 2009

Neiburgs, Uldis, *Resistance Movement in Latvia during Nazi German Occupation (1941–1945)*, Museum of the Occupation of Latvia, 2011

Ney, Gottlieb, *From Scientist to Chekist in The Estonian State and Nation in the Second World War: The Red Year*, Stockholm, 1956

Nikžentaitis, Alvydas, *Germany and the Memel Germans in the 1930s (On the Basis of Trials of Lithuanian Agents before the Volksgerichtshof, 1934–45)*, The Historical Journal, Vol. 39, No. 3, 1996

Nikžentaitis, Alvydas, *The Elections in Memel*, Bulletin of International News, Vol. 15, No. 25, 1938

Parrot, Andrew, *The Baltic States from 1914 to 1923: The First World War and the Wars of Independence*, Baltic Defence Review No 8 Vol. 2, 2002

Piirimai, Kaarel, *Review:* 'Masters of the Baltic'*: Soviet Objectives Towards the Baltic on the Eve of the Second World War*, Journal of Contemporary History, Vol. 47, No. 4, 2012

Plavnieks, Richards, *Nazi Collaborators on Trial during the Cold War: The Cases against Viktors Arājs and the Latvian Auxiliary Security Police*, University of North Carolina, 2013

Potts, Joanna and Berthon, Simon, *Warlords: An Extraordinary Re-Creation of World War II Through the Eyes and Minds of Hitler, Roosevelt, Churchill, and Stalin*, Da Capo Press and Methuen, 2006

Press, B., *The Murder of the Jews in Latvia*, Northwestern University Press, 2000

Rahi-Tamm, Aigi, *Human losses, in: Salo, ed., The White Book, O˜ ispuu, ed., Crimes of Soviet Occupation*

Rei, August, *Nazi-Soviet Conspiracy and the Baltic States*, University of Michigan, 2006

Reichelt, Katrin, *Latvia under German Occupation 1941–1944: The Latvian Part in the Holocaust*, Metropol-Verlag, 2021

Reichelt, Katrin, Lecture at the book presentation *'Lettland unter deutscher Besatzung 1941–1944: Der lettische Anteil am Holocaust' – 'Latvia under German Occupation 1941–1944: The Latvian Part in the Holocaust'*, https://rīga-komitee.eu/en/history/latvia-under-german-occupation-1941–1944

Reichelt, Katrin, *Rescue Knows no Conventions: Help for Persecuted Jews in German-Occupied Latvia 1941–1945*, Lukas Verlag, 2016

Riekstiņš, Jānis, *The 14 June 1941 Deportation in Latvia; The Hidden and Forbidden History of Latvia under Soviet and Nazi Occupation 1941–1991*, Institute of the History of Latvia, University of Latvia, 2005

Rislakki, Jukka, *The Case for Latvia: Disinformation Campaigns against a Small Nation*, Rodopi, 2008

Rodes, Richard, *Maters of Death; The SS–Einsatzgruppen and the Invention of the Holocaust*, Vintage, 2002

Rotundo, Louis, Stalin and the Outbreak of War in 1941, *Journal of Contemporary History*, Vol. 24, No. 2, Studies on War, 1989

Rudashevski, Yitskhok, *Diary of the Vilna Ghetto*, Israel: Ghetto Fighters' House, 1973

Ruutsoo, Rein, *The Estonians: Identity of Small Nation in Past and Present*, Anthropological Journal on European Cultures, Vol. 6, No. 1, 1997

Saburova, Irina, *The Soviet Occupation of the Baltic States Author*, The Russian Review, Vol. 14, No. 1, 1955

Sagatienė, Dovilė, *The Debate About Soviet Genocide in Lithuania in the Case Law of The European Court of Human Rights*, European Humanities University, Vilnius, 2021

Schneider, Gertrude, *Journey Into Terror, Story of the Riga Ghetto*, Westport Praeger, Kindle edition, 2001

Senn, Alfred Erich, *Baltic Battleground: The Hidden and Forbidden History of Latvia under Soviet and Nazi Occupation 1941–1991*, Institute of the History of Latvia, University of Latvia, 2005

Senn, Alfred Erich, *Lithuania in March 1941, An American Diplomat's report*, Journal of Baltic Sudies Vol. 26, 1995

Schalkovsky, Samuel, *The Clandestine History of the Kovno Jewish Ghetto Police*, Bloomington: Indiana University Press, 2014

Schneider, Gertrude, *Journey into Terror, Story of the Riga Ghetto*, Westport Praeger, Kindle edition, 2001

Siliņš, Anderson E., *Latviešu nacionālā pretestības kustība, 1943–1945,* Latvijas Centrālā padome, 1994
Šiušaitė, A. and Landsbergis, V., *Forgotten Soviet War Crime Rainiai in Lithuania 24–25th June, 1941,* AB Baltijos kopija, 2007
Smetona, Antanas, *Antanas Smetona's correspondence 1940–1944,* Vytautas the Great University Publishing House, 1999
Šneidere, Irēne, *The First Soviet Occupation Period in Latvia 1940–1941; The Hidden and Forbidden History of Latvia under Soviet and Nazi Occupation 1941–1991,* Institute of the History of Latvia, University of Latvia, 2005
Šneidere, Irēne, *The Occupation of Latvia in June 1941; The Hidden and Forbidden History of Latvia under Soviet and Nazi Occupation 1941–1991,* Institute of the History of Latvia, University of Latvia, 2005
Snyder, Timothy, *Black Earth,* Random House, Kindle edition, 2015
Snyder, Timothy, *Bloodlands,* Random House, Kindle edition, 2012
Staöaitis, Arûnas, *Lithuania's Struggle against Soviet Occupation 1944–1953,* Baltic Defence Review, No. 3, 2000
Stranga, Aivars, *The Holocaust in Occupied Latvia: 1941–1945; The Hidden and Forbidden History of Latvia under Soviet and Nazi Occupation 1941–1991,* Institute of the History of Latvia, University of Latvia, 2005
Stasiulis, Stanislovas, *The Holocaust in Lithuania: The Key Characteristics of its History, and the Key Issues in Historiography and Cultural Memory,* East European Politics and Societies Vol. 34, Issue 1, 2020
Stolfi, Russel H.S., *Barbarossa Revisited: A Critical Reappraisal of the Opening Stages of the Russo-German Campaign (June-December 1941),* The Journal of Modern History, Vol. 54, No. 1
Strods, Heinrihs, *Resistance in Latvia 1944–1991; The Hidden and Forbidden History of Latvia under Soviet and Nazi Occupation 1941–1991,* Institute of the History of Latvia, University of Latvia, 2005
Strods, Heinrihs, *Sovietisation of Latvia, The Hidden and Forbidden History of Latvia under Soviet and Nazi Occupation 1941–1991,* Institute of the History of Latvia, University of Latvia, 2005
Streim, Alfred, *The Tasks of the SS Einsatzgruppen,* https://museumoftolerance.com/education/archives-and-reference-library
Sužiedėlis, Saulius, *Lithuanian Collaboration during the Second World War: Past Realities, Present Perceptions," in Kollaboration in Nordosteuropa: Erscheinungsformen und Deutungen Im 20. Jahrhundert, ed. Joachim Tauber,* Harrassowitz, 2006
Szarota, Tomasz, *On the Threshold of the Holocaust: Anti-Jewish Riots and Pogroms in Occupied Europe–Warsaw–Paris–The Hague–Amsterdam–Antwerp–Kaunas,* Frankfurt am Main: Peter Lang, 2015
Tenenbaum, Joseph, *The Einsatzgruppen,* Jewish Social Studies Vol. 17, No. 1, 1955
Truska, Liudas, *The Upsurge of Anti-Semitism in Lithuania in the Years of the Soviet Occupation,* downloaded from https://komisija.com
Truska, Liudas and Variekis, Vygantas, *The Preconditions for the Holocaust: Anti-Semitism in Lithuania,* Vilus: Margi raštai, 2004
Tulun, Mehmet Oğuzhan, *Russification Policies Imposed on the Baltic People by the Russian Empire and the Soviet Union,* Başkent University, 2012
Turčinskis, Zigmārs, *The Latvian Armed Resistance Movements against the Soviet Occupation 1944–1957, The Hidden and Forbidden History of Latvia under Soviet*

and Nazi Occupation 1941–1991, Institute of the History of Latvia, University of Latvia, 2005

Valge, Jaak, *Foreign Involvement and Loss of Democracy, Estonia 1934*, Journal of Contemporary History, Vol. 46, No. 4, 2011

Vanagaitė, Rūta and Zuroff, Efraim, *Our People*, Rowman & Littlefield Publishers, Kindle edition, 2020

Vercrumba, Peters J., *Zellis and the Holocaust in Rēzekne, Latvia*, https://academia.edu/49625927/Zellis_and_the_Holocaust_in_Rēzekne_Latvia, 2023

Vīksne, Rudīte, *Members of the Arājs Commando in Soviet Court Files; The Hidden and Forbidden History of Latvia under Soviet and Nazi Occupation 1941–1991*, Institute of the History of Latvia, University of Latvia, 2005

Vilums, Jānis, *Non-Violent Resistance to the Soviet Occupation Regime in Latvia in 1940–1941*, Symposium of the Commission of the Historians of Latvia, Vol. 29, 2021

Weiss-Wendt, Anton, *Murder Without Fatred: Estonians and the Holocaust*, Syracuse University Press, 2009

Weiss-Wendt, Anton, *Extermination of the Gypsies in Estonia during World War II: Popular Images and Official Policies*, Holocaust and Genocide Studies, Vol. 17, No. 1, 2003

Werth, Alexander, *Russia At War, 1941–1945*, Pan, 1965

Zellis, Kaspars, *The Holocaust in Rezekne: Research, Problems, Questions, Perspectives*, University of Latvia, 2017

Zimmermann, Michael, *Jews, Gypsies and Soviet Prisoners of War: Comparing Nazi Persecutions In: The Roma: a Minority in Europe: Historical, Political and Social Perspectives [online]*, Central European University Press, 2007

INDEX